12-22-76

THE UNITED STATES AND THE DEVELOPMENT OF SOUTH AMERICA, 1945-1975

SAMUEL L. BAILY

THE UNITED STATES AND THE DEVELOPMENT OF SOUTH AMERICA, 1945-1975

New Viewpoints
A Division of Franklin Watts
New York / London / 1976

To Nicholas Newlin Baily and Arlene Mack Baily,
whose curiosity and humanism have always been
an inspiration to me

New Viewpoints
A Division of Franklin Watts
730 Fifth Avenue
New York, New York 10019

Library of Congress Cataloging in Publication Data

Baily, Samuel L
    The United States and the development of South
America, 1945–1975.

    Bibliography: p.
    Includes index.
    1. United States—Foreign economic relations—
South America. 2. South America—Foreign eco-
nomic relations—United States. 3. United States—
Foreign relations—South America. 4. South
America—Foreign relations—United States. I.
Title.
HF1456.5.S62B26   338.91′8′073   76–13895
ISBN 0–531–05387–3
ISBN 0–531–05594–9 pbk.

contents

1943139

preface

Since I first became acquainted with Latin America nearly twenty years ago, three concerns in particular have remained with me. One, that although the standard of living of the overwhelming majority of the people of the area has improved some over the years, it still remains intolerably low. Two, that the difference between the standard of living in Latin America and in the United States has become progressively greater. And three, that United States policy, contrary to popular belief, has probably made it more rather than less difficult for Latin Americans to reduce significantly the level of poverty.

These concerns derive from the fact that I have lived for some time in various parts of Latin America and have experienced what the statistics coldly and abstractly summarize: a baby mutilated by a rat in a small Mexican village, an old woman frantically rummaging through the garbage cans for something to eat in front of a fashionable São Paulo restaurant, a Bolivian child hopelessly deformed by disease and malnutrition, unemployed sugar workers sharing a meal of watery soup in Tucumán, the inhabitants of the shantytowns surrounding Lima looking for pure water to drink.

This book is thus a reflection of my experience with Latin

American poverty and of my intellectual concern with the policies of the United States that seem to contribute to it. My personal convictions generally lead me to focus on what is positive in any situation. In this case, however, I am critical of the United States and dwell at length on its shortcomings because I see no other way to influence a relationship that helps perpetuate intolerable living conditions for so many people. The South American policy of the United States is not, in my opinion, the result of some secret conspiracy among Wall Street bankers, executives of multi-national corporations, and generals in the Pentagon. Rather, it flows naturally from the pursuit of what our leaders believe to be our national interest coupled with ignorance and apathy on the part of the general population. It is my hope that by setting forth the pertinent historical data and raising some of the important questions, I will encourage the reader to evaluate our policy and gain an understanding of its consequences for the average South American. With such an understanding, the possibility of change increases.

The topic is controversial for North Americans. Scholars, journalists, government officials, businessmen, and labor leaders disagree on the past and present state of United States-South American relations, on what United States policy should be in the future, and on what the national interest is. Personal values, assumptions, and ideological preferences come into play at nearly every stage of information gathering and analysis. Yet with recognition of the complexity of the subject, respect for differences in perspective, and a degree of humility, it is possible to eschew blinding dogmatism and emotionalism, and instead focus on understanding.

The book is not a history of United States-Latin American relations and I have not sought to "cover" all countries or all issues. I have focused on the broad outlines of United States-Latin American relations, on representative countries, and on the most important issues. Furthermore, I have concentrated on the period since World War II and on the South American countries.

The concentration on South America can be justified in a number of ways. Certainly many of my observations apply equally to all parts of Latin America, but the United States has treated South America somewhat differently than it has Mexico, Central America, and the Caribbean; South America is located farther from the United States, United States interest in the area developed later and has never been as great as its interest in the more immediate areas of Latin America, and the United States has not directly intervened militarily in South America. Also, many of the South American countries have had closer ties with Europe than have the northern Latin American countries. Finally, while United States relations with Mexico and Cuba have been written about extensively by North American scholars, South America has to a considerable extent been ignored.

One final clarification. Some might question the validity of my comparison of the South American countries with the United States. If one were to compare the quality of life in South America with that in much of Asia and Africa, one could conclude that our southern neighbors had come a long way and were not so badly off. That would, however, do serious injustice to the South American perspective. The South Americans compare themselves to the United States, not to the poorest states of Asia and Africa, and they believe that the United States has something to do with their low standard of living.

A number of people have contributed in various ways to the appearance of this book. Ed Duckles, Herberto Sein, and Von Peacock of the Friends Service Committee in Mexico first exposed me to the reality of Latin America and helped me understand its humanistic dimensions. Robert J. Alexander, Warren Dean, Lloyd Gardner, Gerald Grob, Irving Louis Horowitz, John Lenaghan, Albert Michaels, and Herbert Rowen read the manuscript and, although some of them disagree sharply with certain of my interpretations, generously gave me the benefit of their detailed comments. My wife, Joan, read and reread the many drafts of the manuscript, patiently discussed unclear and illogical passages with me, and continually provided encouragement. The book is much improved as a result of their help, but they, of course, are not responsible for any of the shortcomings that may still remain.

S. L. B.

chapter
1

Poverty and Development
in South America

Most South Americans have lived in poverty as long as anyone
can remember, but in recent years they have become aware that
they are poor while others are rich. Railroads, roads, transistor
radios, and television have brought them into contact with the
opulence of their cities and of the industrialized countries of the
world. They no longer perceive malnutrition, disease, short life expectancy, and subsistence as the inevitable pattern of life, and
they are increasingly demanding a share of the wealth they see.
Poverty, the revolution of rising expectations, and the growing demand for social and economic change make up the present and
the foreseeable future reality of South America.

This study explores how United States relations with South
America have affected the quality of life of the people of that
area. Has the United States helped or hindered South American
efforts to develop and to eliminate poverty? How and why has it
done so? Is current policy toward South America, in the short and
the long term, in the best national interest? Is it, for example, in
our best interests to live in relative luxury, while most South
Americans live in poverty? The United States accounts for about
6 percent of the world population, yet it consumes annually about

CUBA   DOMINICAN
       REP.   Puerto Rico
HAITI   (USA)   Virgin Is. (USA)
(HISPANIOLA)   Guadeloupe (Fr.)
JAMAICA   Martinique (Fr.)
CARIBBEAN SEA   BARBADOS
           Aruba
           (Neth.) Curacao   TRINIDAD
                    (Neth.)   AND TOBAGO

ATLANTIC

OCEAN

Baranquilla   Caracas
PANAMA   **VENEZUELA**   Georgetown
                       Orinoco   GUYANA   Paramaribo
Panama   SURINAM   Cayenne
Canal   (Neth.)   FR. GUIANA
           Bogotá
COLOMBIA
                    Rio Negro   *Amazon*   Belém
Quito   Manaus   Fortaleza
ECUADOR   (Ceará)   Natal

                    Leticia   Recife
                              Madeira   *Tapajós*   (Pernambuco)

PERU   **BRAZIL**   São Salvador
Callao   Lima   (Bahia)
         Cuzco
       Titicaca   **BOLIVIA**   Brasília
Tacna   La Paz   *São*   Belo
Arica   Sucre   *Paraguay*   *Francisco*   Horizonte
                              BRASILIAN
Antofagasta   *GRAN*   *HIGHLANDS*
                         CHACO   São Paulo
                              PARAGUAY   Santos   Rio de
       Tucuman   Asuncion   Janeiro

                    Paraná   Porto
                                          Alegre

PACIFIC

OCEAN

Valparaíso   Mendoza
Santiago   Buenos   **URUGUAY**
                        Aires   Montevideo
CHILE   **ARGENTINA**   *Rio de*
                         la Plata
Valdivia

           ANDES
           PATAGONIA

       Str. of   Falkland Is.
       Magellan
       TIERRA
       DEL FUEGO
         Cape Horn

SOUTH AMERICA
and the Caribbean

40 percent of the world's resources. Are we prepared to give up some of our luxury in order that others might live a better life? Would we be more secure if we were to do so? Is it in our national interest to support repressive military dictatorships like that in Brazil? If we believe in democracy at home, should we not support all democratic regimes abroad, including socialist regimes like that of the former Allende government in Chile? What kinds of governments and societies in South America would best serve our economic interests and national security?

Development: South America's Goal

The distinct economic and political realities of the United States and the South American countries underlie our differences in goals and perspective. The United States is a "have" as opposed to a "have not" country. It is the most powerful nation on the globe and the leader of the "Free World" or "Non-Communist" bloc of states. Geographically, the United States is isolated by two broad oceans, which until World War II made its people feel secure from foreign attack. Since then, technological developments have destroyed much of the protective value of these oceans and have increased our concern with security. The United States is a large country with rich, though dwindling, natural resources. It is also a capitalist society committed to the sanctity of private property and to the primacy of individual initiative. It is an urbanized and industrialized mass consumer society with a large internal market, the highest per capita gross domestic product (GDP) in the world, and with by far the highest per capita consumption of the world's resources. The people of the United States are, in David Potter's words, a people of plenty. Their heritage is white Anglo-Saxon Protestant modified only somewhat by the presence of more recent and diverse groups of immigrants and by blacks.

South America is, in many important respects, quite the opposite. It is a "have not" area. It lacks military or economic power; it is a follower of others, not a leader of international blocs; and its geographic position, though isolating it from much of the world, has not given it security or freedom from external interference. South America witnessed a number of internal wars in the nineteenth and twentieth centuries and has been vulnerable to outside intervention by Spain, Portugal, Holland, France, England, Germany, and the United States. About 42 percent of its labor force is occupied in agricultural activities, 33 percent in the service sector, and only 25 percent in industry (Table 1–1). It has no mass consumer societies, and although it has enormous natural resources, these resources have not led to the creation of a people of plenty. Poverty is widespread and the distribution of wealth very unequal. Its heritage is Spanish-Portuguese-Catholic mixed in some areas with that of Indians and blacks.

The diversity within the region is enormous. South America consists of thirteen countries. Among these countries there is great variety in climate, geography, fertility of soil, natural resources, political systems, social structures, and levels of economic development. The population is nearly equivalent to that of the United States, and the land area twice the size of that of the United States. Per capita gross domestic product (GDP) ranges from $195 per year in Bolivia to $934 per year in Argentina; literacy from 47 percent in Bolivia to 94 percent in Argentina; and racial composition from predominantly white European stock in Argentina and Uruguay to predominantly Indian in Bolivia and Peru to mixed white, Indian, and black in Brazil.[1] Brazil, Bolivia, Chile, Ecuador, Peru, Argentina, and Uruguay have different forms of military dictatorship, while Colombia, Guyana, and Venezuela have some form of democratic parliamentary government.

In addition, there are significant differences within each of the thirteen South American countries. The northeast of Brazil is a subsistence, drought-prone agricultural area, while São Paulo in the south is a dynamic, modern industrial center. While Lima,

TABLE **1-1**

Size of Agrarian Labor Force
(% of total labor force)

	Latin America	United States
1855		63
1890		42
1930	63	21
1950	50.2	12
1965	43.1	6
1969	42	4.6

Source: Raul Prebisch, *Change and Development—Latin America's Great Task* (New York, 1971), pp. 30–31.

Peru, is a modern coastal city in the middle of a desert, most of the population of the country, descendants of the Incas, barely survives in the cold, barren mountains of the interior. Buenos Aires, Argentina, is a cosmopolitan "Paris of South America," whose culture, density of population, and wealth contrast sharply with the simple life of the gauchos of the pampa.

The point that must be emphasized, however, is that the diversity within South America becomes insignificant when the standard of living of the area as a whole is compared to that of the United States and the other developed countries of the world. The average per capita GDP of the ten major South American countries is $470 per year, while that of the United States is $3,353 per year or seven times higher. The difference between the per capita GDP of Bolivia and Argentina, the lowest and highest respectively in South America, is $738. The difference between the per capita GDP of Argentina and that of the United States is $2,419. If one takes into consideration the highly unequal internal distribution of income in the South American countries, the disparity with the United States for the vast majority of people is even greater. Figures on adult literacy, life expectancy, daily caloric intake, and school population follow the same pattern (Table 1–2).

What makes this even less acceptable to most South Americans is that, although there has been some absolute improvement in the situation since World War II, the gap between the United States and South America has continued to widen. A survey by the United Nations Economic Commission for Latin America (ECLA) shows that during the decade of the 1960s the GNP of the developed countries increased 43 percent, while that of the developing countries increased only 27 percent. Figures on South America as compared with the United States are similar, and the per capita figures show an even larger gap.[2] South America is not only poor, it is becoming poorer in relation to the United States and the rest of the developed world!

It is thus not surprising that there is considerable agreement among the South American governments on goals even if they disagree on the causes of and solutions to specific problems. What almost all South Americans feel acutely is that their countries are poor, that there is a wide gap between the standard of living in South America and in the United States, and that this gap is wid-

TABLE 1-2

Some Indicators of the Quality of Life in South America

	Per Capita Gross Domestic Product			Adult Literacy (15 years old +)			Life Expectancy (at birth)			Daily Caloric Intake		Percent of Population 5–14 in school		Salaries and Wages as % national income	
	1950	1960	1970	1950	1960	1970	1950	1960	1968	1955	1967	1950	1968	1960	1968
Argentina	$684	$758	$934	86%	91%	94%	60.6	65.5	66.3	3,070	2,920	66%	73.1%	—	—
Bolivia	168	142	196	32	40	47	40.9	—	50.0	1,830	1,980	24	54.7	42.6%	43.8%
Brazil	183	263	350	49	61	71	42.3	—	57.0	2,560	2,690	28	45.7	—	—
Chile	442	491	590	80	84	89	54.0	57.2	62.0	2,550	2,890	66	81.4	51.6	50.8
Colombia	260	298	355	49	73	78	52.2	60.2	60.9	1,900	2,200	28	45.5	41.9	43.9
Ecuador	202	241	284	58	68	73	49.9	52.0	57.7	1,890	2,020	41	55.5	52.9	53.7
Paraguay	242	237	284	66	75	78	54.4	—	59.1	2,510	2,520	51	60.2	40.2	43.6
Peru	219	291	360	47	61	71	57.4	—	58.0	2,040	2,340	43	68.7	46.7	47.8
Uruguay	643	683	677	85	90	93	68.8	68.7	68.4	2,960	3,170	61	73.5	48.2	56.8
Venezuela	412	589	666	51	63	70	58.0	66.1	65.6	1,950	2,490	40	63.0	61.2	57.0
U.S.A.	2,218	2,567	3,353	97.3	97.8	99	68.2	69.7	70.0	3,200	3,200	—	97.0	70.7	71.6

Sources: United Nations, Economic Commission for Latin America, Economy Survey of Latin America: 1970 (New York: 1972). pp. 70–71; Organization of American States, Social and Economic Development of Latin America (Washington, D.C.: 1973), pp. 41, 43, 46, 54, 56.

ening not narrowing. Milton Eisenhower, the brother of former President Dwight Eisenhower and one of his top advisers on Latin America, accurately captured the emotional intensity of these feelings in his book *The Wine Is Bitter*. The Latin Americans, he explained:

> . . . are shackled to the past with bonds of ignorance, injustice, and poverty. And they no longer accept as universal or inevitable the oppressive prevailing order which has filled their lives with toil, want, and pain. The terrible realization has dawned upon them that the futility of their lives and of their parents' lives need not have been, that it is the bitter fruit of an evil system of injustice. And so they are filled with a fury and a determination to change the future.[3]

This "determination to change the future" is evident in the effort to develop the area. There is a sense of urgency and concern about the problem that cuts across traditional political and ideological lines. At Viña del Mar, Chile, in May 1969 the foreign ministers of the Latin American countries formulated a consensus on goals and priorities to present to President Richard Nixon. Predictably, they reaffirmed that the central issue in Latin America, and in United States-Latin American relations, was development. As the conservative foreign minister of Brazil summed up: "Our main aim is to bring about a substantial and continuing increase in per capita income, at a rate which will reduce the difference between the standards of living of Latin American countries and the developed world."[4]

Beyond this agreement on the importance of development and of catching up, there is considerable division of opinion as to how it takes place. Brazilian government officials, representing one end of the spectrum, believe that development can best be brought about by a close partnership with the United States, extensive use of foreign private capital, concentration of income in the hands of the elite, and a paternalistic authoritarian political organization. Officials of the former Allende government in Chile, representing the opposite end of the spectrum, believed that development could best be brought about by pursuing an independent foreign policy, eliminating for the most part foreign private capital, increasing state control over the economy, distributing income widely (particularly to the working classes), and supporting the democratic political process. The other countries fall at various points in between: Bolivia, Paraguay, Uruguay, Argentina, and the current government in Chile are closer to Brazil; Venezuela, Guyana, and Peru are closer to Allende's Chile; and Ecuador and Colombia are somewhere in between.

Although there are profound differences among the South American countries on how best to achieve development and who should benefit from it, they are, nevertheless, unanimous in believing that development and catching up is their most important goal.

The Meaning of Development

"Development" and the cluster of associated terms—"modernization," "advanced," "less-developed," "underdeveloped," and "undeveloped"—elude easy definitions for a number of reasons. One is that people often confuse the *process* and the *condition* implied by the word "development." "Development" is a process of change. In this sense the focus is on the actual movement from condition A to condition B or C or D. On the other hand the word "developed" is used to define a fixed state or condition. The interest here is in the description of the condition at a particular moment in a particular place. In this study, the term "underdeveloped" is used to describe the present condition of South America and the term "developed" to describe that of the United States. The main concern, however, is with the process of development.

Another reason "development" is difficult to understand is that it is a relative concept and its precise meaning has changed over time and from place to place. The "development" of the United States during the first decade of its existence bears little resemblance to the "development" of the United States during the 1970s. Similarly, the "development" of Argentina during the 1970s differs quantitatively and qualitatively from the "development" of the United States during the same period. The term is relative and any standards used to measure it must also be relative. If, as is frequently done, one uses such measurable indicators of development as GNP, literacy, energy consumption, percentage of economically active population in agriculture, and miles of roads and railroads, one must adapt them relative to time and place. The World Bank's Pearson Report (1969) acknowledges the arbitrary nature of its definition but nevertheless states that countries with per capita incomes of less than $500 per year are less developed.[5] This definition would have little value applied to the world of 1950 or to that of 1990.

Mindful of the problems of definition, "development" in this study most simply means technologically induced economic growth. But how much, how fast, and for whose benefit? What political and cultural changes are necessary if economic growth is to take place? What values and institutions must be encouraged? Is rapid economic growth, which always involves sacrifices on the part of some groups and people, possible in a democratic society, or is some form of authoritarian political organization necessary? How important is the immediate improvement of the human condition of the mass of society to the development of that society? What are the roles of external forces in the developmental process? In sum, how does development take place?

A number of sharply conflicting theories provide us with at least partial answers to the question. Most of those writing about the problem adopt one of two broad approaches: the "diffusionist" or the "dependency" model. The diffusionist model is based on the belief that development comes about as a result of the diffusion of technology, capital, trade, political institutions, and culture from the "advanced" to the "backward" countries of the world. Its proponents further assume that the underdeveloped countries are dual societies divided into a backward or neo-feudal rural sector and a modernizing capitalist urban sector. Just as the development of the backward country comes about by the diffusion of ideas and capital from the advanced countries, so the development of the backward areas of the country comes about through the diffusion of capital and ideas from the advanced urban centers. The agents of development, according to this theory, are the modern capitalist countries working in alliance with the growing local "middle class" in the developing country. Thus, through the spreading of technology and capital to the backward countries, they are able to move step by step up the ladder from their own backward condition toward that of the advanced countries. As they do, the gap between the standard of living of the developed and the underdeveloped countries, and between the modern and backward sectors of the developing countries, is supposed to narrow and eventually close.

Perhaps the most widely used formulation of this approach is that of the economist W. W. Rostow. In his book *The Stages of Economic Development,* he seeks to demonstrate that all societies go through five stages in the process of transformation from a traditional (undeveloped) to a modern (developed) society in much the same manner that the United States and some of the Western European countries did. A society begins in the traditional stage and, with the aid of the advanced countries, accumulates sufficient savings and technology to progress to the preconditions for takeoff, then to the takeoff stage and the drive for maturity, and finally reaches the stage of high mass consumption and self-sustained economic growth in which real per capita income is such that a large number of people gain "command over consumption which transcends basic food, shelter and clothing." [6]

The dependency model is more difficult to describe accurately because of the large and continually growing number of dependency theorists who often disagree with and contradict each other.[7] However, almost all reject the basic assumption of the diffusionists: that the spread of capital, trade, technology, political institutions, and culture from the developed to the underdeveloped countries will in the long run result in genuine development and the closing of the gap separating the developed from the underdeveloped. Instead, they argue that the diffusion of capital and ideas makes the receiving country dependent on the giving country, slows down its potential growth, and widens the gap between the standard of living of the countries involved. The development of the already industrialized countries and the underdevelopment of the nonindustrialized countries is, according to dependency theorists, part of the same historical process: Western Europe and the United States developed by exploiting the resources of the underdeveloped world and thus contributed to its continuing underdevelopment. Furthermore, according to the dependency theorists, the dependency relationship that exists between countries is duplicated within the dependent country. The backward rural sector and modernizing urban sector are tied together in an internal dependency relationship with the agrarian, commercial, and industrial elites exploiting the rural sector for their benefit and for that of the developed countries of the world.

Thus, from the point of view of the dependency theorists, underdevelopment is not an early stage in the evolution of societies and development the advanced stage of consumer capitalism represented by the United States, as Rostow suggests. Underdevelopment is part of a structural relationship of inequality among different countries and areas of the world. The noted Brazilian economist Celso Furtado explained that underdevelopment is a "creation of development, or rather . . . a consequence of the impact of the technological processes and the international division of labor commanded by the small number of societies that espoused the Industrial Revolution of the nineteenth century." [8]

There are, however, a number of weaknesses in both conceptual models that preclude the wholesale adoption and utilization of either one. Most importantly, Rostow and the other proponents of the diffusion model assume that because Western Europe and the United States industrialized in a particular way this pattern must be the inevitable and universal pattern for all subsequent development. South America, however, had had a very different historical experience from that of the presently developed countries and today is confronted with external forces and restrictions far greater than any similar external influence on the developed countries when they were developing. Furthermore, although there has been some growth in countries such as Brazil, all of the South American countries are faced with an increasing gap between their standard of living and that of the United States, and with an increasing gap between the standards of living of their rural and urban sectors. The diffusion theory helps to explain a great deal about how the United States and some of the Western European countries developed, but it does not seem to offer much insight into the causes of the progressive, relative impoverishment of South America.

The issue becomes clearer when we look at a specific example. Argentina has literacy, caloric intake, life expectancy, and other similar figures comparable with those of the United States, and it has been in this position for half a century. Rostow tells us that Argentina reached the takeoff stage somewhere in the 1930s, yet Argentina has not taken off and is not developed. Its per capita GDP is only $934 per year or one-fourth that of the United States; its growth rate during the past two and a half decades has barely exceeded the population increase; the gap between its standard of living and that of the United States has steadily increased; the gap between the standards of living of its rural and urban sectors has also increased; and the majority of its population has not "gained command over consumption which transcends basic food, shelter, and clothing." [9]

Argentina, like the other South American countries, does not fit the Rostow pattern very well, nor is there any reason to assume that it should. The Argentine and world situations in the twentieth century are simply not the same as were the United States and world situations in the nineteenth century. The diffusionist model, based on the assumption of the universality of the experience of the already industrialized countries, is of limited use in understanding why Argentina and South America are having such difficulty in catching up.

The dependency theory also suffers from certain problems. [10] The concept is vague, difficult to apply, and needs to be defined more precisely in specific historical contexts at specific times. Furthermore, most of its proponents focus on economic variables to the exclusion of important ethical, cultural, and political factors. In addition, dependency theorists frequently assume that dependency explains all development problems. Yet the theory is more a critique of diffusion than a conceptualization of development. Its focus is on what actually happens when the diffusionist model is applied to the underdeveloped countries. It does suggest how the industrialized countries developed—by exploiting the underdeveloped countries—and it helps to explain why the underdeveloped countries have not been able to catch up—because of their dependency on the developed countries—but, beyond advocating socialism, it offers us little specific guidance on how the currently underdeveloped countries can develop.

Although both theories are based on limited empirical evidence and claim too much, they raise important issues and suggest some answers. As such, they provide a convenient starting point for an analysis of hemispheric relations and the impact of the United States on the development process in South America.

The United States and the Development of South America

The diffusionist theory underlies United States South America policy and the traditional liberal interpretation of hemispheric relations. All three—the theory, the policy, and the interpretation —are based on two propositions: one, that the interests of the

United States and Latin America are essentially compatible; and two, that the United States government is capable of defining and pursuing a national interest that is different from and superior to the private interests of any particular group or sector within society. The frequent past difficulties and disagreements between the United States and Latin America, according to this line of thinking, have been caused by neglect, misunderstanding, and the temporary confusion of private with public interest.[11]

The revisionist view of hemispheric relations coincides for the most part with the dependency theory and is accepted by many South Americans. Its proponents reject both basic assumptions of the liberal interpretation.[12] Instead of compatibility they see conflict of interests. Instead of the United States government defining and pursuing a national interest distinct from that of any private sector, they see United States foreign policy primarily serving the interests of United States capitalism. What the liberals see as neglect, misunderstanding, and the temporary confusion of private with public interest, the revisionists see as a rational long-term relationship of dependency.

That the diffusion of technology and capital from the United States has been and still is an important variable in the development process of South America is not disputed; the critical question is, however, on what terms has this diffusion taken place and for whose benefit? It would seem that since the arrival of Columbus, the South Americans have not been entirely free to develop their economies and to raise their standards of living as they might have chosen. To varying degrees they have been weak and vulnerable to the dictates of the politically and economically powerful in the world. The capital, technology, and markets they have needed have been controlled by others, who therefore have been able to influence the nature and pace of development. They have been unable to make critical developmental decisions on the basis of what they have judged to be their best national interest.[13]

In the twentieth century the United States has assumed the position of dominance in South America formerly held by Spain, Portugal, and England. Through a variety of direct and indirect political, economic, and cultural mechanisms, the United States has come to exert enormous influence in the area. It has used this position to defend what policy makers have considered to be the

United States' national interest, but in so doing the United States has frequently distorted, frustrated, and undermined the South Americans' efforts to overcome their poverty.

Many in government circles recognize this "special relationship," although they would not call it a dependency relationship. The "special relationship" is an attitude or assumption that is so implicitly understood by those who refer to it that they never bother to define it. The absence of definition has covered up the real meaning of the term and its changing nature over the years.

In his report to former President Nixon, Nelson Rockefeller wrote: "Historically, the United States has had a special relationship with the other American republics. It is based upon long association, geography, and, above all, on the psychological acceptance of a concept of hemisphere community. It is embodied in the web of organizations, treaties, and commitments of the inter-American system. Beyond conventional security and economic interests, the political and psychological value of the special relationship cannot be overestimated." [14] This statement tells us that the special relationship has something to do with long association, geographic proximity, a sense of community, security, and economic interests, but we do not know what the relationship really is or how it has changed over time.

In fact, during the first half of the nineteenth century, the special relationship between the United States and Latin America was a relationship of the newly emerged nations of the Western Hemisphere, nations that believed themselves set apart from the rest of the world, and particularly from Europe, by their recently established independence. It was a feeling not unsimilar to that of the Third World nations of today, a sense of a special relationship among themselves based on the difference between themselves and the industrialized countries.[15]

As the economic and military power of the United States grew rapidly during the last decades of the nineteenth century and the early decades of the twentieth, the special relationship between the United States and Latin America evolved into one of domination and subordination. No longer were the respective parties more or less equals who favored a certain level of interdependence in the face of a common past and a common external threat. The Latin American states had been drawn into the sphere of influence of the United States. The special relationship became a dependency relationship.

The United States does not bear the sole, nor necessarily the major, responsibility for continued poverty in South America. There are critical internal obstacles to development, which cannot be minimized, that the South Americans themselves must eliminate. Many of these countries have high rates of population growth and illiteracy, poorly developed transportation networks, limited sources of energy, unequal distribution of wealth, inadequate technology, small internal markets, and so on. Also, some segments of their populations are uninterested in or hostile to development. In many cases the traditional elites have lived quite well in the underdeveloped societies of South America and thus have felt no great compulsion to industrialize or to eliminate the poverty of the working classes. Furthermore, small rural property owners and some peasants have frequently opposed industrialization. But the persistence of the internal obstacles to the solution of South America's social and economic problems is often linked to the significant external obstacles. This study is primarily concerned with these external obstacles to development.

NOTES

1. Gross Domestic Product is the "market value of the product, before deduction of provisions for the consumption of fixed capital, attributable to factor services rendered to resident producers of the given country. Domestic product differs from national product by the exclusion of net factor income received from abroad." See Latin American Center, University of California at Los Angeles, *Statistical Abstract of Latin America, 1968* (Los Angeles, 1969), p. 240.

2. United Nations, Economic Commission for Latin America, *Economic Survey of Latin America: 1969* (New York, 1971); *The New York Times,* July 10, 1972.

3. Milton S. Eisenhower, *The Wine Is Bitter* (New York, 1963), p. xi.

4. Chile. *The Latin American Consensus of Viña del Mar* (Santiago, 1969), p. 27. Hereafter referred to as *Consensus.*

5. Lester B. Pearson, *Partners in Development* (New York, 1969), p. 23.

6. W. W. Rostow, *The Stages of Economic Growth* (London, 1960), p. 10. C. E. Black, in *The Dynamics of Modernization* (New York, 1966), looks at the process from a more political perspective, but comes up with

similar general stages of development. The developed society in this case is the integrated society in which "personal power tends to become institutionalized through bureaucracy and the exercise of power is divided into many specialities and shared by many people." Jacques Lambert, in *Latin America, Social Structures and Political Institutions* (Berkeley, Calif., 1967), emphasizes social structure, but adopts a similar scheme. According to Lambert, the social structure of Latin American progresses from archaic groups of small closed communities to a dual structure that combines small closed communities with a developed national community to a developed national social structure.

7. The literature on dependency is abundant and growing. A convenient place to begin is the first issue of *Latin American Perspectives* (Spring 1974). I have found the following works most useful: Susanne Bodenheimer, "Dependency and Imperialism: the Roots of Latin American Underdevelopment," in K. T. Fann and D. C. Hodges (eds.), *Readings in United States Imperialism* (Boston, 1971); F. Bonilla and R. Girling (eds.), *Structures of Dependency* (Palo Alto, Calif., 1973); F. H. Cardoso and E. Faletto, *Dependencia y desarrollo en América Latina* (Mexico, 1969); T. Dos Santos, "The Structure of Dependence," *American Economic Review* (May 1970); J. Cotler and R. R. Fagen (eds.), *Latin America and the United States* (Stanford, Calif., 1974); A. G. Frank, *Latin America: Underdevelopment or Revolution* (New York, 1969); C. Furtado, *Obstacles to Development in Latin America* (New York, 1970); G. A. O'Donnell, *Modernization and Bureaucratic-Authoritarianism* (Berkeley, Calif., 1973); and O. Sunkel, "The Structural Background of Development Problems in Latin America," in C. T. Nisbet (ed.), *Latin America, Problems in Economic Development* (New York, 1969). The linkage politics approach is similar to dependency theory in describing the relationship between the United States and Latin America, but it places less emphasis on the economic aspects. See Douglas A. Chalmers, "Developing on the Periphera: External Factors in Latin American Politics," in James N. Rosenau (ed.), *Linkage Politics, Essays on the Convergence of National and International Systems* (New York, 1969).

8. Furtado, *Obstacles*, xvi.

9. Two Argentine economists who studied with Rostow suggest the difficulty of using this approach to understand development in Latin America. They argue that Argentina reached the takeoff stage during the first decade of the twentieth century and then, because it obviously did not take off as it was supposed to have done, they throw in another stage called the great delay. Rostow argues that Argentina reached the takeoff stage in the 1930s, yet it still has not taken off. See Guido Di Tella and Manuel Zymelman, *Las etapas del desarrollo económico argentino* (Buenos Aires, 1967).

10. David Ray, "The Dependency Model of Latin American Underdevelopment: Three Basic Fallacies," *Journal of Inter-American Studies* (February 1973). The entire issue of the journal is devoted to foreign investment and dependence in Latin America. For an interesting first attempt to measure dependence quantitatively, see Robert Kaufman, Harry J. Chernotsky,

and Daniel S. Geller, "A Preliminary Test of the Theory of Dependency," *Comparative Politics* (April 1975).

11. A good summary of the different ideological approaches to United States-Latin American relations, particularly in regard to the Alliance for Progress period, can be found in Abraham F. Lowenthal, "United States Policy Toward Latin America: 'Liberal,' 'Radical,' and 'Bureaucratic' Perspectives," *Latin American Research Review* (Fall 1973).

12. In addition to the works listed in note 7, see : Lloyd C. Gardner, *Economic Aspects of New Deal Diplomacy* (Madison, Wis., 1964); David Green, *The Containment of Latin America* (Chicago, 1971); Gabriel Kolko, *The Roots of American Foreign Policy* (Boston, 1969); Gabriel and Joyce Kolko, *The Limits of Power* (New York, 1972); Stanley J. and Barbara Stein, *The Colonial Heritage of Latin America* (New York, 1970); William A. Williams, *The Tragedy of American Diplomacy* (New York, 1962); Richard J. Barnet, *Intervention and Revolution* (New York, 1968) and *The Roots of War* (New York, 1972).

13. Stein, *Colonial Heritage.*

14. *The Rockefeller Report on the Americas* (Chicago, 1969), p. 39.

15. Arthur P. Whitaker, *The Western Hemisphere Idea* (Ithaca, N.Y., 1954).

chapter

2

The Creation of a United
States Empire in South
America: 1797–1945

For the past one hundred and fifty years United States government officials have linked the security and prosperity of the
United States with some kind of control over Latin America.
Until the end of the nineteenth century, however, the country was
preoccupied with internal problems (development, slavery, and so
on) and expansion into adjacent territories (Louisiana, Florida,
Texas, California, Northwest Territory), and it lacked the economic and military power to fulfill its aspiration to such extended
influence. England, France, and Spain intervened repeatedly with
impunity in nineteenth-century Latin America. As a result, the
United States could only stake a verbal claim on a Latin American empire, a claim that it would actually take up in the twentieth
century. As the United States gradually made good this claim, it
established its predominance first in northern Latin America
(Central America, Mexico, and the Caribbean) and then in South
America proper.

1797–1889: Staking a Claim on Empire
Regular United States contact with Latin American began in
the last decade of the eighteenth century. In 1797 the Spanish

government decreed that henceforth all neutral countries could trade in Spanish-American ports. The United States was ideally situated to take advantage of this decree, and trade with the Spanish colonies grew enormously after 1797. By 1811, 16 percent of United States foreign trade was with the Spanish-American colonies, and although this figure fluctuated, it was still at 13 percent a decade later.[1]

Latin America's successful struggle for independence (1810–1825) facilitated increased contacts between the two areas. The United States welcomed the Latin American independence movements as efforts to throw off the corrupt monarchical yoke of the European powers and to create a haven of republican liberty throughout the Western Hemisphere. As soon as the United States completed the purchase of Florida from Spain (1821), it recognized the newly independent countries of Latin America and sent official representatives to many of them. By 1824, five of the ten United States diplomatic legations were in Latin America: Buenos Aires, Bogotá, Santiago, Lima, and Mexico. The other five were in Europe.

The early Latin American policy of the United States—set forth by Thomas Jefferson, James Madison, James Monroe, Henry Clay, and John Quincy Adams—developed around the idea of an economic and political American system: America must be for the Americans and Europe should keep out. The United States government must devote its efforts to the promotion and maintenance of the political independence of the Western Hemisphere and to the development and protection of commerce and trade within the hemisphere.[2]

The Monroe Doctrine was the crystallization of a number of ideas that had developed over the preceding quarter of a century. Specifically, President Monroe and his Secretary of State John Quincy Adams were concerned about Russia's attempts to colonize the northwestern portion of the continent and about the Holy Alliance's efforts to move into the vacuum being created by the loss of Spain's American empire. Thus, in his annual message to Congress in 1823, President Monroe brashly asserted that Europe must not interfere in the Americas and that in return the United States would not interfere in Europe. To deal with the Russian threat he enunciated the non-colonization principle: "The American continents, by the free and independent conditions which they have assumed and maintain, are henceforth not to be considered as subjects for future colonization by any European powers." To warn the Holy Alliance, he set forth the principle of non-interference:

> We [the United States] should consider any attempt on their part [the European powers] to extend their system to any portion of this hemisphere as dangerous to our peace and safety. With the existing colonies or dependencies of any European power we have not interfered and shall not interfere. But with the governments who have declared their independence and maintained it, and whose independence we have, on great consideration and on just principles, acknowledged, we could not view any interposition for the purpose of oppressing them, or controlling in any other manner their destiny, by any European power, in any other light than as the manifestation of an unfriendly disposition toward the United States.[3]

President Monroe and the other formulators of the Doctrine were as concerned with European commercial and economic expansion as they were with colonization, and they viewed the Doctrine as a positive statement of America's claim to supremacy in the hemisphere; expansion of the United States into Latin America was not only inevitable, it was necessary for the security and prosperity of the country. The Monroe Doctrine was a unilateral statement of United States policy toward Latin America, a "manifestation of American empire," to use William Appleman Williams' words, an option on empire. The United States presumptuously spoke on behalf of Latin America when it told Europe to keep hands off. The Doctrine, in contrast, set no limits on United States colonization in Latin America.[4]

In spite of the strong language of the Monroe Doctrine, the frequent cases of European intervention in nineteenth-century Latin America reveal clearly the inability of the United States at the time to exercise its self-proclaimed option on the area. Initially the Monroe Doctrine did not even theoretically apply to South America, because the United States, with its internal preoccupations and its limited military power, could not possibly enforce it at such a great distance. For example, when England occupied the Islas Malvinas (Falkland Islands) in the early 1830s, Argentina contended that this constituted a violation of the Monroe Doctrine. The United States, however, said the Monroe Doctrine did not apply to the situation and refused to get involved. Similarly, the United States declined to invoke the Doctrine between 1838 and 1850, when the French and English repeatedly blockaded the Rio de la Plata. In his annual message to Congress in 1845 President James Polk formally confirmed the geographical limitations of the Doctrine:

> The present is deemed a proper occasion to reiterate and reaffirm the principle avowed by Mr. Monroe. . . . The reassertion of this principle, *especially in reference to North America,* is . . . but the promulgation of a policy which no European power should cherish the disposition to resist. Existing rights of every European nation should be respected; but it is due alike to our safety and our interests, that the efficient protection of our laws should be extended over our whole territorial limits, and that . . . no future European colony or dominion shall, with our consent, be planted or established *on any part of the North American continent.*[5]

Even on the North American continent the United States had difficulty enforcing the Monroe Doctrine. During the 1830s and 1840s England continued to expand her already considerable influence in Central America with little regard for United States aspirations. Yet the logistics of the situation favored the United States, and in 1850 the two contenders worked out a compromise in the Clayton-Bulwer Treaty. Both agreed that they would not seek exclusive control over an isthmic canal or railroad, nor would they occupy, colonize, or exercise dominion over any part of Central America. English influence in Central America declined somewhat after 1850, but England remained a formidable rival of the United States in the area throughout the second half of the nineteenth century.

Several European powers took advantage of the Civil War in the United States to intervene in northern Latin America. In May 1861 Spain annexed the strife-torn Dominican Republic with the consent of the shaky government of that country. Secretary of State William H. Seward strongly protested this action but was forced to back down when Spain informed him that the annexation "is a *fait accompli,* which Spain will maintain by all the means in her power." [6] In 1865, after four years of frustrating and costly rule and with the Civil War in the United States coming to a close, Spain withdrew. The Dominican Republic became "independent" under the effective tutelage of its increasingly powerful northern neighbor.

Even closer to the border of the United States, the French intervened in Mexico and set up a European noble as emperor. At the end of 1861 the French, along with the English and the Spanish, occupied the Mexican port of Veracruz to collect outstanding debts in default. England and Spain quickly settled with Mexico and withdrew. The French under Napoleon III, however, refused to settle with the government, supported the conservative faction in a bloody Mexican civil war, eventually captured Mexico City, and in 1864 set up Archduke Maximilian of Austria as emperor of Mexico. During the American Civil War the United States could do little to oppose this operation, but with the end of the war the United States successfully exerted pressure on the French to withdraw. Maximilian, no longer supported by French soldiers, was shortly overthrown and executed by the liberal Mexican faction under the leadership of Benito Juárez.[7]

In retrospect, the successful removal of the Spanish from the Dominican Republic and the French from Mexico seems to have been a significant turning point regarding the ability of the United States to apply the Monroe Doctrine on the North American continent. With the Civil War over and an increasingly powerful northern industrial elite in control of the country, the United States was ready and able to exercise its option on a Latin American empire. United States influence increased so rapidly during the decades after 1865 that in 1881 the United States Consul in Cuba could report that "Cuba has become commercially a dependency of the United States, while still remaining a political dependency of Spain."[8]

Nevertheless, United States influence was still for the most part confined to northern Latin America. When the United States attempted to mediate between Chile on the one hand and Peru and Bolivia on the other during the War of the Pacific (1879–1883), it failed. Believing that England was supporting Chile, the United States backed Peru and Bolivia in order "to gain for American capitalists the opportunity to challenge British preeminence in the west coast countries of South America." United States efforts came to naught and the conflict was settled without its participation. The United States suffered a humiliating loss of prestige and influence. The English gained even more influence by backing the winner and the dominant power in the area, Chile.[9]

1890 to 1933: Exercising the Option

The 1890s represent something of a turning point in the history of United States-Latin American relations in that the United States seriously began to exercise the option on empire staked out nearly seventy years before. By 1890 the United States had successfully developed a dynamic industrial economy but was finding that such an economy created new problems as well as new wealth. Cyclical expansion and contraction, depressions, unemployment, surplus capital, and surplus goods combined to produce serious tensions within society. Furthermore, there was a widespread belief that the internal frontier—the escape valve—no longer existed. Gradually important segments of the economic and political elite developed the conviction that foreign expansion—new foreign markets and investment opportunities—could solve the social, political, and economic problems created by rapid industrialization.[10] The tradition of expansion—the acquisition of Louisiana, Florida, Texas, California, and Alaska—went back to the earliest years of the country's existence, but the dislocations associated with rapid industrialization during the decades following the Civil War gave a sense of urgency and special meaning to this process.

There was widespread agreement among government officials and businessmen on the need for foreign expansion, but they did not agree on how to pursue this objective or how best to protect overseas commercial interests. Some argued that the United States must obtain formal colonies in various parts of the world. Others believed that a series of strategic bases would enable the country to compete successfully with the government-supported European enterprises in Asia and Latin America. Nevertheless, there was a broad consensus that the United States, in one form or another, should expand abroad.

To carry out its expansionist policy, the United States developed its navy. After the Civil War the size of the navy declined, but in 1883 the government began to reverse this trend, and in 1890 Congress authorized the construction of a battleship. During the 1890s the revival of the navy was in full swing.

One of the first tasks for the new navy was to protect United States commercial interests during the 1893–1894 Civil War in Brazil. The Brazilian conflict broke out in September 1893, and, as President Grover Cleveland stated in his annual message to Congress in January 1894, the conflict "found the United States alert to watch the interests of our citizens in that country [Brazil] . . . with which we carry on important commerce. . . ." [11] At the time of the outbreak of conflict, there were a half dozen foreign, but no American, warships in the harbor at Rio. The United States government immediately sent three ships to Rio and they proceeded to break a blockade of the harbor.

The United States alone among the foreign powers used its navy to protect its growing commerce with Brazil. And as Thomas L. Thompson, the United States representative in Rio, reported at the end of the conflict: "Business is improving, and now that the war is ended, I shall be able to give more particular attention to the development and expansion of our commercial relations with Brazil. The field is a profitable one and I hope in time to be able to cultivate it to the satisfaction of the Department."

At the same time the United States initiated the Pan American movement to facilitate its economic expansion. James G. Blaine, while secretary of state in the Garfield Administration, saw that the increasing accumulation of domestic capital would necessitate a search for foreign investment opportunities and that industrialization had produced and was continuing to produce large surpluses of goods. Latin America was, in Blaine's vision, an ideal area for United States economic expansion. The vision was partially transformed into reality some years later when Blaine, as William Henry Harrison's secretary of state, presided over the first Pan-American Conference in Washington in 1889. Blaine urged the Latin Americans, among other things, to form a customs union with the United States. Although the Latins rejected Blaine's idea, the growing economic and political power of the United States enabled it to dominate succeeding conferences and to focus the meetings on economic matters. [12]

The Venezuelan-British Guiana boundary dispute of 1894–1895 revealed more clearly than any other situation that the United States had established its control over northern Latin America and much of South America. When the English rejected United States arbitration, Secretary of State Richard Olney sent a strong note to London insisting that the Monroe Doctrine applied to the dispute. The Monroe Doctrine, Olney wrote, had to be respected because

> . . . the safety and welfare of the United States are so concerned with the maintenance of the independence of every American state as to justify and require the interposition of the United States whenever that independence is endangered. . . . Today the United States is practically sovereign on this continent, and its fiat is law upon the subjects to which it confines its interposition. Why? It is not because of the pure friendship or goodwill felt for it. It is not simply by reason of its high character as a civilized state, nor because wisdom and justice and equity are the invariable characteristics of the dealings of the United States. It is because, in addition to all other grounds, its infinite resources combined with its isolated position render it master of the situation and practically invulnerable as against any or all other powers. All the advantages of this superiority are at once imperiled if the principle be admitted that European powers may convert American states into colonies or provinces of their own.[13]

The importance of this confict is that the United States intervened on the basis of the Monroe Doctrine, and although the British initially challenged the right of the United States to intervene, they later backed down and accepted arbitration of the dispute. In so doing the British acknowledged United States supremacy in Latin America at least as far south as Venezuela. Since by this time England was the only European power capable of challenging the United States in the area, English recognition of United States supremacy was tantamount to general recognition of this fact. In future situations, such as the Venezuelan crisis of 1902–1903, the European powers sought and obtained prior approval of the United States before they intervened in a Latin American country.

The war between Spain and the United States in 1898 was an important step in the expansion of United States control over Latin America. The war and its aftermath resulted not only in the United States' annexation of Hawaii, the Philippines, and Puerto Rico, and the substitution of United States for Spanish control over Cuba, but also marked the end of the phase of expansion via the acquisition of territory. Henceforth, United States policy makers operated on the assumption that regarding Latin America the country could expand its influence, control markets, support investment, and protect its security without direct colonization.

United States imperial expansion did not stop; it simply changed its form. During the first three decades of the twentieth century the United States did not seek colonies in Latin America, but it exercised its influence in Mexico, the Caribbean, and northern South America through a policy frequently referred to as "dollar diplomacy"; it resorted to such things as the Platt Amendment, enormous capital investments, the separation of Panama from Colombia, and frequent military interventions in Cuba, the Dominican Republic, Haiti, Mexico, and Nicaragua.

The Roosevelt Corollary of 1904 formalized the new imperialism by proclaiming that the United States had the responsibility under the Monroe Doctrine to intervene in Latin America in order to avoid any pretext for European intervention in the hemisphere. President Theodore Roosevelt, obviously shouldering the white man's burden, justified such preemptive intervention in the following imperious and moralistic terms:

> If a nation shows that it knows how to act with reasonable efficiency and decency in social and political matters; if it keeps order and pays its obligations, it need fear no interference from the United States. Chronic wrongdoing, or an impotence which results in a general loosening of the ties of civilized society, may in America, as elsewhere, ultimately require intervention by some civilized nation, and in the Western Hemisphere the adherence of the United States to the Monroe Doctrine, may force the United States, however reluctantly, in flagrant cases of such wrongdoing or impotence, to the exercise of an international police power.

World War I greatly facilitated United States economic expansion in Latin America and also significantly reduced English influence in the area. As World War I cut off Europe from Latin America, the Latin Americans were forced to turn to the United States for vital supplies and to trade on terms dictated by the United States. The figures on trade and investment clearly demonstrate the growing influence of the United States and its replacement of England as the leading financial power in Latin America. United States investments in northern Latin America (mostly in Mexico and Cuba) increased nearly five times from 1897 to

1913–1914 (from $266 million to $1,276 billion) and increased another 85 percent (to $2,356 billion) by 1928–1929. Furthermore, during World War I United States investments in northern Latin America surpassed those of England.

More dramatic, however, was the increase in United States investments in South America during the same period. In 1897 United States investments in South America totaled an insignificant $38 million. By 1913–1914 this figure had jumped nearly ten times to $366 million (mostly in Chile) and increased nearly ten times again to just over $3 billion in 1928–1929 (mainly in Argentina, Chile, Brazil, and Venezuela). Since the British had increased their already substantial investments in South America only slightly during the period, the United States had by 1928–1929 gone a long way toward catching up with them (Table 2–1).

The trade figures reveal a pattern that is essentially the same (Table 2–2). United States trade with Latin America increased enormously between 1913 and 1927, particularly its trade with South America. At the same time, English trade with the area, which already was considerable, increased only slightly. The result was that by 1927 the value of United States trade with northern Latin America was seven times that of the British, and the value of its South American trade had surpassed that of the British.

The growth of foreign branches of United States banks in Latin America confirms the dramatic pattern of United States economic expansion during and after World War I. Frank A. Vanderlip, president of the National City Bank of New York from 1906 to 1919, led the fight to establish United States banks in Latin America. Latin America was a desirable field for such expansion, Vanderlip believed, because it was underdeveloped: it could absorb large quantities of United States manufactured goods and provide needed agricultural products and raw materials; it exported more to the United States than it imported from it; and its local banks were not involved in financing foreign trade and promoting foreign investment. The two major barriers to such expansion were the powerful English and German banks and the laws of the United States which prohibited national banks from establishing foreign branches. World War I, by cutting Latin America off from Europe, resolved the first problem. The passage of the Federal Reserve Act in 1913, which permitted United States

TABLE 2-1

Private Foreign Investment in Latin America
(in millions)

Year	United States				English				Latin America as % of Total Private Foreign United States
	South America	%	Northern Latin America	%	South America	%	Northern Latin America	%	
1890					$1,540* (Argentina)	73	$479 (Mexico)	23	
1897	$38	12.5	$266 (Mexico)	87.5					
1913–14	$366 (Chile)	22	$1,276 (Mexico, Cuba)	78	$3,588 (Argentina, Brazil)	73	$1,104 (Mexico)	22	
1928–29	$3,014 (Argentina, Brazil, Chile, Venezuela)	56	$2,356 (Mexico, Cuba)	44	$4,349 (Argentina, Brazil)	75	$1,228 (Mexico)	22	
1929**	$1,543	45	$1,919	55					47
1939–40	$1,542 (Argentina, Brazil)	57	$1,154 (Mexico, Cuba)	43	$3,910 (Argentina, Brazil)	78	$1,000 (Mexico)	20	39

									Chile, Venezuela)
1949–50	$2,957 (Argentina, Brazil, Chile, Venezuela)	67	$1,488 (Mexico, Cuba)	33	$1,342 (Brazil)	65	$668 (Mexico)	32	40
1960	$5,940 (Brazil, Venezuela)	79	$1,545	21					23
1970	$8,572 (Argentina, Brazil, Venezuela)	70	$3,631	30					16

* Figures include direct and portfolio investment in millions of U.S. dollars. The British pound was converted to dollars at $4.86/pound up to 1939–40, at $4.44/pound for 1939–40, at $3.68/pound for 1949–50.
** United States investment figures include direct investment only from 1929 on.

Sources: United Nations, Economic Commission for Latin America, *External Financing in Latin America* (New York, 1965); J. Fred Rippy, *British Investments in Latin America, 1822–1949* (Minneapolis, 1959); Max Winkler, *Investments of U.S. Capital in Latin America* (Boston, 1929); U.S. Department of Commerce, *Statistical Abstract of the United States* (Washington, D.C., 1961, 1971).

TABLE 2-2

Latin American Foreign Trade

(Combined value of exports and imports—in millions)

Year	South America			Northern Latin America			%* United States	%** World
	Total	United States	England	Total	United States	England		
1913	$2,313	$381 (Argentina, Brazil)	$595 (Argentina, Brazil, Chile)	$688	$436 (Cuba, Mexico)	$83 (Cuba, Mexico)	21	
1927	$3,825	$991 (Argentina, Brazil)	$742 (Argentina)	$1,314	$792 (Cuba, Mexico)	$113 (Cuba, Mexico)	20	
1938	$2,523	$561 (Argentina, Brazil, Venezuela)	$475‡ (Argentina)	$693	$394 (Cuba, Mexico)	——	19	6.5

1948	$9,500	$3,472 (Argentina, Brazil, Venezuela)	$1,163‡ (Argentina)	$2,949	$2,125 (Cuba, Mexico)	——	29	10.3
1958	$11,558	$4,520 (Brazil, Venezuela)	$1,184‡ (Argentina)	$4,790	$3,191 (Cuba, Mexico)	——	25	7.4
1970	$20,326	$6,009 (Brazil, Venezuela)	——	$9,138	$4,441 (Mexico)	——	12.6	4.6

* United States-Latin American trade as percent of total United States trade.

** Latin American trade as percent of world trade.

‡ Total Latin American trade with England listed under South America.

Sources: Max Winkler, *Investments of U.S. Capital in Latin America* (Boston, 1929); U.S. Department of Commerce, *Statistical Abstract of the United States* (Washington, D.C., various years); United Nations, *Yearbook of International Trade Statistics, 1970–1971* (New York, 1973); Brian R. Mitchell and H. G. Jones, *Second Abstract of British Historical Statistics* (Cambridge, 1971).

banks to establish foreign branches, resolved the second. By 1920 the National City Bank had established fifty-six branches in Latin America: twenty-one in South America, thirty-four in the Caribbean, and one in Central America. However, with the resumption of British competition after the war and the postwar depression, National City Bank was forced to close some of its Latin American branches. The efforts of Vanderlip, nevertheless, had helped undermine European economic predominance in Latin America and had supported the enormous expansion of United States trade and investment in the area.[15]

Latin American concern over the dramatic expansion of United States economic and political influence in the area grew steadily throughout this period. In 1893, at the same time United States warships arrived in Rio to protect United States commercial interests, a Brazilian, Eduardo Prado, published *The American Illusion*. This book was immediately suppressed by the Brazilian government because it attacked the government's slavish imitation of everything American, the economic aggressiveness of the United States, the Pan-American movement, and the Monroe Doctrine.[16]

In Argentina Manuel Ugarte wrote a series of books between 1910 and 1917 critical of the growing United States influence. He cited as examples the war with Mexico, the separation of Panama from Colombia, the seizure of Cuba and Puerto Rico from Spain, and the interventions in Cuba, the Dominican Republic, Haiti, Mexico, and Nicaragua. The unification of Latin America and the concomitant rejection of Pan-American unity, he argued, was the only way to protect the political, economic, and cultural independence of Argentina and the other Latin American countries. Furthermore, Ugarte was one of the first Latin Americans to urge government protection for national industry. "The country that exports only raw materials and imports foreign manufactured products," he warned in 1910, "will always be a country in the intermediate stage of its evolution." [17]

Others, such as the Argentines José Ingenieros and Alfredo Palacios, the Peruvians José Carlos Mariátegui and Victor Raul Haya de la Torre, the Cuban José Martí, the Nicaraguan Rubén Darío, and the Uruguayan José Enrique Rodó, also voiced the mounting criticism of United States expansion. Furthermore, opposition to the United States was manifested at the various Pan-

American Conferences in 1901, 1906, 1910, 1923, and 1928, but the United States was easily able to thwart any efforts to curb its actions.

1933–1945: Modifications to Preserve the Empire

During the early decades of the twentieth century the United States gained sufficient economic and political power to establish its control over northern Latin America and most of South America. The United States used its growing economic power and alliances with sympathetic local elites to secure its influence in the area. But the dominant method of maintaining control was military force or the threat of force. By the 1920s, however, it became increasingly clear that there were serious limits to the use of force to maintain influence in Latin America.

In the first place, force was not particularly effective in resolving the problems that prompted its use. Military intervention frequently became more necessary every time it was used. The United States intervened in Cuba from 1898–1901, 1906–1909, and 1917–1922. Between 1898 and 1920 it felt compelled to intervene militarily twenty separate times in the Caribbean area alone. Second, for logistical reasons, military intervention was difficult, if not impossible, in much of South America. Third, the traditional rationale for military intervention no longer seemed applicable. By the 1920s the United States was unchallenged in northern Latin America and was the dominant power in most of South America. There no longer existed any external menace to justify the policeman role. And finally, the reliance on force to control Latin America had undesirable implications for American interests in other parts of the world. How, for example, could the United States condemn Japanese intervention in Manchuria if it did the same thing in Latin America? Thus, toward the end of the 1920s and during the early 1930s United States policy makers came to reject the use of force and sought to develop more tactful and sophisticated alternatives to influence Latin America.[18]

The Good Neighbor Policy resulted from these efforts. Its first stage was essentially negative—renouncing military intervention. At the Seventh International Conference of American States, which met in Montevideo in December 1933, Secretary of State Cordell Hull accepted the Latin American proposition that "no state has the right to intervene in the internal or external affairs of another," with the only qualification being that the United States reserved its rights under the law of nations as generally recognized. Three years later President Franklin Roosevelt personally attended the Inter-American Conference for the Maintenance of Peace in Buenos Aires at which the American states reaffirmed, unequivocally, the non-intervention doctrine adopted at Montevideo.[19]

At no point was intervention defined. To the United States, intervention simply meant the use of armed force, and non-intervention therefore meant the rejection of the use of armed force. Intervention, however, had a broader meaning for most of the Latin American states; to them it meant the use of *any means* to exert pressure on a state to change a policy against its will. This difference in definition, for the most part ignored or unnoticed at the time, was to be the source of future difficulties.

——The second and positive stage of the Good Neighbor Policy emerged gradually in the 1930s and early 1940s. This was a policy of reciprocity, of exchanging favors; the United States would do something the Latin Americans wanted and in return the Latin Americans would do something the United States wanted. It was based on the recognition that the United States' rejection of intervention was not sufficient in and of itself to bring about full Latin American cooperation.

The idea germinated at Montevideo where Hull reaffirmed and strengthened Hoover's renunciation of the Roosevelt Corollary. In return he obtained support for the so-called Montevideo Program, a program that facilitated bilateral Latin American-United States trade agreements based on the exchange of raw materials for manufactured goods. The newly established United States Export-Import Bank would provide the dollar credits necessary for such trade and thus, for the first time, brought the government directly into such arrangements. The Montevideo Program was followed by the Reciprocal Trade Agreement Act of 1934 which mitigated the crippling effect of existing tariff legislation on United States-Latin American trade by allowing the President to raise or lower tariffs by as much as 50 percent in exchange for similar concessions. During the next few years the United States signed trade agreements with ten Latin American countries.

Trade was only part of the problem for the Latin Americans. They not only wanted support for increased trade but also aid to industrialize and develop their economies. The 1930s was the first period of sustained industrialization in Latin America. The protection offered by World War I had given temporary stimulus to local industry in some countries, but it was not until the depression decade that industry became permanently important. A number of writers have pointed out that the industrialization of the 1930s was "accidental," "a by-product of contingencies originating outside the Latin American economies and their centers of decision." "The protectionist instruments used were not principally directed toward the encouragement of industry, but towards the defense of the balance of payments." Yet if industrialization originally came to Latin America more as the result of historical accident rather than of conscious design, its importance for the Latin American elites once it has been introduced must not be underestimated. The urban middle classes and increasingly the commercial and agricultural elites personally profited from industrialization, and "they had a vague hope that industrialization would perform painlessly and automatically the social transformation [of their societies] they had not been able to bring about themselves." Thus, they sought United States help to develop their industry.[20]   1943139

The fact that Latin America's bargaining position vis-à-vis the United States was good during the late 1930s facilitated such efforts. The United States was concerned about growing economic nationalism in the area; Bolivia expropriated the holdings of Standard Oil in 1937, Mexico expropriated American-owned oil properties in 1938, and Venezuela and Colombia threatened to do the same. Most importantly, Germany and Japan were competing with the United States for Latin American cooperation, and the approach of the war added a security dimension to this competition. Franklin Roosevelt thus embarked on a new phase of reciprocity that gave Latin Americans an increased share in economic decision making and in the profits of trade and investment. As he explained in January 1940: "That is a new approach that I am talking about to these South American things. Give them a share. They think they are just as good as we are, and many of them are." [21] A few months later the United States Export-Import Bank agreed to finance equipment for the Volta Redonda steel mill in Brazil. The United States had extended the concept of reciprocity to include development loans through the Export-Import Bank.

United States officials had gradually come to accept limited government support for Latin American development on the grounds that this was in the best interests of the United States. As one author summarized, the assumptions of the new policy were: (1) trade will develop more rapidly with countries where the production of semi-finished and finished manufactured goods (light industry) as well as raw materials is encouraged; (2) direct and portfolio investment will increase more rapidly in relatively prosperous as opposed to subsistence economies; and (3) the creation of a strong middle class will promote stability and security.[22]

The assumptions underlying the "give them a share" policy are of particular significance because they have continued to underlie United States-Latin American policy ever since. Yet the emergence of these assumptions and the new policy did not mean that the United States believed it any less necessary to maintain its control over Latin America. The United States did renounce the use of armed intervention and it did give Latin America an increased share in economic decision making and domestic profits. But it was the United States acting unilaterally upon Latin America and not two equal or nearly equal partners negotiating mutual concerns. The Good Neighbor Policy embodied new indirect methods of influence, but it remained a policy of control.

How the United States operated in a specific situation to exercise and maintain its influence depended on three things: the strength and stability of the government involved, international competition, and particularly on the availability of alternatives. Thus, the United States might use a combination of financial incentives (trade agreements, aid, and so on) and discriminatory practices (withheld aid, quotas, non-recognition) to achieve its objectives and at the same time remain always mindful of the alternatives open to the government involved.

The situations surrounding the expropriation or threat of expropriation of United States-owned oil companies in Latin America during the late 1930s provide a good example of how the United States operated during the Good Neighbor period and of how United States policy evolved more sophisticated mechanisms of control. On March 13, 1937, the Bolivian government expropriated the holdings of Standard Oil and made no effort to compensate the company for its former property. The United States government, well aware that Bolivia lacked political stability or an alternate source of financial and technological aid, proceeded to apply various forms of pressure on the Bolivian government to settle the matter favorably for Standard Oil. The United States tried to prevent Bolivia's immediate neighbors (Argentina, Peru, and Chile) from helping it to exploit and market the oil and refused to extend the loans and technical assistance essential to the production and marketing of the oil. In time, United States policy helped produce the desired results. The recalcitrant Bolivian government was overthrown and the new administration quickly reached a settlement with Standard Oil. The next day, new United States economic aid to Bolivia was announced.[23]

In 1938 Mexico expropriated the holdings of American and British oil companies. The United States oil companies instituted a marketing and shipping boycott of Mexican oil and a general boycott by United States firms trading with Mexico. The Mexican government, unlike the Bolivian government, had widespread popular support for its action and it also threatened to sell oil to Germany. As a result, a settlement favorable to the Mexicans was reached.

The United States had "won" in Bolivia and "lost" in Mexico, but in both cases United States concerns had lost their property and the situations had strained United States-Latin American relations. With the coming of World War II, for which it needed the support and cooperation of Latin America, the United States therefore developed a new policy toward expropriation. Essentially the policy consisted of increased government involvement in the potential conflict to assure a negotiated settlement before expropriation took place.

In 1935 Juan Vicente Gomez, dictator of Venezuela since 1909 and protector of the foreign-owned oil companies, died. The new president, Gomez's last minister of war, Eleazar López Contreras (1935–1941), although by no means a radical reformer, permitted labor unions to function, Congress to pass a law establishing an eight-hour day and collective bargaining procedures, and the passage of a constitutional amendment that enabled the imposition of an export tax. Furthermore, he sought to make the oil companies pay their back taxes and to give Venezuela a greater share of the oil profits. The oil companies became alarmed and defensive. As United States Ambassador to Venezuela Frank P. Corrigan noted in late 1939, "the situation has now developed into one in which the government keeps pressing to obtain more revenues while the companies keep fighting a bitter rearguard action against what they feel are unfair attacks." [24] Mindful of the recent Bolivian and Mexican actions, the United States government became concerned that Venezuela and even other Latin American countries might follow suit. Thus, the United States government became actively involved in the situation and initiated negotiations to prevent expropriation before it happened. The oil companies made significant concessions to Venezuela, there was no expropriation, and United States-Venezuelan relations improved.

The United States response to Brazil's efforts to build a steel mill also reveals the evolution of United States policy during the late 1930s. Brazil, anxious to develop its economy, sought to construct its own steel mill. The United States, however, was not enthusiastic about the idea because it believed Brazil would do better if it exported raw materials and agricultural products and bought manufactured steel abroad. After an extended series of negotiations with private United States concerns had failed to produce the necessary financial and technological assistance to build the mill, Brazilian President Getulio Vargas issued an ultimatum to the United States: either the United States would support Brazil's efforts to build a steel mill, or Brazil would go to the Germans. Shortly thereafter, the Export-Import Bank issued a $17 million credit to Brazil for equipment to construct and operate the mill.[25]

By the time the United States became involved in World War II it had evolved more subtle and sophisticated methods of exercising its control over South America. World War II, like World War I, gave the United States an opportunity to extend its influence in Latin America. The United States believed it essential to its security to hold Latin America in line, but the Latin Americans were ambivalent in their response to the United States. On the one hand, most saw the necessity of cooperating with the United States for the security of all. On the other hand, many feared the extension of United States influence.

As in World War I, the economic options open to Latin America were severely curtailed, and the United States took full advantage of the situation to strengthen its influence in the region. The economic dislocations caused by the war were serious; Chile, for example, lost the important Italian market for its major export, copper, and Argentina lost its main sources of coal in Europe. As a result, the United States was able to replace Europe as the major supplier and customer of Latin America. In 1938 approximately 55 percent of Latin American exports went to Europe and 44 percent of its imports came from Europe. In 1944, however, the figures had dropped to 20 percent and 7 percent respectively. At the same time, the United States accounted for more than half of Latin American exports and imports.[26]

— The United States needed Latin American help and support during the war (raw materials, prevention of Axis infiltration, military bases, and so on) and therefore had to prevent the collapse of the Latin American economies. It thus provided Latin America with limited supplies of essential materials and absorbed some of the unmarketable surpluses. But the United States' primary concern was with the countries directly involved in the war, so Latin America received little help for economic development. Most enjoyed a favorable balance of trade with the United States and Europe, but there were few goods they could buy and the dollar and sterling credits they received simply accumulated in the national treasuries. Furthermore, Latin America's percent of United States aid was very small. Before the war, Latin America had received nearly 50 percent of all Export-Import Bank loans. During the war it received only one percent of these loans. In addition, it received only one percent of Lend-Lease aid.[27] To make matters worse for the Latin Americans, United States aid was channeled into the production of raw materials and not into economic diversification and industrialization. The war-created shortages stimulated local consumer industries, but there was little aid to help create heavy industry and to develop a balanced economy.

Despite misgivings regarding increased United States influence, economic dislocations and shortages, and a lack of substantial financial aid, the Latin American countries did support the United States during the war. They did so not only because of the obvious Axis threat, but also because they believed they would be rewarded with aid for development after the war was over. During the two years preceding Pearl Harbor, many Latin American governments, and particularly those of South America, sought to maintain an officially neutral stance and avoid involvement in the deepening world confrontation. At the same time they cooperated with the United States in a number of areas. At the Panama Foreign Ministers Conference in 1939 the representatives of the Latin American countries established the Inter-American Economic and Financial Advisory Commission and the Inter-American Development Committee to coordinate efforts to deal with some of the major economic problems confronting the hemisphere. At Havana a year later they agreed to prohibit the transfer of European colonies in America from one power to another, and they permitted the United States to establish bases on their territory and cooperated in the effort to eradicate Axis infiltration.

After Pearl Harbor the threat of the Axis was perceived by all except Argentina as a threat to the entire hemisphere, and as long as the threat continued, the Latin Americans went along with the United States. Old enemies, such as Manuel Seoane of Peru and Ramón Grau San Martín of Cuba, supported the United States. At Rio in January 1942 all of the Latin American countries except Argentina and Chile severed relations with the Axis. Chile severed relations in 1943 and Argentina in 1944. The war represented a high point in Inter-American solidarity as was concisely expressed by Guatemalan President Juan José Arévalo in March 1945: "Thanks to the power of the United States the war is being kept far away from our soil." [28]

The Chapultepec Conference: A Frustrated Call for Development

The Inter-American Conference on the Problems of War and Peace (the Chapultepec Conference), which met in Mexico City from February 21 to March 8, 1945, represented something of a watershed between the past and the future. It met just before the death of Roosevelt and at a time when all knew that the Allies would win the war with Germany and Japan. The conference was, on the one hand, the culmination of the wartime unity and collaboration between the United States and Latin America for mutual protection. One author summed up with only slight exaggeration: "During World War II the New World attained the high point of solidarity which had been envisioned for it by Henry Clay a century and a quarter earlier. . . . It [solidarity] now came to include not only expanded trade relations but also financial, military, political, and particularly moral cooperation." [29]

Yet the Chapultepec Conference also manifested the division between the United States and Latin America. As victory approached and the external threat receded, the unity so often verbalized seemed to be slipping away. The United States was concerned primarily with global problems, such as the creation of an international organization to keep the peace and the reestablishment of the prewar trading structure. Its priorities were the reconstruction of Europe and the international free trade economy.

— Latin America, on the other hand, was concerned about its own economic development and particularly about protecting and expanding the local industry established during the war. The Latin Americans were distrustful of the intentions of the big powers both on political and economic issues. They wanted a say as to the nature of the postwar world and did not want the United States or any other big power to be able to undermine or restrict their efforts to develop. Their concerns were essentially regional and economic. They believed they had sacrificed a great deal during the war for the common cause (supplied raw materials to the United States and the Allies, accepted shortages of goods, and postponed major economic development) and were now entitled to their just rewards. Thus, the stage was set for a clash of interests that has continued for the most part to this day.

As the end of the war approached, Latin America began to push hard for the recognition of regional organizations in the postwar order. Most reasoned that a strong regional organization in the Western Hemisphere would give Latin America a priority claim to United States help. Secretary of State Cordell Hull, however, favored the creation of a strong world organization with all regional organizations subordinated to it. He thus insisted that an Inter-American Conference to discuss postwar international organizations be postponed until the big powers could meet and settle the issue among themselves. The Chapultepec Conference was in accordance postponed until after the Moscow meeting of the Big Four foreign ministers (the United States, Russia, England, and France) in November 1943 and the Dumbarton Oaks Conference in mid-1944. When the conference was finally convened, the Latin Americans were annoyed at the long delay and frustrated because they had not previously been consulted on matters so important to their future.

On the second day of the conference, United States Secretary of State Edward R. Stettinius, Jr., set forth the basic objectives of United States foreign policy for the coming years. The United

States wanted the earliest possible defeat of the Axis and "to in-sure that neither Germany nor Japan will ever again have the mil-itary or industrial capacity to make war," to build a world "in which the right of every nation to develop free institutions accord-ing to its own desire will be upheld," to create an international or-ganization to insure the peace of the world and thus to use the power of the great nations "in the interests of peace and freedom of all nations," and to build a peace that offered all peoples assur-ances of "freedom from fear and want." The latter objective, Stet-tinius emphasized, is not a "rhetorical assertion of vague inten-tions. . . . We cannot, of course, accomplish this purpose overnight . . . . [but] the United States intends to propose and support meas-ures for closer cooperation among us [the American states] in public health, nutrition and food supply, labor, education, science, freedom of information, transportation, and in economic develop-ment, including industrialization and the modernization of agriculture." [30]

In these general terms it was difficult for the Latin Americans to disagree with Stettinius' objectives. Yet as the conference pro-ceeded, it became quite clear that there was considerable disagree-ment over the specific meaning of these objectives and the priority given to each of them. Of the 155 draft resolutions submitted to the conference, 61 final resolutions, compromise statements, were hammered out by six separate committees. A close examination of the draft and final resolutions reveals the wide area of disagree-ment between the United States and Latin America.

Committee I, which dealt with cooperation in the war effort, had little difficulty reaching agreement. Essentially, it reaffirmed and extended the agreements regarding the war that had been reached three years before at Rio. It recommended that a perma-nent inter-American military agency be created in the future and that the existing Inter-American Defense Board continue until such an agency might be established. It also made suggestions on control of arms, war crimes, and subversive activities. [31]

Committee II, chaired by Stettinius, dealt with the establish-ment of a world organization. The main work of this committee was *Resolution XVI: On the Establishment of a General Interna-tional Organization,* which, as the United States wanted, accepted the Dumbarton Oaks proposals as the basis for setting up the new international organization. It also included seven points of agreement among the Latin American states that the United States was not particularly anxious to include, but which the Latin Americans insisted be taken into consideration in the final formulation of the organization. The Latin Americans' greatest concerns were to make the General Assembly of the new organization truly representative, to allow for the effective continuation of inter-American methods and procedures, and to assure adequate Latin American representation on the Security Council. Although the Latin Americans were resentful because they had not been consulted regarding the Dumbarton Oaks proposals and were concerned about their role vis-à-vis the big powers in the future world organization, there was little open controversy in the proceedings of this committee.

Committee III, which discussed the inter-American system, produced two important resolutions. The first, known as the *Act of Chapultepec* and entitled *Reciprocal Assistance and American Solidarity,* provided for mutual defense against internal or external aggression. The other resolution strengthened the inter-American system by providing for regular conferences and for upgrading the Pan-American Union. As was true in the proceedings of the two previous committees, there was little conflict between the United States and Latin America.

Significantly, the basic disagreements between the United States and Latin America emerged during the sessions of Committees IV and V, which dealt respectively with economic and social problems. The two committees met jointly a number of times and discussed many common matters. The disagreements were so serious and time-consuming that Committee IV did not finish its business until March 7, just one day before the end of the conference. The American delegation reported: "These resolutions [of Committee IV] are the result of protracted discussions which were made necessary by very considerable sentiment among the other American Republics in favor of many restrictive measures designed to protect their war developed industries together with industries which they hoped to see developed in the future." [32] The major conflicts that arose concerned the issues of economic development, industrialization, and trade.

The conflict on these issues was anticipated in the pre-conference memos between United States officials in Mexico City and those in Washington. There was some difference of opinion be-

tween officials in the two cities, but it was a difference of emphasis rather than one of substance. At the end of January 1945, less
than a month before the conference was to open, economic adviser Merwin L. Bohan sent two memos to Washington attempting
to "crystallize" the thinking of the State Department regarding the
economic well-being of Latin America. Bohan argued that the
United States definitely had "more than a minimum responsibility
in the interim and in the early postwar period. We asked for and
obtained the help of Latin America in the prosecution of the war
—Latin America will ask, and we must give, help in the transition from war to peace." [33]

The kind of help Bohan had in mind was to "furnish the leadership in a cooperative effort to assure Latin America of at least
its prewar exports of products essential to the economic life of the
countries of this hemisphere." The United States, he argued,
would have to coordinate the effort to help Latin America rees-
tablish its prewar markets in Europe because "Latin America cannot prosper in peace times without an equitable share of the European market." Nevertheless, Bohan suggested limits to this
cooperation; he believed that the United States had to "assure
Latin America of at least its prewar exports" of twenty basic
commodities, and no more. Thus, he argued, "collective responsibility ends when Brazil is assured of a reasonable market at reasonable prices for its coffee, cotton, meats, hides, and corn. Hot-
house, war-induced industries—such as rubber—are the
responsibility of Brazil alone. . . ." [34] Bohan recommended recog-
nizing the necessity for economic diversification and industrialization in Latin America, but the essential thrust of his position
was to work out commodity agreements to support the *status quo
ante*.

Washington's responses during the next few weeks emphasized
two general points: first, "the reduction of barriers to the free
flow of trade and commerce," and second, the United States government's willingness to assist Latin America in "cushioning the
shock from the termination of war purchases and in meeting internal economic and social problems." The United States Ambassador to Mexico, George Messersmith, and Bohan warned Washington that trade and industrialization were important but delicate
issues. "The Mexicans," said Bohan, "are going to be very disappointed if the United States comes to the Conference prepared

only to discuss the reaffirmation of liberal trade principles. They are looking for something more. . . ." Messersmith argued that the United States could secure support for liberal trade policies at the conference, "but if nothing further is offered by way of a program, it will cause the keenest disillusionment. . . ." [35]

The same message was conveyed to Washington by the United States delegation. Commenting on Mexican Foreign Minister Ezequiel Padilla's opening address to the conference, the delegation noted: "He was warmly applauded throughout, and his reference to the desirability of the industrialization of the American Republics evoked considerable applause. In this latter connection he said that it was vital for the Americas to do more than produce raw materials and live in a state of semi-colonialism." [36] Nevertheless, the United States pursued liberal trade policies without offering much else and the conflict inevitably emerged.

Several resolutions and draft resolutions reveal more precisely the area of disagreement. The best known resolution of Committee IV, *An Economic Charter of the Americas,* was a broad statement of economic objectives plus the principles for achieving them. The objectives were: continued mobilization of economic resources until total victory; orderly transition from a war to a peace economy maintaining economic stability; and sound economic growth through the development of natural resources and infrastructure, industrialization, and modernization of agriculture. These objectives, which were accepted essentially as written in the United States draft proposal, were stated in such broad terms that there was little room for disagreement. [37]

The ten principles that accompanied the objectives were more specific and some provoked sharp disagreements. Those that were adopted essentially as they appeared in the United States draft proposal related to the improvement of the standard of living, to the prevention of private agreements that might restrict international trade, to the creation of the International Monetary Fund, the International Bank for Development and Reconstruction, and so on, to the distribution of production surpluses, and to the protection of labor.

Most significantly, the Latin Americans demanded and obtained changes in the other five principles as proposed in the United States draft. To the principle on the equality of access to the trade and raw materials of the world, the Latin Americans insisted on adding "a reciprocal principle of equal access to the producers' goods which are needed for their [the Latin Americans'] industrial and economic development." [38]

The principle of international commercial policy produced considerable debate. The United States draft sought to "reduce barriers of all kinds to the flow of international trade," whereas the final resolution, modified by the Latin Americans, sought to "reduce all barriers detrimental to trade between nations in accordance with the proposition of assuring the peoples of the world high levels of living and the sound development of their economies. . . ." The change came about because many Latin Americans argued that the unqualified acceptance of the United States draft would expose existing and nascent industries in Latin America to unfair competition with the industrialized nations. Some argued that a protective tariff was indispensable for industrialization. As State Department adviser Laurence Duggan put it: "The provision on tariffs was more satisfactory to the United States than to Latin American countries. To the latter, it seemed disingenuous that the United States should first build up its own industries under tariff protection and then frown on other countries for doing likewise." [39] The United States was pursuing an open door policy in Latin America, but Latin America, mindful that such an open door would hurt its efforts to develop and industrialize, insisted on protection for its infant industries.

The Latin Americans also objected to the principle that called for the "elimination of economic nationalism in all of its forms." [40] The final draft of the resolution focused on the *excesses* of economic nationalism and thus implicitly recognized the validity of some forms of economic nationalism; specifically, it sought to "eliminate the excesses which may result from economic nationalism," and it also sought to terminate "excessive restriction of imports and the dumping of surpluses of national production in world markets." Again, the Latin Americans were demanding something in return for their support and cooperation; they would try to limit excessive economic nationalism, but the United States would have to limit excessive import restrictions and dumping.

The principle entitled the *Just and Equitable Treatment of Foreign Enterprise and Capital* was of particular concern to the United States in light of the expropriation of oil companies in Bolivia and Mexico. In its draft resolution the United States argued for measures to "assure just and equitable treatment and encouragement for enterprises, skills and capital brought from one country to another." The final version, however, included another sentence, which placed the public interest of all countries above the "just and equitable" principle: "The American Republics will undertake to afford ample facilities for the free movement and investment of capital giving *equal treatment to national and foreign capital, except when the investment of the latter would be contrary to the fundamental principles of public interest.*" [41]

And finally, the principle dealing with private enterprise was modified. The original United States version called for the promotion and encouragement of private enterprise, the removal of obstacles that discourage economic growth, and a commitment "to refrain from the establishment of state enterprises for the conduct of trade." The Latin Americans believed that the state was an important vehicle of their economic development and were anxious to be able to involve the state in the conduct of trade or anything else. As a result, they insisted that the commitment "to refrain from the establishment of state enterprises for the conduct of trade" be dropped.

Several other resolutions complemented the Economic Charter, the most important of which was one on industrial development. The United States draft of this resolution, entitled *Maintenance and Development of the Internal Economies of the American Republics,* did not mention industrialization! Instead, it reaffirmed the importance of eliminating obstacles to trade and of strengthening private enterprise. The final draft, reflecting Latin American thinking, was strikingly different. Retitled *Industrial Development,* it stated that industrialization was critical to the economic development and to the national interests of the Latin American countries. It called for the promotion of "new branches of industry and the improvement and enlargement of those now in existence." It further stated the desirability that "such industries survive without the necessity of permanent, high restrictive protection, since that would be prejudicial to the legitimate interests of the consumers." It reiterated the desire to avoid "insofar as possible the competition of governments with private enterprise except where it is essential in the public interest." And finally, they resolved that "the investment of foreign capital in private enterprises in the American Republics should be made in such a manner as to assure to

national capital a just and adequate participation, not only in the
establishment of such enterprises, but also in their management." [42]

The Chapultepec Conference was indeed a watershed of past
and future United States-Latin American relations. On the one
hand it symbolized the close cooperation of the countries of the
hemisphere in the effort to defeat the Axis powers. On the other
hand, however, it clearly revealed the differences between the
United States and Latin America regarding the future economic
development of the area. The United States was interested in open
door policies for Latin America: free trade, export of raw materials, low tariffs, return to the *status quo ante,* and so on. Latin
America, however, wanted to claim its reward for helping the
United States during the war and this meant United States assistance to develop and industrialize. Latin America wanted economic development, industrialization, protection, and rapid movement beyond the *status quo ante.* The conflict of these two
fundamental points of view has remained basic to much of United
States-South American relations since World War II.

NOTES

1. Arthur P. Whitaker, *The United States and the Independence of Latin
America, 1800–1830* (New York, 1964), pp. 116–117.

2. *Ibid.,* pp. vii, 35.

3. The full text of the document can be found in James W. Gantenbein,
The Evolution of Our Latin American Policy (New York, 1950), pp.
323–325. For an analysis of the development of the document, see J.
Lloyd Mecham, *A Survey of United States-Latin American Relations* (Boston, 1965), pp. 38–52.

4. William A. Williams, *The Contours of American History* (Chicago,
1966), pp. 215–216.

5. The full text of the message can be found in Gantenbein, *Evolution,*
pp. 328–329. Emphasis added.

6. Mecham, *Survey,* p. 59.

7. For an analysis of the French in Mexico, see Ralph Roeder, *Juárez
and His Mexico* (New York, 1968).

8. Mecham, *Survey,* p. 293.

9. *Ibid.*, p. 417. For an analysis of the War of the Pacific, see Herbert Millington, *American Diplomacy and the War of the Pacific* (New York, 1948).

10. The interpretation set forth in this and the two subsequent paragraphs is based on Walter LaFeber, *The New Empire; An Interpretation of American Expansion, 1860–1890* (Ithaca, N.Y., 1963). For the traditional interpretation, see Ernest May, *Imperial Democracy* (New York, 1961) and *American Imperialism* (New York, 1968).

11. United States, Department of State, *Foreign Relations of the United States, 1894*, p. 61. This and the following paragraph are based on *ibid., 1893*, pp. 26–149, and *ibid., 1894*, pp. 57–87. Hereafter cited as *Foreign Relations*. See also Michael B. McCloskey, "The United States and the Brazilian Naval Revolt, 1893–1894," *Americas* (January 1946).

12. Mecham, *Survey*, pp. 93–117. See also Dana G. Munro, *Intervention and Dollar Diplomacy in the Caribbean, 1900–1921* (Princeton, N.J., 1964).

13. Gantenbein, *Evolution*, pp. 340–354.

14. *Ibid.*, pp. 361–362.

15. Robert Mayer, "The Origins of the American Banking Empire in Latin America," *Journal of Inter-American Studies* (February 1973), pp. 60–76. See also Harry Magdoff, *The Age of Imperialism* (New York, 1969), pp. 74–75.

16. Eduardo Prado. *A ilusão americano* (São Paulo, 1961), third edition.

17. Manuel Ugarte, *El porvenir de América Latina* (Buenos Aires, 1953), p. xxv.

18. Bryce Wood, *The Making of the Good Neighbor Policy* (New York, 1961).

19. Gantenbein, *Evolution*, pp. 761, 778–779; Cordell Hull, *The Memoirs of Cordell Hull* (London, 1948), Vol. 1, pp. 308–341.

20. Claudio Veliz (ed.), *Obstacles to Change in Latin America* (New York, 1969), pp. 4–6, 10–12; Eldon Kenworthy, "Argentina: the Politics of Late Industrialization," *Foreign Affairs* (April 1967).

21. Quoted in Green, *Containment*, p. 38.

22. Gardner, *Economic Aspects*, p. 105.

23. Wood, *Good Neighbor*, pp. 168–201.

24. *Ibid.*, p. 266.

25. John Wirth, *The Politics of Brazilian Development, 1930–1954* (Palo Alto, Calif., 1970); Frank D. McCann, Jr., *The Brazilian-American Alliance, 1937–1945* (Princeton, N.J., 1973), pp. 193–199.

26. Donald M. Dozer, *Are We Good Neighbors?* (Gainesville, Fla., 1959), pp. 128–129.

27. *Ibid.*

28. Quoted in *Ibid.*, p. 147.

29. *Ibid.*

30. *The New York Times*, February 23, 1945. See also Thomas M. Campbell, *Masquerade Peace, America's U.N. Policy, 1944–1945* (Tallahassee, Fla., 1973), Chapter 5.

31. For the texts of the resolutions, see United States, Department of State, *Report of the Delegation of the United States of America to the Inter-American Conference on Problems of War and Peace, Mexico City, February 21–March 8, 1945* (Washington, D.C., 1946). Hereafter referred to as *Report on Chapultepec.*

32. *Foreign Relations,* 1945, p. 148.

33. *Ibid.,* pp. 64–65.

34. *Ibid.,* pp. 64–65, 68–71.

35. *Ibid.,* pp. 83, 105, 111.

36. *Ibid.,* p. 123.

37. *Report on Chapultepec,* pp. 277–280.

38. *Ibid.,* pp. 120–124.

39. Laurence Duggan, *The Americas* (New York, 1949), p. 155.

40. *Report on Chapultepec,* p. 279.

41. *Ibid.,* p. 123. Emphasis added.

42. *Ibid.,* pp. 118–120.

chapter

3

Maintaining a South
American Empire in the
Cold War Era: 1945–1960

The United States emerged from World War II as the most powerful nation in the world and assumed England's mantle of responsibility for the welfare of the world capitalist system. Self-interest seemed to dictate such a role; United States prosperity depended on expanding foreign markets for growing domestic production. United States exports had grown from a low of $1.6 billion per year in 1932 to $15.3 billion in 1944, and the war, which had not damaged the country's industrial plant, increased the capacity to produce. As President Harry Truman explained, the objectives of peace and freedom "are bound up completely with a third objective—reestablishment of world trade. In fact the three—peace, freedom and world trade—are inseparable." [1] The United States therefore used its enormous power to develop and maintain a postwar global structure that would guarantee peace, stability, and free access to markets necessary for expanded trade.

Very quickly United States policy makers came to perceive Russia, and by extension all varieties of communism, as the major threat to the achievement of this kind of world. At the same time, Russia became skeptical of United States intentions and fearful of the consequences of United States policy for its future.

As a result, Russia refused a $1 billion United States loan, rejected membership in the newly formed World Bank and the International Monetary Fund, instituted a campaign to eliminate Western influence within its borders, and began to consolidate and defend its interests in Eastern Europe. The United States viewed these among other acts as efforts to destroy the vital open world economy and as the beginning of postwar Russian expansionism. Thus, from the perspective of Washington, the world was reduced to two hostile and competing blocs: the United States, which, as leader of the capitalist world, was trying to further world peace, political democracy, and an open world trading system; and Russia, which, as leader of the communist world, was seeking to divide and disrupt the world, to impose its "totalitarian" system on the weak, and to prevent the creation of an open world trading system.[2]

Having defined the postwar world in bipolar terms, the United States government accordingly developed and pursued a policy designed to contain communist expansion and to preserve as much of the world as possible for capitalist development. United States policy emerged in a series of steps, most of which bypassed the newly created United Nations organization. The clearest statement of the new policy was the Truman Doctrine. On February 21, 1947, England informed the United States that it could no longer assume responsibility for maintaining stability and order in Greece and Turkey. The United States was alarmed because the pro-Western regimes in these countries were on the verge of collapse. The situation in Greece was of particular concern since the country was in the midst of a bitter civil war, which pitted strong, popular revolutionary forces against an increasingly ineffective and predominantly conservative anti-communist regime. The United States believed that if it did not immediately assume England's traditional role in these two countries, the communists, or groups sympathetic to the communists, would take over and permit Russia to dominate the Middle East.

On March 12, 1947, President Truman spoke before a joint session of Congress and made the case for United States intervention. He argued that United States survival depended on the survival of free institutions throughout the world, and that United States security therefore demanded helping those seeking to maintain such institutions in the face of a communist threat. He then asked Congress to appropriate $400 million for economic and military aid to Greece and Turkey and to authorize the commitment of United States civilian and military personnel. Congress acted favorably on the President's requests, and the United States embarked on the first stage of its containment policy.

United States intervention in Greece established a precedent for future United States intervention in similar circumstances and the criteria for determining success or failure. The United States would support any anti-communist regime threatened by internal groups dedicated to fundamental change of the *status quo,* because it perceived any such effort as part of the international communist conspiracy to undermine the world capitalist system. Popular challenges to the *status quo* might overthrow or weaken anti-communist regimes, and since communism was a threat to United States security, the communists had to be opposed at all costs.

The United States took additional steps to contain communism in the years following the enunciation of the Truman Doctrine. The Marshall Plan provided billions of dollars to reconstruct the war-devastated economies of capitalist Europe, and the North Atlantic Treaty Organization established a mutual defense system for that area. The Point Four Program provided technical assistance to underdeveloped countries to help them resist communism and to "open up new sources of materials and goods which we [the United States] need, and new markets for the products of our farms and factories." The commitment of United States troops to Korea was an effort to limit communist expansion in the Far East. And the landing of troops in Lebanon under the Eisenhower Doctrine was designed to contain communist expansion in the Middle East.[3]

United States policy toward South America during the decade and a half following World War II was an integral part of its overall foreign policy. Since the United States already exercised effective control over South America, its concern was one of maintaining rather than of gaining influence in the area. To do this the United States pursued two general policy lines. First, it sought to impose its diffusionist view of economic development on South America. As the Chapultepec Conference revealed, the United States believed that South America could best develop by utilizing domestic and foreign private capital to exploit and export its vast reserves of raw materials and to import manufactured goods from the industrialized capitalist countries. Such a policy would provide the United States with an important market for its surplus industrial production and a source for vital raw materials. Second, the United States sought to keep international communism out of South America. This meant that the United States supported anti-communist regimes whether or not they were representative, opposed socioeconomic change that might undermine the power of anti-communist regimes, and attacked independent or neutral policies that might restrict its influence.

The frequent use of the word "neglect" to describe United States South American policy during this period has created considerable confusion regarding the nature of that policy. It is true that the United States focused most of its attention on Europe and other parts of the world, that South America received only minimal amounts of United States aid, and that only a major crisis—usually involving some potential communist threat—aroused the interest of the United States in the area. But to describe United States South American policy as one of neglect is misleading. The United States was not particularly interested in South American development and at times actively opposed it. It thus refused to provide significant resources for that task. The important point, however, is that the United States was very much interested in maintaining its influence in South America and did not in any sense neglect this task. Indeed, precisely because the ties binding South America to the United States were strong and only infrequently challenged, the United States did not need to devote much attention to the area. The analysis that follows illustrates how the United States managed to maintain its South American sphere of influence during the cold war era with minimal effort.

The Truman Administration: 1945–1952

South America's initial response to the Truman Administration was one of cautious optimism. The disillusion with United States policy that had developed toward the end of the war and the fear that the United States did not want South America to industrialize remained a part of South American thinking, but there was the possibility that a new administration might bring about positive change. Truman's initial statement to Congress on April 16, 1945, encouraged some hope: "The responsibility of the great state,"

Truman said, "is to serve and not to dominate the people of the world." [4] Yet the actions of the new administration quickly led to widespread feelings of frustration, resentment, and disillusionment.

United States concern with the reconstruction of Europe, the defense of capitalism and free trade, and the "Russian menace" had severe consequences for South America. In the first place, South America was a low priority for economic assistance; while Europe received $25 billion from the United States in economic and military aid during the Truman Administration, Latin America, with a slightly smaller population and a larger land area, received less than $1 billion (Table 3–1). Furthermore, South America suffered from the abrupt termination of war purchases by the United States, shortages of machinery and other goods, an unfavorable balance of trade, and United States opposition to rapid industrialization, nationalization, state corporations, and fundamental social and economic reform.

A few examples will illustrate the specific nature of United States South American policy during the immediate postwar period. The San Francisco Conference to set up the United Nations (April 1945) revealed the dismay of the South Americans and their fear of United States domination. Although all the South American states had broken relations with the Axis powers by the beginning of 1945, President Roosevelt told them that they had to declare war on the Axis powers if they wanted to participate in the San Francisco Conference. All, except Argentina, obliged, but they felt that breaking relations and cooperating with the United States was essentially the same thing as declaring war, and that this last-minute insistence on the part of the United States made it appear to the world that the South American countries were mere puppets of the United States. As State Department adviser Laurence Duggan observed: "They [the Latin Americans] felt that in the eyes of the world they had been forced to obey the orders from the United States under penalty of exclusion from the United Nations." [5]

The issue was not simply a question of saving face; the major concern of South America at San Francisco was to insulate itself as much as possible from the control and influence of the big powers. South Americans went to the conference determined not to rubber-stamp what the Big Four had already agreed to at the previous wartime conferences (Moscow, Dumbarton Oaks, and so

TABLE 3-1

United States Foreign Economic and Military Aid, Fiscal Years 1946–1973

(All figures in billions of United States dollars)

Countries	Truman Administration (1946–1953)	Eisenhower Administration (1954–1961)	Kennedy Administration (1962–1964)	Johnson Administration (1965–1969)	Nixon Administration (1970–1973)
All	43.6	44.6	20.5	37.5	40.5
(per year)	(5.5)	(5.6)	(6.8)	(7.5)	(10.1)
Developed	30.7	11.9	2.2	2.8	4.3
(per year)	(3.8)	(1.5)	(.72)	(.56)	(1.1)
Less Developed	10.6	31.1	18.4	34.7	36.2
(per year)	(1.3)	(3.9)	(6.1)	(6.9)	(9.0)
Latin America	1.3	4.1	3.6	6.6	4.5
(per year)	(.16)	(.5)	(1.2)	(1.3)	(1.1)

Europe	29.4	13.7	2.3	2.4	3.0
(per year)	(3.7)	(1.7)	(.76)	(.48)	(.75)
Near East, Southeast Asia	3.7	11.1	6.7	8.8	7.1
(per year)	(.47)	(1.4)	(2.25)	(1.76)	(1.77)
East Asia	6.9	12.9	4.7	13.6	19.0
(per year)	(.9)	(1.6)	(1.56)	(2.7)	(3.8)
Africa	.07	1.2	1.4	2.0	1.9
(per year)	(.008)	(.15)	(.47)	(.4)	(.48)
Other	2.3	1.64	1.65	4.2	5.0
(per year)	(.3)	(.21)	(.55)	(.84)	(1.25)

Sources: Agency for International Development, *U.S. Overseas Loans and Grants, 1961, 1971, 1972, 1973* (Washington, D.C.). There are discrepancies in the figures cited from edition to edition resulting from the withholding of military and other items that are then reported later. I have used the latest figures available in every case.

on). According to Duggan, they were startled and resentful when they found that most Europeans believed the war had been an "unmixed blessing" for South America and that they were satellites of the United States.

At the conference, the South Americans supported the United States on the critical Polish question, but found themselves disagreeing with the United States on many of the important issues. Their chief concerns were the elimination of the big power veto in the Security Council and the viability of the inter-American system set forth at Chapultepec, for which they fought strenuously. Thus, the most important resolution of San Francisco for the South Americans was Article 51 of the United Nations Charter, which permitted regional organizations to act in self-defense without the specific authorization, and therefore the possible Big Four veto, of the Security Council. The South Americans' persistence so annoyed Secretary of State Stettinius that he told the United States delegation "the time has arrived when we must not be pushed around by a lot of small American republics who are dependent on us in many ways—economically, politically, militarily; . . . we must provide leadership." [6]

Brazil's efforts to obtain United States financial aid for development during the early postwar years illustrates the low priority of South American development for the United States. In May 1946 a delegation of Brazilians met State Department officials in Washington to discuss possible economic assistance. The United States turned down the requests. The head of the Brazilian delegation, obviously upset by the rejection, noted that "Brazil had been led to believe that immediately after the war would be a most favorable time to undertake its development program, and that conversations with industrialists in this country [the United States] had tended to bear out this impression. . . . In the course of . . . official discussions it seemed that Brazil, however, had been mistaken." State Department officials quickly, if lamely, explained that if the United States did not help Brazil exactly as it wanted, this was due only to the "multitude of demands" confronting the government.[7] In other words, the development of Brazil, the largest and most populous country in South America and an important ally during the war, was not very important to policy makers in Washington.

Another dimension of United States policy was revealed by a

dispatch from the United States ambassador to Colombia. "Colombia," he pointed out, "is in great need of materials, equipment and machinery from the United States but is now faced with [the] unpleasant prospect of paying more for these purchases while being denied a better price for its principal export product [i.e., coffee]." He went on to suggest that continuation of the established price ceiling on coffee seemed prejudicial to United States interests in expanding export markets and world trade.[8] The issue was essentially the same for all of the South American countries exporting raw materials to the United States. The United States was successful in holding down the price on the raw materials it purchased, yet the price on United States-manufactured items necessary for the growth and development of South American industry continually increased.

The United States did not always refuse to grant economic aid. United States-Chilean relations in 1946 and 1947 suggest the circumstances under which the United States might help a South American country. Chile needed capital for industrial development. The United States wanted to protect its Chilean investments and to eliminate any external or internal threat to its preeminence. It therefore used requests for financial assistance as leverage to bring about its desired goals. Chile already had received some financial assistance, but no new loans were forthcoming until Chile settled a strike against Kennecott copper and put its financial house in order according to traditional financial standards. Furthermore, no loans were made that might have enabled Chilean industry to compete with United States industry either for Chilean or foreign markets.

What finally brought about even restricted amounts of aid to Chile was the threat of help from Argentina and the fear of a communist take-over. United States Ambassador Claude Bowers summed up the Argentine threat as follows: "Should it be necessary to abandon plans for industrialization or take credits from Argentina, public opinion here [in Chile] would make it impossible for any Government to abandon the projects. And should this situation develop I am afraid that it would throw Chile, against her will, into the Argentine orbit." [9]

The communist threat in Chile came to the fore during the first two years of the presidency of Gabriel González Videla (1946–1947). González Videla, a member of the middle-of-the-road Radical Party, was elected president with the support of the Communist Party and therefore gave Communist Party members several seats in his cabinet. Alarmed by this, the United States government put increasing pressure on González Videla to get rid of the communists. The Chilean president was annoyed, because he continually had to deny that his government was a communist government and because the United States did not understand his difficult political situation. The Communist Party had considerable influence among the Chilean masses and had helped elect him. Thus, in order to avoid protests and strikes by the working classes, he had to handle the matter with the utmost caution. The United States, however, remained impatient.

Strikes in the United States-owned copper mines in 1946 produced considerable friction between the United States and Chile, but the coal strike of 1947 brought the two together. González Videla, after months of haggling with the striking coal miners and supported by the United States, attacked the Communist Party and attempted to conscript the striking miners into the army. To do this he needed coal from the United States. Because of the shortage of coal in the world at the time, the United States was reluctant to give Chile what it requested. On October 13, however, Bowers wired the Secretary of State as follows:

> The strike is Communist and revolutionary and result will have inevitable effect throughout South America. . . . In view of the world contest between Communism and democracy it seems incredible that we should be indifferent to the major battle Communism is waging in Chile, and that we cannot do better than heretofore indicated [i.e., the amount of coal offered]. Unless we can and do we may prepare ourselves for a grave Communist triumph in our backyard and which will spread to other American nations.[10]

The telegram produced the desired results; United States aid in the form of coal and the long-sought-after credits were immediately forthcoming.

All of these issues were brought out at Bogotá in March 1948, when delegates gathered for the Ninth International Conference of American States, the first regular meeting of the American states since before the war. The conference did give permanent treaty form to the association of American states (Charter of the Organization of American States). It also coordinated and unified existing treaties and conventions for the peaceful settlement of disputes (Pact of Bogotá). Yet the South Americans received no support for what they considered to be the essential issue: economic development. As the report of the United States delegation noted: "It was not possible to reach agreement on the most difficult questions in this field [economic development], which were referred to the Economic and Social Council for further study." The United States opposed an Inter-American Bank, an Inter-American Development Corporation, and an Inter-American Institute of Commerce, action to "compensate for the disparity that is frequently noted between the prices of raw materials and the prices of manufactured products," and obligatory joint participation of foreign and national capital in Latin America. Instead, the United States, reiterating its view that private investment could do the development job, begrudgingly announced that President Truman had requested Congress to increase the lending authority of the Export-Import Bank by $500 million and presented the presidents of the Export-Import Bank and the World Bank to discuss loans.[11]

Secretary of State George Marshall summed up the United States position in his address to the conference.[12] He emphasized the fact that the burden on the United States in bringing about world recovery was "far heavier than seems to be realized." He then reviewed the history of the development of the United States and emphasized the role of private foreign and domestic capital in the process. He assured the delegates that the United States was willing to help. But, he concluded, "it is beyond the capacity of the United States Government itself to finance more than a small portion of the vast development needed. The capital required through the years must come from private sources, both domestic and foreign. . . . As the experience of the United States has shown, progress can be achieved best through individual effort and the use of private resources."

For the South Americans, disillusionment was practically complete. The area was to be left to private capital to bring about economic development. The United States government would be active only to protect the investments and trade of its citizens and to make sure that South America remained anti-communist.

The Argentine Problem. The communist threat quickly became one of the important issues for the United States in post-World War II South America, but the Argentine threat also demanded considerable attention during much of the Truman Administration. Officially the United States was concerned about the pro-Axis sympathies of the military government that had come to power in June 1943 and of the government of Juan D. Perón, who was elected in February 1946. During the latter years of the war and at Chapultepec the United States had sought to expose and eliminate the "fascist threat in Argentina." When Spruille Braden was United States ambassador to Argentina and then under assistant secretary of state for Latin America (1946 and 1947), he had carried on an intensive campaign against "Argentine fascism" and against Perón. Thus, among other things, the United States had published an exposé of Nazi penetration into Argentina and its alleged connection with Perón just two weeks before the presidential election of February 1946. Nevertheless, Perón had been elected president by a substantial majority.

The real Argentine problem for the United States was its economic nationalism and its independent foreign policy. During the war there had been reason for concern about German infiltration and influence in Argentina, but the military government had belatedly declared war on the Axis, and after the war the so-called "fascist threat" ceased to have any basis in fact. What mattered to the United States was that Argentina under Perón nationalized public utilities and the railroads, built up the merchant marine, and greatly increased state control over credit and marketing. In addition, Argentina pursued an independent foreign policy and attempted to form an independent bloc of South American states (Bolivia, Paraguay, Uruguay, Chile, and Peru) to counterbalance the influence of the United States.

In July 1946, Braden, rather candidly, summarized the position of the United States:

> The essence of the long-term problem is that Argentine governments have long aspired to create and control an anti-United States bloc of Latin American states and to become the dominant power in South America. Perón's aim, already partially accomplished, of forming a totalitarian-type state, with almost absolute power in his hands, increases the danger which this traditional Argentine policy represents to the Inter-American system. There is no quick, easy way to change this attitude which is the root cause of Argentina's obstructionist role in every phase of Inter-American politics and of Argentina's so-called "neutrality" in both World Wars.[13]

George Messersmith, who replaced Braden as United States ambassador to Argentina early in 1946, sought to modify the hard-line approach of his predecessor and to bring Argentina into the inter-American fold. In one of his first dispatches as ambassador (June 15, 1946), Messersmith suggested that the United States pursue two objectives. First, it should "get the Argentine to turn her eyes away from Europe, to which they have always been directed in practically every field, and to turn them to this hemisphere." And second, the United States should "get the wholehearted and loyal collaboration of the Argentine Government and people, in the political, economic, social and defense fields." Messersmith correctly perceived Perón as a pragmatist who was willing to reach some kind of rapprochement with the United States. Therefore he supported a bilateral defense pact between the two countries and other forms of assistance that might lead to the realization of his objectives.

Messersmith thought the issue of a southern bloc much less serious than Braden, and he thought it subject to negotiation. In the first place, he argued, the southern bloc was not an invention of Perón; in the second place, the government was preoccupied with the domestic situation; and in the third place, it had no source for military equipment and industrial machinery except the United States. He summed up by noting that,

> . . . the question is not now an active one, although it is one which we must always bear in mind. Such a regional bloc of course would be disadvantageous for American unity and cannot be tolerated and it is just as dangerous as the idea that Latin American collaboration comes first and American collaboration second. These are ideas which must be combatted by all of the American republics, but if we carry through the defense pact . . . any thoughts which anyone in the Argentine may have with regard to a Southern Bloc are out.[14]

United States concern with Perón's independent foreign policy and his creation of a bloc was matched by its concern for his economic nationalism. Even though Perón compensated the owners of nationalized utilities, the United States was bothered by the example of nationalization of private concerns. Furthermore, the United States was concerned about Argentina's efforts to build up its merchant marine. Early in 1947, the Moore-McCormack Shipping Company became alarmed about Argentine competition on the New York-Buenos Aires run. It complained to the United States government that Argentina was discriminating in favor of Argentine ships for unloading berths in Buenos Aires. The issue became more serious when the United States Maritime Commission refused to permit the nearly bankrupt Newport News Shipbuilding Company to sell three ships to a private Argentine shipping company. As Ambassador Messersmith reported:

> Rightly or wrongly, the feeling is that we do not want the Argentine to build up her merchant marine. Rightly or wrongly, the feeling here is the Moore-McCormack interests have been very active with the Maritime Commission, etc., and are responsible for this refusal of the Maritime Commission to approve the sale. . . . The feeling is that we are trying to keep Argentine ships out of the River Plate-New York trade so as to keep it for Moore-McCormack.[15]

Messersmith did manage to improve relations with Argentina, but the issues of the Argentine problem were to endure and to trouble the United States in the future. South Americans, with the exception of the Uruguayans, never really understood the great concern of the United States over Perón's "fascism" after the war, and indeed most perceived this issue for what it was—a guise for United States opposition to Perón's independent foreign policy and to his domestic economic nationalism. The dangerous ideas that Messersmith referred to—neutralism and nationalism—were not the creation of Perón nor was he the last to articulate them. Fidel Castro of Cuba, Janio Quadros and Jango Goulart of Brazil, and Salvador Allende of Chile were to set forth similar ideas and would also be opposed by the United States. The Argentine problem became the Cuban problem, the Brazilian problem, and then the Chilean problem, and most certainly will reappear in other South American countries in the future.

The Inter-American Defense System. During World War II all of the South American countries, except Argentina and to some extent Chile, had worked closely with the United States to build up the inter-American defense system and to defend the hemisphere from the immediate threat of the Axis. The war conferences, particularly the Rio Conference of 1942, and a series of bilateral agreements between the United States and the individual South American countries had established the procedures for mutual defense. Under these arrangements, the South American governments had eliminated German propaganda and subversive activity, had seized German-controlled airlines and businesses, had granted the United States strategic military bases, and had cooperated in the effort to standardize military supplies, organization, and training.

When the war was over, the embryonic inter-American defense system quickly broke down. The Axis had been defeated and the immediate security threat removed. The South American governments insisted that the United States give up its South American military bases, and they turned their attention toward the economic development that they felt had been postponed by the war effort. In the United States the first postwar Congress (1946–1948), controlled by Republicans determined to cut down government spending, refused to pass the legislation necessary to build up the inter-American defense system. In addition, the State Department initially opposed any efforts to build up the South American military establishments.

There was, however, a significant division of opinion within the United States government that led ultimately to the reversal of the immediate postwar defense policy. The War and Navy Departments believed that a strong, coordinated inter-American defense system under the leadership of the United States was essential to national security. Thus, to insure continued United States influence within the South American military establishments, the War Department fought tirelessly to make permanent the defensive alliances established during the war, to complete the standardization of equipment, organization, and training, and to become the sole supplier of South American military hardware.

The difference of opinion between the State Department and the War Department focused on legislation to underwrite the cost of building up the South American military establishments. Under Secretary of State Dean Acheson at first opposed the Inter-American Military Cooperation Act on the grounds that its passage would undermine democratic government in South America and impose economic hardship on the governments of the area. If the United States built up the Latin American military establishments, Acheson argued, it "would lose much of the support and friendship of those people of Latin America who are devoted to the cause of peace and of stable democratic government." In addition, he noted, "the economic handicaps imposed by the proposed arms program would perpetuate and aggravate conditions of economic and political instability which already constitute a serious security problem for this government in Latin America." [16]

The War Department countered the arguments of the State Department by noting that the South Americans would build up their military establishments regardless of what the United States did and that United States support for these military establishments was the best way to fight communist expansion in the area. In a series of memoranda to Acheson in March and April 1947 Secretary of War Robert P. Patterson suggested that

> . . . the majority of the sovereign states of the Western Hemisphere will insist upon maintaining such military establishments as *they,* not *we,* feel they require and which *they,* not *we,* feel they can support financially. Thus, the question we face in Latin America is not, "Shall they have arms?" The basic question, which is the vital crux of the whole subject, is, "Shall they have United States or foreign arms?"

Most importantly, Patterson argued that the sale of arms, the standardization of equipment, the military missions, and visits to the United States would assure United States influence and prevent communist infiltration. Thus, he explained, "will our ideals and way of life be nurtured in Latin America, to the eventual exclusion of totalitarianism and other foreign ideologies." The inter-American arms program, he continued, is a preventative measure. "It is designed to prevent the very type of crisis which has arisen in Turkey and Greece where we are now desperately attempting to lock the stable door while the horse is almost in the process of being stolen. In Latin America, we must lock the stable door before the danger ever arises." A month later he summed up the case by stating: "It would seem that we are playing into the hands of the Communists if by our own decisions we disable ourselves from the tender of military assistance." [17]

The crises in Greece and Turkey, the growth of communist activity in Chile and other Latin American countries, and the general intensification of the cold war led Acheson to change his mind, to overrule objections within his department, and to join the War Department in supporting the Inter-American Military Cooperation Act. As a result, a clear and consistent United States military policy toward Latin America unfolded and was gradually implemented. The United States would seek permanent defensive alliances with all Latin American countries and would effect close collaboration with the Latin American military establishments. Such a policy would not directly strengthen Western military capability in the event of a conflict with the Soviet Union, but it would guarantee United States predominance and lessen Soviet and European influence in the area. The military would be cultivated as the most effective Latin American ally in the cold war struggle.

In September 1947 the American states met in Rio de Janeiro and accepted the Inter-American Treaty of Reciprocal Assistance. The conference had been delayed because of the Argentine problem, but with the heightening of the cold war and the shift in State Department policy, the United States decided to proceed. The treaty made permanent the wartime Act of Chapultepec; it established a permanent defensive alliance in which the American states agreed to help each other in the event of external or internal aggression.

Close and effective collaboration with the South American military establishments was not achieved until the Korean War, because the United States Congress would not support grants for military equipment. The Mutual Defense Assistance Act of 1949 provided for the sale of arms to Latin America but had little impact since there was no economic aid to pay for the arms. The Mutual Security Act of 1951, however, did authorize grant-aid transactions with Latin America and established a permanent institutional framework for an effective military assistance program. In so doing, it established the basis for intimate United States-South American military collaboration designed primarily to maintain United States access to strategic materials, to insure sufficient South American military capability to respond to small air and submarine attack from abroad, and to lessen the commitment of United States forces to the defense of the area.[18]

By the end of the Truman Administration, the basic postwar pattern of United States-South American relations was well established. To maintain its position—to guarantee access to South American markets, investments, and raw materials and to keep communist influence at a minimum—the United States used its economic and political resources to oppose not only communism, but neutralism, economic nationalism, state capitalism, and "excessive" industrial development. Washington singled out the South American military as the most viable and effective group to further its interests and gradually worked out a program to build it up and to make it increasingly dependent on the United States.

The Eisenhower Administration: 1953–1960

By 1953 most of the Western European countries had recovered from the devastation of World War II and were once more functioning members of the world capitalist system. Their recovery, however, did not bring an end to the cold war. Rather, the primary focus of the competition between the capitalist and communist powers shifted from Europe to the countries of the Third World. The Eisenhower Administration therefore channeled increased resources to the underdeveloped countries. While the Truman Administration had granted $3.8 billion per year in aid to the developed countries (mainly Western Europe) and only $1.3 billion per year to the underdeveloped countries, the Eisenhower Administration reversed the situation. It granted $3.9 billion per year in aid to the underdeveloped countries and only $1.5 billion per year to the developed countries (Table 3–1).

United States aid to Latin America followed the general pattern of aid to the underdeveloped countries. During the Truman Administration Latin America had received only $.16 billion per year in aid from the United States, while during the Eisenhower Administration it received $.50 billion per year or three times as much. Furthermore, the value of United States direct investment in Latin America (two-thirds of which was in South America) increased from $4.4 billion in 1950 to $7.5 billion in 1960 (Table 2–1).

Milton Eisenhower, President Eisenhower's brother and principal Latin American adviser, argued on the basis of this evidence that the Eisenhower Administration brought about a major change in United States policy toward Latin America. Nevertheless, the most striking thing about this policy is that it was essentially the same as that of the Truman Administration.[19] At Caracas and Rio in 1954, at Buenos Aires in 1957, and at other Inter-American conferences, the United States opposed any effort to establish a Latin American development fund, to stabilize the prices of raw materials, to strengthen national development corporations, to permit greater Latin American access to the United States market, and so on. In private meetings with Latin Americans, Milton Eisenhower and other Washington officials continued to attack what they called "excessive industrialization." "Latin Americans," the President's brother pointed out, "often wave aside caution, such as my repeated reminder in conversations with business leaders that it took the United States several centuries to reach its present stage of economic development. . . . Latin Americans do not want to wait; they want to absorb this experience in a decade or two. Misled into believing that the Soviet Union under a Communist dictatorship has done this, they think they can too." [20]

Equally important, United States economic and military aid figures show quite clearly that while the absolute amount of aid to Latin America increased dramatically under Eisenhower, Latin America was still a low priority area of the world. The biggest portion of all aid continued to go to Western Europe, with East Asia and the Near East-South Asia in second and third place respectively. Latin America was a distant fourth (Table 3–1). Furthermore, most Latin American aid was in the form of loans rather than grants and the total amount was inadequate for the task of rapid development.

The Eisenhower Administration consolidated and in some cases extended Truman's policies toward Latin America, but it did not fundamentally change the pattern of United States-Latin American relations. Eisenhower, like Truman, promoted the interests of United States investment and trade, defined Latin American development in traditional economic terms (private capital can do the job, create and maintain a good investment climate, maintain monetary stability at all costs, follow the United States example, be patient, and so on), assumed traditional United States paternalism toward Latin America, cultivated the military, and kept foremost in mind the containment and eradication of communism.

The Anti-Communist Crusade. President Eisenhower and his Secretary of State John Foster Dulles, like their predecessors, associated neutralism, economic nationalism, state capitalism, and "excessive" industrialization with the spread of communism and devoted considerable energy and resources to fight them all. But the intensification of the cold war and the shift of its main focus to the underdeveloped areas gave the new administration's anti-communist program the aura of a crusade. President Eisenhower's primary interest in Latin America was the elimination of communist influence; maintaining United States influence and protecting United States economic interests in Latin America would be impossible unless the battle against communist penetration was first won. Thus, for example, in the seven-hundred-page first volume of his *Memoirs,* covering the years 1953 to 1956, President Eisenhower's only real discussion of Latin America was a ten-page section on the communist threat in Guatemala.[21]

When Eisenhower was inaugurated in January 1953, there was trouble brewing in Bolivia, British Guiana, and Guatemala, a fact that heightened and focused the administration's fear of communist penetration in the hemisphere. In Bolivia in April 1952 the slightly left of center Movimiento Nacional Revolucionario (MNR), led by Víctor Paz Estenssoro and supported by radical left-wing miners and peasants, had come to power in a major revolutionary upheaval. At the end of October the new government had nationalized the tin mines (United States investors had only a minor share in one of them) and pressure had mounted for major land reform. The Truman Administration had not recognized the MNR government for six weeks and, because of its concern about nationalization and land reform, withheld economic aid indefinitely.

By 1953 things had settled down considerably in Bolivia. With the moderates in control, a settlement was reached with the former owners of the tin mines. The United States, fearful that its refusal to support the moderate government might pave the way for a radical take-over, decided to purchase Bolivian tin and to grant the country substantial economic aid. The government soon became dependent on United States aid for its survival and the United States was able to exert pressure to guide the revolution into channels acceptable to it.[22]

In April 1953 British Guiana held elections under a new constitution designed to bring independence to that colony in the near future. The People's Progressive Party, led by the Marxist Cheddi Jagan, won 51 percent of the popular vote and eighteen of the twenty-four seats in the legislature. The British government retained ultimate veto power until independence became a reality. In September 1953, just five months after the election, the British landed troops in the colony and suspended the constitution. The basic issue was the alleged communist sympathies and programs of the Jagan government, although the British were unable to produce any evidence of outside infiltration, interference, or control. With the constitution suspended, the colony reverted to full and direct colonial rule, and independence was postponed indefinitely. The United States had a number of interests in British Guiana. The location of the colony on the Caribbean next door to mineral-rich Venezuela gave it strategic importance. During World War II it had been a critical source of bauxite and other metals, and it had permitted the United States to establish an airbase on its soil. By 1953 a number of United States-owned or -controlled companies (Reynolds Metals, Kennecott, Harvey Aluminum, and so on) had extensive investments in the colony. Thus, with the election of a Marxist prime minister in April 1953, the United States became alarmed. The British government emphatically denied that there had been any United States pressure on it to intervene, but given United States interests in the colony it is difficult to believe that the two governments did not discuss the matter and that the United States did not urge action to eliminate Jagan. Jagan himself made a fairly good case that United States pressure was the decisive factor in the British decision to intervene. At any rate, the United States was quick to support the British action and to applaud the removal of Jagan from power.[23]

In the midst of the developing problems in Bolivia and British Guiana, Guatemala presented what the United States perceived as the most serious security threat. In 1944 the Guatemalans had overthrown the dictator Jorge Ubico and had elected the nationalist reformer Juan José Arévalo as their president. Arévalo's successor in 1951, Jacobo Arbenz, a colonel in the army and a former member of the Arévalo cabinet, had carried on the nationalist reform programs of his predecessor. In June 1952 he had introduced an agrarian reform law that, although not radical, caused considerable fear on the part of the politically powerful United States-owned United Fruit Company.

In February 1953, shortly after the inauguration of Eisenhower, Arbenz announced the expropriation of 255,000 acres of unused United Fruit land for distribution among the peasants. The United States government, urged on by United Fruit, increasingly assumed that Arbenz was under the influence of international communism and began to press the Latin American countries to take collective action against the Guatemalan government. The United States prepared itself to undermine Arbenz in a variety of ways. It brought in a new ambassador, John E. Peurifoy, a former ambassador to Greece, presumably because he understood how to fight communist subversion. But the main thrust of United States activity was to get the Latin Americans to condemn Guatemala at the forthcoming Caracas conference and thus to legitimize any future direct action.[24]

The Tenth Inter-American Conference was held at Caracas, Venezuela, in March 1954.[25] Once more the Latin Americans attended seeking to gain United States acceptance of fixed international commodity prices, increased Latin American access to the United States market, and substantial economic and technological assistance for development. None of this was forthcoming. Instead, the United States single-mindedly focused its efforts on gaining support for a declaration condemning Guatemala. Most of the Latin American countries were more concerned about United States rather than Russian intervention in the hemisphere, and since they saw the conflict as one between the United States and Guatemala, they opposed any collective action against Guatemala. Many openly supported Guatemala's defiance of the "Colossus of the North." Thus, they cheered the Guatemala foreign minister when he accused the United States of interfering in the internal affairs of Guatemala to foment a counterrevolution.

At the beginning of the conference only a handful of countries supported United States efforts to bring about collective action against Guatemala, but the United States was determined to have its way. In his three major statements before the conference, United States Secretary of State John Foster Dulles focused on the communist issue. He made several passing references to economic problems, emphasizing the importance of private initiative to resolve them, but spoke at great length on the dangers and horrors of the international communist system "operated by the leaders of the Communist Party of the Soviet Union." He condemned "extreme nationalism" as a tool of the communists, attacked "international front organizations designed to enable its [Russia's] agents to get popular backing from special groups such as labor, youth, women, students, farmers, etc.," and denounced communism because it "enslaved rather than liberated people."

The verbal offensive plus implicit and explicit economic and political pressure enabled the United States to win the vote of seventeen countries for a compromise resolution condemning international communism. Guatemala voted against the motion. Mexico and Argentina abstained. The resolution did not specifically mention Guatemala, nor did it specify the steps to be taken in the event of a communist threat. The main part stated only that "the domination or control of the political institution of any American state by the international communist movement . . . would constitute a threat to the sovereignty and independence of the American states . . . and would call for a Meeting of Consultation to consider the adoption of appropriate action in accordance with existing treaties." [26]

The United States managed to obtain enough support to pass this resolution, but in so doing it further antagonized most of the Latin Americans. Not only were they resentful at the pressure exerted by the United States, but Dulles left the conference as soon as the resolution was passed, the United States decorated the Venezuelan dictator Pérez Jiménez, and the United States once more refused to do anything to support economic development.

Armed with this resolution, the United States moved quickly to overthrow the Arbenz regime. In June 1954 Carlos Castillo Armas, with CIA help, overthrew the government, forced Arbenz to flee the country, and established a pro-United States anticommunist regime.

As United States actions in Guatemala imply, one of the most important features of the Eisenhower anti-communist crusade was to build up the Latin American military establishments, to make them an increasingly influential factor in the political life of the area, and to increase their ties with the United States. The figures in Table 3–2 reveal the extent and nature of this buildup. The United States, which had given Latin America practically no military aid during the Truman Administration, gave it $387.8 million during the Eisenhower Administration. South America received 91 percent of the total, and four South American countries—Brazil, Peru, Chile, and Colombia—received 70 percent! And, more than 90 percent of this military aid, compared to only 10 percent of economic aid, was in the form of grants.

United States policy toward Bolivia illustrates how the Eisenhower Administration attempted to strengthen the military in South America. In mid-1952 Bolivia was weak, divided, poor, and vulnerable to outside pressure. The ruling Movimiento Nacional Revolucionario consisted of radical, moderate, and conservative factions, all competing for control of the revolution. The government of Víctor Paz Estenssoro needed large quantities of food just

TABLE 3-2

U.S. Economic and Military Aid to Latin America, Fiscal Years 1946–1974
(All figures in millions of U.S. dollars)

Year	Economic Aid (A) Latin America	South America	Military Aid (B) Latin America	South America	(B) as % of (A)
1946-1948	274.6	164.1			
(per year)	91.5	54.7			
1949	70.6	40.8			
1950	197.0	173.4			
1951	219.2	62.3			
1952	105.8	86.0	.2	.2	
1953	410.1	393.1	11.2	10.8	2.7
1954	62.5	36.8	34.5	33.0	55.0
1955	325.5	280.3	31.8	27.4	9.7
1956	342.8	203.5	30.4	26.1	8.9
1957	642.4	536.9	43.9	38.9	6.8
1958	377.0	221.5	47.9	43.1	12.7
1959	621.0	456.2	54.0	51.6	8.7
1960	380.4	188.0	53.7	47.7	14.1
1961	981.7	838.3	91.6	87.8	9.3
1962	1,015.9	698.9	174.0	162.2	17.1
1963	987.7	682.1	122.5	106.2	12.4
1964	1,204.7	854.0	112.3	101.9	9.3
1965	1,213.8	597.0	89.1	80.2	7.3
1966	1,266.0	737.3	126.2	115.1	10.0
1967	1,352.0	759.4	87.8	79.8	6.5
1968	1,361.7	652.3	76.2	69.6	5.6
1969	1,000.9	416.2	44.8	36.1	4.4
1970	1,070.4	508.7	23.1	16.6	2.2
1971	647.3	433.0	74.6	59.4	11.5
1972	1,169.9	715.3	90.6	82.4	7.7
1973	1,349.5	491.0	81.9	72.9	6.1
1974	1,493.4	736.8	135.6	129.3	9.1

Sources: Same as Table 3-1.

to keep the people from starving, substantial capital to develop the economy and to carry out the extensive social program of the revolution, and markets for tin. At the time, the United States was the only available source of redress for all of these needs, and Washington was thus able to exert influence over the government of Bolivia.

The United States used this leverage, among other things, to encourage Bolivia to build up its army. The revolution destroyed the 18,000-man army and replaced it with the popular militia and the police, who had been instrumental in the overthrow of the old regime. But pressure from the unarmed middle and upper classes living in the cities reinforced by pressure from the United States led Paz Estenssoro in July 1953 to reconstitute a much reduced army of 5,000 men.

During the next four years the United States as well as the moderate and conservative elements in Bolivia became increasingly alarmed about the militancy of the left and the ability of the government to maintain order. As a result, the government gradually increased the size of the army. By 1958 the army approximated its prerevolutionary size, the officers purged after the 1952 revolution were reinstated, and the United States initiated a military aid program to the country. The Bolivian military, rebuilt with the support and blessing of the United States, seized power in 1964 and has run the country ever since.[27]

Forced Readjustment. The anti-communist crusade of 1953 and 1954 continued throughout the Eisenhower years, but by the end of 1954 Latin America seemed relatively secure from communist intervention, and there were no serious challenges to United States economic interests. Nevertheless, mounting discontent, frustration, and hostility toward the United States during the late 1950s forced the Eisenhower Administration to reevaluate and readjust its Latin American policy.

Underlying much of the growing Latin American pressure for change was the fact that the export boom enjoyed by the area as a consequence of the Korean War came to an end. The value of Latin American exports (excluding Venezuelan) reached a peak of $6.5 billion in 1951. It did not again obtain this level during the eight years of the Eisenhower Administration. Furthermore, during the 1950s the value of Latin American exports (excluding Venezuelan) increased only 10 percent, while the value of world exports increased 141 percent. The per capita value of Latin American exports decreased and prices on their predominantly raw material exports fluctuated drastically.[28]

A number of other developments paved the way for a readjustment in policy. For one, Soviet policy toward Latin America changed somewhat after the death of Stalin in 1953. Previously, the main thrust of Soviet policy had been to support communist parties in Latin America. Under Nikita Khrushchev, however, the Soviet Union developed a more flexible policy of supporting popular non-communist as well as communist parties and sought to extend economic and technical assistance to many Latin American governments. The Russians never made available large sums of money, but the existence of any alternate source of assistance not restricted by the precepts of traditional United States policy presented a challenge to Washington.

In addition, important policy makers in Washington began to change some of their ideas. Milton Eisenhower gradually came to realize that private capital alone could not bring about meaningful development in Latin America and that social changes had to accompany economic development if the latter was to be effective. He argued that at the beginning of the Eisenhower Administration no one in Latin America or in the United States had thought of development in any other than orthdox economic terms, and that the turning point for him and other government officials had been the meeting of the American presidents at Panama in 1956. There, according to Milton Eisenhower, President Eisenhower reflected the change by suggesting the establishment of an inter-American committee to consider ways to improve "the welfare of the individual." [29]

The forces for change were further strengthened in 1957 when Douglas Dillon became under secretary of state for economic affairs. Dillon, who had little knowledge of Latin America, was nevertheless involved in the Inter-American Conference at Buenos Aires and was much disturbed by the negativism of the United States position on development. Dillon joined Milton Eisenhower in the effort to bring about a readjustment.

Latin American antagonism toward the United States also helped stimulate the policy readjustment. Most notably, the United States government was stunned by the hostility shown Vice President Richard Nixon in May 1958 when he visited a number of Latin American countries en route to and from the inauguration of President Arturo Frondizi of Argentina. In Caracas, Montevideo, and Lima, Nixon was the object of bitter denunciations and demonstrations attacking United States policy.

As a result of the hostility shown Nixon, President Juscelino Kubitschek of Brazil suggested a thorough review of all inter-American policies and proposed a joint development program, including an inter-American bank, called Operation Pan America. President Eisenhower responded in several ways. First, at the urging of Dillon, he ended the long-standing United States opposition to an inter-American bank, and in July 1958 the United States proposed the establishment of such a bank. Second, and again as a result of Dillon's efforts, he accepted the establishment of price-stabilization study groups. And third, he sent his brother Milton to Central America to evaluate the situation and to make recommendations for changes in policy.

Even with the change in Soviet policy, the change in personnel, and the jolt of the Nixon trip, there was little immediate change in United States-Latin American policy. For example, after his trip to Central America, Milton Eisenhower had proposed that the United States show its commitment to "the welfare of the individual" in Latin America by funding a model low-cost housing project in Panama. The proposal was dropped because the Treasury Department felt it was economically unsound and too costly.

The Eisenhower Administration made no major policy modifications until provoked by the Cuban Revolution. In January 1959 Fidel Castro overthrew the dictatorship of Fulgencio Batista in Cuba. Over the next two years Castro brought about significant urban and agrarian reform, initiated a major effort to end illiteracy and disease, nationalized foreign-owned companies, established trade relations with Russia and China, and embarked on an arms buildup. The United States became increasingly concerned that Castro was a communist and that the Cuban Revolution was becoming an attractive alternative to its free enterprise model for development in Latin America. Under this pressure, the United States began to support social reform and an increased role for governments in economic development in exchange for opposition to Castro.

In 1960, the last year of the Eisenhower Administration, the new policy began to emerge. Late in February President Eisenhower visited Argentina, Brazil, Chile, and Uruguay for the first time during his administration. He assured the respective governments that he supported social change and economic development and that the United States government was anxious to make new resources available to them. But he also stressed his anti-communist, anti-Castro, and pro-private investment philosophy. For example, he was particularly upset by signs in Rio that said "We like Ike. We like Fidel too," because he felt support for both Ike and Fidel was impossible. In addition, he reminded the four presidents with whom he spoke that "if Latin America is to progress, it must attract increased private investment from overseas, a flow that is certain to dry up unless foreign investors believe that Castroism is to be repudiated by the nations of the Latin American continent." [30] In other words, we will help you, but only if you repudiate Castro.

As the conflict between the United States and Cuba intensified, the Eisenhower Administration increased its efforts to undermine the Castro regime, to destroy the Cuban appeal to the Latin American countries, and to strengthen its own image as the friend of those seeking democratic change and economic development. In July the United States cut Cuba's sugar quota. At the meeting of hemisphere foreign ministers in San José, Costa Rica, in August, the United States sought to win the support of the Latin American states for some kind of collective action against Cuba. There, the United States, in a manner reminiscent of Caracas in 1954, charged the Russians with interfering in the Americas, but the Latin Americans saw the conflict as one between the United States and a revolutionary and nationalistic regime in Cuba. Thus, the Declaration of San José condemned all types of extracontinental intervention in the Americas, but, significantly, it also stated that no American state could intervene in another to impose "ideologies or policies, economic or social principles." [31]

During the summer of 1960 the United States also took steps to establish a special hemisphere fund to be administered by the recently established Inter-American Bank, which would make available soft loans for housing, health, literacy, and other social projects. Dillon was the prime mover in this effort and persuaded Eisenhower and the Congress to contribute half a billion dollars to a new Social Trust Fund. At the Bogotá meeting of the Organization of American States (OAS) Dillon announced the contribution of the United States. Furthermore, the United States also reversed its previous opposition to a Latin American common market and helped establish the Latin American Free Trade Association and the Central American Common Market.

Thus, by the end of the Eisenhower Administration the United States had begun a readjustment of its post-World War II policy toward Latin America. The Truman Administration had developed the basic policy designed to maintain the South American empire during the cold war era—vigilant anti-communism and opposition to neutralism, planned economies, state capitalism, and "excessive industrialization," which the United States associated with communism; support for United States economic interests in the area; support for and development of the military establishments as the local groups most able to defend United States interests; and development via private enterprise. The Eisenhower Administration did not abandon these policies, but a series of circumstances, particularly the Cuban Revolution, forced it to make something of a readjustment or modification of traditional policy, to support social development, and to permit an increased governmental role in economic development. However, the change produced by the Eisenhower Administration was belated and of inadequate dimensions.

NOTES

1. United States, Department of Commerce, Bureau of Census, *Statistical Abstract of the United States, 1950* (Washington, D.C., 1950), p. 840; *The New York Times*, March 7, 1947.

2. One of the best presentations of the official view of the development of the cold war is John W. Spanier, *American Foreign Policy Since World War II* (New York, 1968), third edition. Among the best revisionist analyses of the origins of the cold war are: Barnet, *Intervention* and *Roots*; Lloyd C. Gardner, *Architects of Illusion* (Chicago, 1970); Kolko, *Roots* and *Limits*; and Walter LeFeber, *America, Russia and the Cold War, 1945–1971* (New York, 1972).

3. Barnet, *Intervention*, pp. 132–152; Spanier, *American*, pp. 43–141; Senate Committee on Foreign Relations, *Hearings on the Act for Interna-

tional Development, March 30, 1950 (Washington, D.C., 1950), pp. 1–25.

4. Quoted in Dozer, *Good Neighbors*, p. 191.

5. Duggan, *The Americas*, p. 108. See also *Foreign Relations*, 1945, p. 759.

6. Duggan, *ibid.*, p. 118. Quote taken from Campbell, *Masquerade Peace*, p. 171.

7. *Foreign Relations*, 1946, pp. 492–494.

8. *Ibid.*, pp. 154–155.

9. *Ibid.*, p. 613. This account of United States-Chilean relations is based on *ibid.*, p. 596 ff. and *Foreign Relations*, 1947, p. 497 ff.

10. *Foreign Relations*, 1947, p. 506.

11. For the documents of the conference see United States, Department of State, Ninth International Conference of American States, Bogotá, Colombia, March 30–May 2, 1948, *Report of the Delegation of the United States of America* (Washington, D.C., 1948).

12. For text of address, see *ibid.*, pp. 309–317.

13. *Foreign Relations*, 1946, p. 270. See also Robert H. Potash, *The Army and Politics in Argentina, 1928–1945* (Palo Alto, Calif., 1969), Chapters 7 and 8.

14. *Foreign Relations*, 1946, pp. 256–258.

15. *Foreign Relations*, 1947, pp. 260–261.

16. The debate can be found in *Foreign Relations*, 1946, pp. 86–110, and *Foreign Relations*, 1947, pp. 101–136.

17. *Ibid.*, 1947, pp. 106–112.

18. House Committee on Foreign Affairs, *Hearings on The Mutual Security Program, July 25, 1951* (Washington, D.C., 1951).

19. Milton S. Eisenhower, *The Wine Is Bitter* (New York, 1963), pp. xi, 72–76.

20. *Ibid.*, pp. 128–129. See also Milton S. Eisenhower, "United States-Latin American Relations, Report to the President," Department of State *Bulletin*, XXIX, 752 (November 23, 1953), pp. 695–717.

21. Dwight D. Eisenhower, *Mandate for Change* (New York, 1965), pp. 503–512.

22. Robert J. Alexander, *The Bolivian National Revolution* (New Brunswick, N.J., 1958); James M. Malloy, *Bolivia: The Uncomplete Revolution* (Pittsburgh, 1970); James W. Wilkie, *The Bolivian Revolution and U.S. Aid since 1952* (Los Angeles, 1969).

23. Cheddi Jagan, *Forbidden Freedom* (New York, 1954), pp. 86–91, and *The West on Trial* (London, 1966), pp. 145–169; United Kingdom, *British Guiana, Suspension of the Constitution* (London, 1953), Command No. 8980.

24. Guillermo Toriello Garrido, *La batalla de Guatemala* (Mexico, 1955); Ronald M. Schneider, *Communism in Guatemala, 1944–1955* (New York, 1959); David Wise and Thomas B. Ross, *The Invisible Government* (New York, 1964), pp. 177–196; Mecham, *Survey*, pp. 213–221.

25. For the documents of the conference, see United States, Department of State, Tenth Inter-American Conference, Caracas, Venezuela, March

1–28, 1954, *Report of the Delegation of the United States of America* (Washington, D.C., 1954).

26. *Ibid.,* pp. 156–157.

27. Alexander, *Bolivian;* William H. Brill, *Military Intervention in Bolivia* (Washington, D.C., 1967); Willard F. Barber, C. Neale Ronning, *Internal Security and Military Power* (Columbus, Ohio, 1966); Wilkie, *Bolivian.*

28. United Nations, Economic Commission for Latin America, *The Economic Development of Latin America in the Post-War Period* (New York, 1964), pp. 122–125. Venezuela is excluded from the calculations because its large exports of oil make it unique and distort the Latin American averages.

29. Milton Eisenhower, *Wine,* pp. 199–203.

30. *Ibid.,* pp. 128–129.

31. Department of State *Bulletin* (September 12, 1960), pp. 395–412.

chapter
4

Maintaining a South
American Empire in the Era
of Inevitable Social and
Economic Development:
1961–1975

When John F. Kennedy assumed the presidency in January 1961,
it was clear to most policy makers in Washington that the post-
World War II techniques of maintaining a South American empire
were no longer adequate. Since 1945 the South American countries had been seeking above all else to industrialize and to develop their economies. The Truman and Eisenhower administrations had successfully delayed rapid movement in this direction,
because they believed that "excessive industrialization," development, economic nationalism, and state capitalism in South America
would undermine the economic and security interest of the United
States. But the factors that had stimulated the policy adjustment
during the last year of the Eisenhower Administration continued
in force during the early 1960s and led to a new approach in
maintaining the South American empire.

The new approach, the Alliance for Progress, was based on the
assumption that development was not only inevitable but necessary for the economic and security interests of the United States.
The Alliance was primarily a response to the "Soviet challenge"
and particularly to the Cuban Revolution. It was a reactive policy

of social, political, and economic reform designed to provide Latin America with an attractive alternative to Castroism and to immunize it from communism. Because Washington officials now recognized that socioeconomic change was inevitable, they supported it in order to control and channel it along lines acceptable to the United States. The social and economic revolution envisioned by the Alliance was probably not sufficiently valid in and of itself for the United States to support it without the threat of Castroism. Had there been no Cuban Revolution, there is little evidence to suggest that there would have been an Alliance for Progress of such magnitude.

The Alliance committed the United States to support political democracy as well as development within a capitalist framework. Very quickly, however, Washington officials began arguing that Latin America lacked the necessary social and economic systems to sustain political democracy, that development designed to create such underpinnings of democracy required political stability, and that the United States commitment to democracy thus assumed a prior commitment to support political stability. Once this line of reasoning was generally accepted, the United States increasingly supported the Latin American military as the force best able to bring about orderly development. The commitment to democracy was a long-range goal that rationalized short-term support for authoritarian anti-communist military governments. They, in turn, were supposed to create the social and economic conditions necessary to sustain political democracy in the unspecified future.

As the Castro threat dwindled and Vietnam and the balance of payments problems emerged, the commitment to political democracy and social reform receded into the background and support for the authoritarian anti-communist military governments and for economic development within a capitalist framework came to overwhelm the foreground. The high levels of aid initiated by Kennedy continued throughout the Johnson years, but the rhetoric of social change and political democracy was for the most part dropped. Nixon and Ford took the policy one step further; they cut back aid to Latin America but increased support for the military and business and relied on these two sectors to protect United States economic and security interests. Yet throughout the period, the idea of accepting and controlling development initiated by Kennedy remained the underlying policy for maintaining the South American empire.

John F. Kennedy and the Emergence of the Alliance: 1961–1963

The Kennedy Administration introduced some new ideas into United States Latin American policy. As Arthur Schlesinger, Jr., pointed out, "Though Kennedy was deeply concerned with the conflict between the United States and the Soviet Union, he did not consider that conflict the source of all mankind's troubles." Poverty was a major source of mankind's troubles, and poverty could only be overcome by economic development. Furthermore, Kennedy believed development in Latin America required not only capital and technology, but political and social reforms to eliminate the bottlenecks of economic development.[1]

The Alliance for Progress embodied these new ideas, but as time passed the new ideas were swallowed up by the pragmatism of the President and his advisers. In the end, order and security became the priority and economic development was secondary. Thus, the administration decided that its first commitment was to stable Latin American regimes that were anti-communist, and these regimes were often military dictatorships defending the socioeconomic privileges of the traditional elites. As Kennedy summed up his pragmatic philosophy shortly after the assassination of longtime dictator Rafael Trujillo in the Dominican Republic: "There are three possibilities in descending order of preference: a decent democratic regime, a continuation of the Trujillo regime, or a Castro regime. We ought to aim at the first, but we really can't renounce the second until we are sure that we can avoid the third." [2] Kennedy's Latin American policy included the rhetoric of fundamental change and with it a widespread hope that such change was possible, but by the time of the President's assassination, the traditional anti-communist and essentially pro-*status quo* policy of Truman and Eisenhower was again in effect.

Kennedy's policy emerged from a number of sources. The new President had a deep personal interest in the area that was kindled by the hostility shown Vice President Nixon during his 1958 Latin American trip, by his own visit to Puerto Rico in 1958, and by his realization that the rigid positions of United States cold war policy were becoming increasingly ineffective. In addition, Kennedy was influenced by Brazilian President Kubitschek's Operation Pan America and the Eisenhower Administration's readjustment of policy during its last year. Indeed, Douglas Dillon, a prime mover in the Eisenhower readjustment, became secretary of the treasury under Kennedy and headed the United States delegation to the Punta del Este Conference, which created the Alliance for Progress. And Kennedy was also influenced by Richard Goodwin, who joined his staff in 1959 and became his major adviser on Latin America.

The most important source of the Kennedy Latin American policy, however, was the January 4, 1961, *Report* of his Latin American Task Force. The members of the task force—Adolf Berle, Chairman, Harvard professor Lincoln Gordon, Rutgers professor Robert Alexander, University of Pennsylvania professor Arthur P. Whitaker, and Puerto Ricans Teodoro Moscoso and Arturo Morales Carrion—combined knowledge of Latin America and experience with previous United States efforts to bring about economic recovery and development. As Jerome Levinson and Juan de Onis concisely summed up, the task force

. . . pulled together the main strands of American liberalism as they applied to Latin America. Berle represented a continuation of the Good Neighbor Policy and a link with many progressive Latin American political figures. Gordon brought the operational experience of the Marshall Plan and a professional competence in development economics. Moscoso and Morales Carrion added the Puerto Rican development experiences and a Latin feel for political issues and personalities. Alexander and Whitaker provided some experience and perspective on Latin American history. Goodwin, who sat with the group, provided a link to the White House and represented the New Frontier. . . . [3]

The *Report* affirmed the importance of Latin America to the United States and argued that the "greatest single task of American diplomacy in Latin America is to divorce the inevitable and necessary Latin American social transformation from connection with and prevent its capture by overseas Communist power politics." To meet the communist challenge, one which "resembles, but is more dangerous than, the Nazi-Fascist threat of the Franklin Roosevelt period," the United States must make "an even bolder and more imaginative response." The United States, the *Report* continued, cannot "stabilize the dying reactionary situation" and should instead support the democratic-progressive movements, including the Catholic and moderate democrats on the right and the Christian Socialists and non-communist socialists on the left, but excluding any united front parties.[4]

Furthermore, the task force recommended supporting the Bogotá program, since it "contains the essential elements of the kind of program the new Administration should support," and also a new multilateral programing body. It recognized the importance of agrarian reform, because 70 percent of Latin America's population consisted of agrarian laborers. And finally, the *Report* rejected the Eisenhower Administration's laissez-faire philosophy of economic development and noted that this philosophy "amounted to saying that whatever was good for General Motors would be good for the Latin American countries." The United States, the *Report* summed up, must "withdraw our doctrinaire opposition to loans and technical assistance for Latin American government enterprises in mineral, oil, and industrial fields." Furthermore, the *Report* recommended that while there should be no blanket support for market stabilization of all major Latin American exports, the United States must be willing to discuss such arrangements when necessary.[5]

The task force thus set forth the basic assumptions of the Alliance: the Latin American *status quo* could no longer be maintained; the social transformation of the area was necessary and inevitable; the United States, working with the predominantly middle-class democratic left, must assume leadership in bringing about this transformation in order to make sure that development proceeded within a capitalist framework.

The Puerto Rican development program known as Operation Bootstrap was a source of practical experience for the Alliance for Progress.[6] Operation Bootstrap had been initiated by the Puerto Rican Popular Democratic Party of Luis Muñoz Marín and directed by task force member and the future deputy for Latin America of the Agency for International Development (AID) Teodoro Moscoso. When Muñoz Marín was first elected governor of Puerto Rico in 1940, he had been supported by a broad coalition of the left that had sought agrarian reform, state ownership of public services, and industrialization under the tutelage of the state as the best way to transform the stagnant sugar economy. In power, however, Muñoz Marín adopted an increasingly "pragmatic" philosophy and pursued more conservative policies. Most significantly, Operation Bootstrap, which got under way during the late 1940s, committed Puerto Rico to industrialization via United States private capital and technology. A program of liberal tax incentives and a Development Bank, which pursued conservative lending policies coupled with political stability, cheap labor, and easy access to the United States market, attracted hundreds of United States firms to the island. The government sold the state-owned cement and bottle industries to private concerns once they demonstrated that they were profitable. Agrarian reform was given little attention. Government planning and control gave way to government promotion and support of United States private investment.

Since the Alliance for Progress incorporated much of its basic philosophy and approach, the results of Puerto Rico's "industrialization by invitation" are important. On the one hand, industrial production increased dramatically and the annual growth rate climbed to a remarkable 6 percent. By 1960 industry had replaced agriculture as the major income-producing sector of the economy. Per capita income grew from $122 in 1940 to $341 in 1950 and to $677 in 1960. On the other hand, Puerto Rico became more closely integrated into the United States economic structure, unemployment increased, tens of thousands of Puerto Ricans migrated to the mainland, the distribution of wealth became more unfavorable to the working class, and the unionization of workers remained low.

Perhaps most importantly, Puerto Rico increasingly lost control of economic decision making. Three out of four firms doing business in Puerto Rico belonged to non-Puerto Rican stockholders. Four out of five top management personnel were non-Puerto Rican. Profits were high and, since there were no guarantees that the profits would be reinvested, capital increasingly flowed out of the island. And finally, capital was available mainly for the manufacturing and processing of export commodities and thus prevented the development of a balanced economy. Operation Bootstrap dramatically stimulated the industrialization of the island and increased the wealth of the few. But it also increased Puerto Rico's dependency on the United States, removed important parts of the decision-making process from the island, and did little to improve the quality of life of rural peasants and the majority of the urban poor.

None of the South American countries were prepared to accept Puerto Rico as a model for their development. Many felt that Puerto Ricans could speak neither for the United States nor for South America. Roberto Campos, the Brazilian economist and government adviser, made this point when he commented on the appointment of Moscoso as AID deputy for Latin America. The official reaction of the Brazilian government to the appointment of Moscoso was favorable, Campos explained, but in private, many Brazilians expressed doubts about it. They felt, he continued, that a Puerto Rican, all of whom were believed to be second-class citizens of the United States, would not carry sufficient weight in the United States to be effective and, since Puerto Ricans had "developed a rather passive mind in relation to the United States," that the Puerto Rican experience was not the best for understanding the problems of South America.[7]

In the early days of the Kennedy Administration, policy makers in Washington did not apparently perceive the potential conflict involved in simultaneously pursuing their goals of development and anti-communism and therefore felt no need to establish a priority between them. From the beginning, all of the members of the administration agreed that no other Latin American state could be permitted to follow the Cuban path and that capitalist development under the tutelage of the United States was the best way to eliminate poverty and the appeal of Castroism, but there was a division of opinion among them regarding the best way to proceed.

Delesseps S. Morrison, a prominent New Orleans businessman-politician and Kennedy's ambassador to the Organization of American States, was representative of the "conservatives" or "realists" within the administration. Latin Americans were, according to Morrison, illiterate and lacked a democratic tradition.[8] The communist threat was widespread in Latin America and demanded firm opposition on the part of the United States. Development, Morrison believed, was now inevitable, but the process of

development was inherently so disruptive that the first require-
ment of policy was to insure the maintenance of order. The military, he argued, was the most realistic and reliable force within
the Latin American countries and the only one capable of maintaining order. Therefore, the United States must be ready to work
with it. While he opposed military coups, Morrison hastened to
point out that not all military coups were bad and should be condemned. If such a coup was anti-communist and kept communists
and their sympathizers out of power, the United States should
support it. Each military coup had to be evaluated in terms of the
specific situation.

While he urged support of the anti-communist military in Latin
America, Morrison denounced the democratic left as romantic,
unrealistic, and soft on communism. He attacked Kennedy advisers Arthur Schlesinger, Jr., and Richard Goodwin, who he believed viewed the democratic left as an extension of the Americans for Democratic Action and as the group most capable of
bringing about Latin American development. For Morrison, Argentine President Arturo Frondizi and his advisers and Brazilian
Presidents Janio Quadros and Jango Goulart and their advisers
were "undercover agents or dupes of Castro" and intolerable
"neutrals," who refused to vote with the United States on every
issue before the Organization of American States.

Arthur Schlesinger, Jr., a Harvard historian and a member of
Kennedy's White House staff, was representative of the "liberal"
view toward Latin America within the administration.[9] Schlesinger complained bitterly about the conservative bureaucracy of the
State Department, which he felt was uncritically committed to the
concepts of the 1950s: rigid anti-communism, reliance on the military, and development via private investment and technical assistance (development "as an act of immaculate private concep-
tion"). Schlesinger believed that by 1961 the military interests in
the United States threatened to undermine United States-Latin
American policy just as business interests had undermined it thirty-
five years before. The significance of Kennedy, according to
Schlesinger, was his attitude toward the Third World in general
and Latin America in particular. Dulles, he pointed out, had
viewed neutralism as immoral, while Kennedy saw it as a position
similar to that of the United States in an earlier period. Schlesin-

ger believed that Latin America was a critical battleground between democracy and communism, but Dulles' definition of neutralism would drive the Third World closer to Moscow.

The Alliance for Progress, Schlesinger argued, was designed not only to provide capital and technology in greater quantities than had previous administrations, but also to destroy the internal Latin American social and political barriers to economic development. The only Latin American group that was anti-communist and capable of carrying out a program of democratic development was the democratic left. Therefore, according to Schlesinger, the United States must support the democratic left.

Kennedy's Latin American policy thus encompassed two goals —development within a capitalist framework and the prevention of any Latin American country from following the example of Castro—and two approaches to achieve these goals—support for the military and support for the democratic left. Initially the administration pursued both goals with equal fervor, but as time passed it increasingly gave priority to the containment of communism—the maintenance of order and internal security—and to support for the military.

During the first year of the Kennedy Administration, the United States pursued its developmental and anti-communist aims simultaneously. On March 11, 1961, Kennedy rekindled the frustrated hopes of most Latin Americans when he promised to help them "strike off the remaining bonds of poverty and ignorance" with a ten-year United States-supported development program, economic integration, stabilization of commodity prices, and the sharing of technology. Less than a month later Kennedy permitted the ill-fated invasion of Castro Cuba at the Bay of Pigs.

Similarly, the United States pursued its developmental and anti-communist goals at the two Inter-American Conferences in Punta del Este, Uruguay. At Punta del Este I (August 1961), the Alliance for Progress was formally launched and the United States committed itself to support the "democratic modernization" of Latin America. At Punta del Este II (January 1962), the United States set forth the "indispensable supporting policy for the containment of Castro," the expulsion of Cuba from the OAS.[10]

What is significant about these examples is that the United States pursued its goals ignoring the fact that while the majority of Latin American governments supported the Alliance and were anti-communist, they rejected the United States approach to the containment of Castroism and their primary concern was development. Most Latin Americans criticized the Bay of Pigs fiasco as an example of unnecessary and unjustified United States intervention in the internal affairs of a Latin American country. At Punta del Este II Cuba was expelled from the OAS by a vote of 14–6, exactly the two-thirds necessary, but the largest, most populous, and most democratic countries (Argentina, Brazil, Mexico, Chile, Bolivia, and Ecuador) abstained in protest. Furthermore, to get the vote of Haiti, the fourteenth vote, the United States "yielded to blackmail and agreed to resume our aid to the airport at Port-au-Prince." [11]

Increasingly, however, the Kennedy Administration believed that it was forced to choose, at least in the short run, between democratic development and anti-communism, and in every case it chose the latter. Kennedy was very much upset by Russian Prime Minister Khrushchev's January 1961 speech, which predicted the triumph of communism in the underdeveloped world through internally based wars of national liberation. This concern was intensified by his two-day confrontation with Khrushchev in Vienna five months later. The anti-communism of the Eisenhower Administration had depended on nuclear bombs for the most part. The new anti-communism of the Kennedy Administration relied instead on special United States anti-guerrilla forces (the Green Berets) and on local military counterparts throughout the underdeveloped world. Thus, in South America, Khrushchev's challenge, plus a fear of Castro, frustration with the operation of the inter-American security system, doubts about the assumption that increased economic aid would produce political stability, and distress at the apparent inability of civilians to provide effective leadership, led the pragmatic Kennedy to resort to covert subversive operations and to increased support for the military as the only sure way to contain communism and create an environment suitable for development.[12]

United States relations with British Guiana clearly illustrate the administration's preoccupation with internal security and its willingness to employ covert subversive activity to eliminate even the slightest possibility of communist penetration in South America. As mentioned in the preceding chapter, during the early years of the Eisenhower Administration, when the United States government was deeply involved with the communist threat in Bolivia and Guatemala, the Marxist Cheddi Jagan was elected local leader of British Guiana. Five months later Jagan was removed from office when the British, encouraged by the United States, suspended the constitution of the colony and landed troops. A similar election was held in British Guiana in September 1961, less than a year after Kennedy's inauguration. Jagan again won.

Kennedy adviser Arthur Schlesinger did not think British Guiana was very important to the world political situation, but he did see it as a target of convenience for the communists in South America.[13] The main targets were Venezuela and Brazil. Nevertheless, Schlesinger felt, the United States had to meet the Russian challenge even in tiny British Guiana. England, on the other hand, saw Jagan as an independent and a nationalist as well as a Marxist and, most importantly, the choice of the people of the country. Thus, England believed that both London and Washington should support him.

In October 1961, one month after his reelection as prime minister, Jagan came to Washington seeking $40 million in aid for development. He talked with Kennedy and made it clear that he was a socialist and a nationalist and that he believed a considerable degree of state planning and control was essential to develop his country. Kennedy responded by saying:

> We are not engaged in a crusade to force private enterprise on parts of the world where it is not relevant. If we are engaged in a crusade for anything, it is national independence. That is the primary purpose of our aid. The secondary purpose is to encourage individual freedom and political freedom. But we can't always get that: and we have often helped countries which have little personal freedom, like Yugoslavia, if they maintain their national independence. This is the basic thing.[14]

Nevertheless, "national independence" in British Guiana did not in fact seem to be the "basic thing" for the Kennedy Administration. Schlesinger explained that the administration was concerned because Jagan admired the Marxist *Monthly Review* and he was ideologically "fuzzy." Kennedy concluded that "Parliamentary democracy is going to be damn difficult in a country at this stage of development." Thus, the United States government decided against granting any aid at the time but agreed to send a face-saving mission to British Guiana to look into the matter. The State Department at first favored granting aid to Jagan, but then Secretary of State Rusk personally intervened and reversed this decision because he feared congressional criticism and the possibility that such aid might damage the entire AID program.

Seven months later Forbes Burnham, a former leader of Jagan's People's Progressive Party but by that time his chief political rival, came to Washington. He was a socialist and a nationalist like Jagan, but unlike Jagan he was a fervent anti-communist and strongly pro-United States. Schlesinger commented that he quickly developed the feeling that "an independent British Guiana under Burnham would cause us many fewer problems than an independent British Guiana under Jagan."

The administration's concern, apparently, was not to develop British Guiana and improve the quality of life of her people, but to minimize problems, and to minimize problems meant supporting Burnham rather than Jagan. In October 1963 the British, again pressured by the United States, changed the election rules in British Guiana to favor Burnham. The critical elections of December 1964 proved the effectiveness of the change; Jagan's party won a clear majority of the popular vote (46 percent) but only twenty-four seats in the legislature, while Burnham's party won twenty-two seats, and a third party won seven seats. By combining his votes in the legislature with those of the third party, Burnham was able to oust Jagan as prime minister. In 1966 British Guiana became the independent state of Guyana under the leadership of Burnham.

Schlesinger's account does allude to the parliamentary manipulation that permitted Burnham to oust Jagan, but it leaves out the covert role played by the United States in bringing this about. The vehicles of United States operations in British Guiana were an American labor union and the CIA. Between 1959 and 1964 the American Federation of State, County and Municipal Employees, under the leadership of Arnold Zander, permitted two CIA agents to join its International Affairs Department and accepted approximately $60,000 per year to support its international activity. The CIA agents, working under cover of the Government Employees Union, joined pro-Burnham unions in instigating riots, racial strife, and strikes in British Guiana in 1962 and 1963 for the purpose of embarrassing Jagan and undermining confidence in his ability to control and rule the country. The CIA provided money and food to keep the strikes going every time they appeared to be faltering.[15]

It is impossible to measure the precise relationship of the strikes to Burnham's victory, but clearly the strikes did not help Jagan. Most important, however, was the fact that the Kennedy Administration felt compelled and justified to resort to such covert operations. Jagan was the most popular leader in the country and had been democratically elected prime minister several times. It thus seems reasonable to conclude that the "basic thing" was not "national independence" as Kennedy had told Jagan in October 1961. The basic thing was the new pragmatic anti-communism.

In addition to its willingness to engage in covert subversive activity, the Kennedy Administration also relied increasingly on the South American military to fight what it perceived as real or potential communist threats. For the most part this involved strengthening the South American military organizations and developing an even closer working relationship with them. Thus, under Kennedy, the United States more than doubled the annual amount of military aid to Latin America (Table 3–2), substantially expanded its officer exchange training programs, and intensified the advisory activities of the United States military missions in the area.[16]

There were, however, several problems associated with such a policy. First, Kennedy officials perceived a change in the nature of the security threat, and this required a corresponding change in the nature of the response. Until 1960 hemispheric defense doctrine had, for the most part, focused on external threats to the area. With Khrushchev's talk of wars of national liberation and Castro's increasingly radical actions, however, policy makers in Washington became preoccupied with the potentialities of guerrilla warfare. The Kennedy Administration thus shifted its attention from external to internal security. To carry out this policy, it had to work out ways to convert military establishments primarily prepared to fight external conflicts and conventional internal uprisings into fighting forces capable of eradicating highly mobile and hard-to-find guerrilla bands.

A second problem for the Kennedy Administration was that it was committed to a democratic transformation of the existing South American socioeconomic structure at the same time that the

South American military it supported had the image of being a defender of the *status quo*. The Kennedy Administration thus set about to change the activities and the image of the South American military, to transform it from an impediment to democracy into a force associated with the kinds of reform and progress envisioned by the Alliance for Progress. The central focus of this effort was the doctrine of civic action.[17] The Civic Action Program attempted to involve the military in highly visible non-military projects—transportation, health, housing, and so on—which would benefit the general public. This involvement of the military establishments in the process of development, it was assumed, would soon create the desired new image for them.

Administration officials recognized the risks involved in pursuing the new policy, but they nevertheless came to believe that there was no alternative. The South American military was an active political force in most countries and increased United States support would strengthen its position vis-à-vis civilian democratic political forces. Most of Washington believed that since order and security were essential to the success of the Alliance for Progress, the military was the only force capable of providing the necessary order and security. As Secretary of Defense Robert McNamara summarized: "The essential role of the Latin American military as a stabilizing force outweighs any risks involved in providing military assistance for internal security purposes."[18] The Kennedy Administration, in the name of creating and preserving the proper environment for development, gradually adopted the "pragmatic" views of Morrison and his supporters and made anti-communism (order and security guaranteed by the military) its number one priority.

United States reaction to military coup d'etats in Argentina and Peru illustrates the nature and implications of this policy. In March 1962, just a few months after Punta del Este, the democratically elected pro-United States president of Argentina, Arturo Frondizi, was overthrown by the military. He was overthrown because he had permitted the followers of former President Juan D. Perón to participate in a free election (which they won) and because Argentina refused to support the expulsion of Castro from the OAS at Punta del Este II. The State Department wanted Kennedy to condemn the coup as unconstitutional and in conflict with the principles and goals of the Alliance for Progress and to suspend aid to Argentina. Morrison, who opposed such action, went to Senators Wayne Morse and Burt Hickenlooper and convinced them of the correctness of his position. The senators saw Kennedy and there was no condemnation or suspension of aid. "As it turned out," Morrison noted, "condemnation would have been most unfortunate. The military in Argentina had brought about the severance of relations with Cuba." [19]

In July 1962 the Peruvian military, led by officers trained in the United States and using equipment supplied by the United States, overthrew the government in order to keep the democratically elected president from assuming office. The United States suspended diplomatic relations, cut off economic aid, and condemned the coup. But this policy increased political tensions and the possibility of internal disorder within Peru and so, after extracting a promise to hold elections, the administration reversed itself and recognized the military government. "Though Kennedy was criticized at the time," Schlesinger noted, "for seeming to begin one policy—nonrecognition—and then to go back on it, the fact was that the suspension of relations produced exactly the desired result. There were no reprisals, civil freedom was restored, free elections were guaranteed. While most American businessmen in Peru wanted unconditional recognition of the regime, the United States government showed its independence of business pressure and its opposition to military dictatorship." [20] A year later elections were held, but in 1968 the military staged another coup and has remained in power since then.

Kennedy's Latin American policy, which initially committed the United States to support and guide the "inevitable and necessary Latin American social transformation" in order to "prevent its capture by overseas Communist power politics," gradually evolved into pragmatic anti-communism. Order and security became the prerequisites for development and the military became the most viable and reliable force to further United States interests in the area. In the process, the socioeconomic reforms and the democratic politics envisioned by the Alliance for Progress were for the most part relegated to a distant and perhaps nonexistent future.

Some Friendly Critiques

At Punta del Este I (August 1961), Cuban Economic Minister Che Guevara denounced the Alliance for Progress as an "instru-

ment of [United States] economic imperialism," but criticism of
Kennedy's Latin American policy was not confined to Cubans or
to Marxists. A number of more conservative Latin Americans,
who considered themselves friends of the United States, also were
bothered by many aspects of Washington's new approach to the
area. One of the most perceptive of these critics was the Brazilian
economist and diplomat, Roberto Campos. Campos had been
managing director of the Brazilian Development Bank under Juscelino Kubitschek, roving ambassador to Europe under Janio
Quadros, ambassador to Washington under Jango Goulart, and in
1964 was made planning minister under the military government
of Humberto Castello Branco. His views are of particular significance because of his high level of participation in so many different Brazilian governments, his belief in an essentially conservative
economic policy (monetary discipline, credit containment, private
enterprise both foreign and domestic, and so on), his anti-communism and anti-Castroism, his distrust of "extreme nationalism,"
and his great friendship and admiration for the United States.

In an extensive interview with a representative of the Kennedy
Library on May 29, 1964, Campos began by noting the dissatis-
faction in Brazil because of the Eisenhower and Kennedy administrations' rejection of Operation Pan America. Nevertheless, he
believed that the Alliance for Progress, which for the first time
committed the United States to support target rates of growth and
long-range planning and financing, was a good thing. The novelty
of the Alliance, Campos believed, was its insistence on social and
structural reform and its emphasis on social investment.[21]

However, it is important to note that the emphasis on social reform, which Milton Eisenhower, Douglas Dillon, Kennedy, and
others saw as so significant, was treated with some suspicion and
skepticism by Campos. He pointed out that the architects of Operation Pan America regarded social development as something
that "would flow inevitably from economic development itself,
while the premature emphasis . . . on social development might
decrease the needed concentration of investment on basic industry
and basic economic projects." At the time of the Alliance, Campos continued, many Brazilians also believed that the emphasis on
social reforms might in fact be a delaying tactic of the United
States to avoid a major financial commitment to Latin America;
that inaction on social reforms, which would be difficult to bring

about and would take a long time to achieve, would provide the
United States with an excuse to withhold funds. Furthermore, he
pointed out, many thought that the "emphasis on social reforms
might be a convenient way of slowing down the possible pace of
industrialization, thereby affording United States industry more
time to get ready for competition from an industrialized Latin
America." [22]

At Punta del Este I (August 1961), Campos noted, Brazil differed with the United States on a number of points. Brazil was
more concerned with industrialization and stable raw material
prices, while the United States placed a lot more emphasis on
monetary stabilization "than we thought possible or desirable."
Such emphasis on monetary stabilization, Campos continued,
might have increased the influence of the International Monetary
Fund and might have made it the clearinghouse for financial aid
to Latin America. [23]

His analysis of Janio Quadros' independent foreign policy is
particularly insightful. This policy, Campos explained, was partly
a reaction to the domestic political situation in Brazil. Quadros
was supported by the conservative National Democratic Union
(UDN) and opposed by the sizable Brazilian left. He thought he
could increase his support among the left if he demonstrated that
he was not "automatically aligned with the United States." Quadros also believed, Campos went on, that a neutral foreign policy
was a useful weapon in dealing with the United States because it
"has a sort of masochistic bent and at times it seems more understanding and forthcoming to enemies that offer some promise of
reconciliation than to staunch and traditional friends." Most importantly, Campos pointed out that the independent foreign policy
"was merely a desire to affirm the Brazilian personality in world
affairs, for there was a deep national desire for affirmation in foreign policy." [24]

Brazilian suspicion of United States intentions continued
throughout the brief presidency of Janio Quadros. United States
Ambassador to Brazil Adoph Berle, Jr., who was also chairman
of Kennedy's task force, offered Brazil financial assistance at the
same time he sought to sound out Quadros on Cuba. Quadros, according to Campos, felt that the amount of aid offered was "ridi-
culously small" and "to some extent . . . an ill-disguised bribe."
This sort of diplomacy, the refusal to understand and respect his

independent foreign policy, and the Bay of Pigs irritated Quadros enormously, but, Campos insisted, Quadros still believed that Brazil's destiny was linked to that of the United States.[25]

Despite some tension and concern, the Kennedy Administration supported Quadros. In August 1961, however, when Quadros resigned and the populist nationalist leader Jango Goulart became president, Brazilian-United States relations began to deteriorate. At Punta del Este II (January 1962), Campos was personally frustrated by his inability to convey the Brazilian viewpoint to the United States, a viewpoint "which was really much more severe to Cuba than appeared on the surface. But I found that Saxons are not as rational as they claim to be. In this particular instance of Cuba they were extremely emotional and quite irrational." Brazilian Foreign Minister San Tiago Dantas was unfairly judged by the United States, Campos argued, because his position and Brazil's position was realistic. (Morrison and others branded him a Communist and referred to him as San Tiago de Cuba.) Brazilian officials recognized, "without liking it, the fact that there was a Communist regime in Cuba and that short of invasion it would stay for a long while." What was needed, Campos continued, was to impose a structure of limitation, and although the United States eventually saw this, the Brazilians were disappointed and bitter at the out-of-hand rejection of their position.[26]

Goulart visited the United States shortly thereafter (April 1962) and was very much impressed by the liberal rhetoric of Kennedy and his advisers. Goulart was so taken in that Campos believed for a time that the Brazilian president might become a liberal leader of the Alliance for Progress in Latin America. This never came to pass because, as Campos explained, internal circumstances coupled with Washington's insensitivity led Goulart to believe that a close alliance with the United States would be fatal to his regime.[27]

The event that proved most decisive, according to Campos, was the Bell-Dantas Agreement of March 1963. Armed with the three-year anti-inflationary Furtado Development Plan, Foreign Minister San Tiago Dantas went to Washington to seek the necessary extensive financial aid to support a program of simultaneous monetary stabilization and economic development. As Campos pointed out, Dantas was handicapped by the misrepresentation of his role at Punta del Este II. The United States position was one of limited and cautious cooperation. What the Brazilian government needed, Campos believed, was either an internal or external victory to succeed with its difficult stabilization-development plans. An internal victory was impossible because austerity measures would be unpopular. Therefore, Brazil's only hope was an external victory, "a demonstration of foreign confidence, of foreign support and assistance, that would strengthen politically the hand of those that were seeking stabilization."

The Kennedy Administration, responding to conservative domestic political pressure, was anxious to demonstrate that it could be tough. Brazil got only a small amount of the aid it had sought and it never got the external victory it needed. "My view was," said Campos, "that if the United States Congress was not willing to understand that Brazil is a sufficiently large [and important] risk to justify major financial effort, then there was no hope for salvation in Latin America." Goulart, Campos concluded, saw the agreement as a defeat for Brazil and "proof of United States mistrust and that embittered him and further diverted him from the mood of cooperation." [28] United States-Brazilian relations deteriorated rapidly from then on. Dantas was fired in June and Goulart, who turned increasingly to the left for support, was overthrown by the military at the end of March 1964.

One comes away from the Campos interview with a sense of tragedy. Campos, the friend of the United States, saw the United States as insensitive, rigid, and unable to grasp the nature of Brazilian politics, which in the end contributed to the overthrow of a democratically elected reform-minded regime and its replacement by a harsh military dictatorship. What Campos failed to see was that what he labeled insensitivity, rigidity, and misunderstanding was part of a policy—based on the fear of Goulart's independent foreign policy, his domestic reforms, and his left-wing support—to encourage the president's domestic enemies to replace him (see Chapter 5). The result, nevertheless, was clear: Brazil, the largest and most populous country of South America, became one of the most repressive military dictatorships in the area, a questionable victory, one would think, for the Alliance for Progress.

An incident related to me personally by a conservative Argentine friend of the United States sheds additional light on the Kennedy Administration's Latin American policy.[29] The incident revolved around Argentina's cancellation of contracts with United

States oil companies on November 15, 1963, just a week before the assassination of President Kennedy. In 1958 Arturo Frondizi had been elected president of Argentina on a highly nationalistic platform, but in July of that year he had reneged on his campaign promises and had entered into a series of contracts with foreign firms, mostly from the United States, to explore and develop Argentina's oil reserves. He also had signed an investment guarantee agreement with the United States. As a result, approximately $175 million of United States money had flowed into Argentine oil development during the next three years. By 1962 total United States investment in the country had reached about $1 billion. In March 1962 the military had overthrown Frondizi and in the next elections (July 1963) Arturo Illia had been elected president. Illia vowed to cancel the contracts with the foreign oil companies because he believed they were illegal and unconstitutional; they had never been approved by the Argentine Congress as required by law. Illia was a friend of the United States and hardly a radical, but he was a legalist who believed the contracts were illegal and had to be canceled.

In late August 1963 Ricardo Pueyrredon, a member of Illia's People's Radical Party and a prominent businessman, went to Washington as an unofficial ambassador to deliver a message from Illia to Kennedy. On August 27 and 28 Pueyrredon met various officials, including Under Secretary of State Edwin Martin and White House aide Ralph Dungan. All of the conversations focused on Illia's pledge to cancel the oil contracts with United States firms. Pueyrredon explained his country's position; the contracts were illegal because they had never been submitted to the Argentine Congress. He pointed out that, although the investment guarantee agreement would have to be modified, Argentina wanted foreign capital and that foreign capital had the guarantee of the Argentine constitutional system and of Argentina's good record on paying debts. Dungan said that the United States was interested only in getting more capital into Argentina and insisted that "we never had any intention of violating your constitution." He told Pueyrredon that he would inform the United States ambassador in Argentina, John McClintock, to go along with Illia and to set up a United States-Argentine group to work out an agreement.

Pueyrredon went on to Chicago and New York, where he had

business matters to attend to. In New York a young woman who claimed she worked for *Newsweek* sought him out and said she wanted to do a story on him. She attempted to seduce him, presumably to blackmail him, and although Pueyrredon learned that she did not work for *Newsweek*, he never found out who she was, for whom she worked, or if she had any connection, as he supposed, with those who sought to reverse Argentina's position on the oil contracts.

On September 5 Pueyrredon received a call from a Mr. Cutler, a lawyer for the Kaiser Company, which had large investments in Argentina, on behalf of Seymour Peyser of the State Department. He was calling to see if Pueyrredon would come to Washington again. The next day Pueyrredon was met at the Washington airport by an assistant of Cutler's and driven to the State Department. At the meeting, which lasted about an hour and fifteen minutes, were Cutler and his assistant, Peyser, and several other State Department people. The critical part of the conversation, as recorded by Pueyrredon, went as follows:

They: Sixty-three countries have accepted the investment guarantee agreement.

Pueyrredon: Probably the agreement doesn't violate their constitutions.

They: We don't want to violate the Argentine constitution.

Pueyrredon: I know. If not, I wouldn't be here. But IKA [Kaiser] does.

They: American investors need guarantees.

Pueyrredon: They have them in our constitution.

They: What happens if the government expropriates an American company?

Pueyrredon: The Constitution states that every expropriation must be paid for.

They: An international court will determine this?

Pueyrredon: Argentina has competent courts. There cannot be organizations with special privileges in my country.

Jandreau [a State Department official, interrupted the conversation]: But you aren't an official ambassador of Illia. This is a waste of time.

Pueyrredon: I am not an official ambassador because Illia isn't officially president until October 12.

Jandreau: You are a friend of Illia's?

Pueyrredon: Yes, and also a friend of the United States.

Jandreau: I don't understand. We are wasting time.

Pueyrredon: If you are wasting your time, so am I. And I am not even being paid. [He stood up to go. Peyser stopped him and appeared annoyed. He gave a nasty look to Jandreau and Jandreau apologized.]

They: Argentina stands to lose $483,000 in new investments ready to come to your country. I'm going to give you this list [of potential investors] to study.

Pueyrredon: [He refused to look at the list since as an advertising man on business for the government this wouldn't be correct.] Argentina laments the loss of this money, but it must preserve its Constitution. We prefer honor and poverty. You know we are right. Put yourselves in our position. Would you accept this kind of control?

They: But you aren't opposed to foreign capital?

Pueyrredon: No, we need it. Foreign capital is like a river. It comes from outside, passes through and benefits a country, and continues on.

They: McClintock will talk with Illia in the near future. I am sure we can work everything out.

By the end of October it became clear that Illia would indeed cancel the contracts of the foreign oil companies and this prompted the Senate Foreign Relations Committee to add the Hickenlooper amendment to the pending foreign aid bill. This amendment stated that within sixty days of the annulment or suspension of contracts with United States investors in foreign countries, all aid would be cut off unless significant progress toward prompt and adequate payment of compensation was being made. The Hickenlooper amendment stirred up considerable opposition in Latin America, since it set the United States government above the courts of the countries in question as the sole arbiter of what was prompt and adequate compensation.

Early in November 1963 Under Secretary of State Averell Harriman visited Argentina and warned that the cancellation of the oil contracts would imperil aid. His main concern, however, was compensation. The Argentine position was that the companies would be compensated in accordance with Argentine justice, but this did not satisfy the United States. On November 15 Argentina canceled fourteen oil contracts, the majority of which were with United States companies. The decree did not specifically mention compensation since this would be taken care of under existing laws.

The United States Congress demanded the termination of aid to Argentina. Kennedy was reluctant to do this and urged negotiations to obtain fair compensation. As *The New York Times* explained: "Congress was frustrated over Latin America's apparent failure to recognize the importance of private investment for economic growth and for the success of the Alliance." Senate Majority Leader Mike Mansfield urged that aid be "suspended pending a just settlement," and if no settlement were reached, the Hickenlooper amendment should be applied. "This practice of seizure of American properties," Mansfield argued, "has got to be stopped or adjudicated on a reasonable basis. We have got to face up to this issue and make the best of it, even though it involves a serious blow to the Alliance for Progress." Senator Hubert Humphrey echoed similar sentiments; the time has come "to emphasize that we cannot continue to tolerate the use of foreign aid money to help confiscation of American property." [30]

The Hickenlooper amendment was never formally applied, but United States aid to Argentina dropped from an all-time high of $135 million in fiscal year 1963 to only $21 million in fiscal year 1964. A settlement was eventually reached, but not until the continuing lack of United States financial assistance had further weakened the already critical economic position of Argentina. This contributed to the unstable environment that led to the eventual overthrow of Illia in June 1966 and his replacement by a military dictatorship very much like that of Brazil.

The Pueyrredon and Campos interviews clarify the real priorities of Kennedy's Latin American policy. These two men, both conservatives and friends of the United States, tried to win the understanding and support of the United States for the progressive and democratic programs of their respective governments. But the United States ignored the demands of internal politics, the laws, and the courts of the two largest South American countries. In so doing, Washington further weakened already unstable but democratic reform regimes that were attempting to carry out some of the ideals set forth in the Alliance for Progress, and thus contributed to the emergence of military dictatorships in both Argentina and Brazil.

Johnson and the Consolidation of the Alliance for Progress, 1964–1968

The Johnson Administration's Latin American policy was the logical extension of Kennedy's Latin American policy. Johnson consolidated the new approach he had inherited and updated it as the changing circumstances seemed to dictate. Washington officials continued to accept the necessity of United States support for and control of development in order to protect its economic and security interests. Under Johnson, United States economic and military aid to Latin America exceeded the high levels initiated by Kennedy (Table 3–2). Naturally, the policies of development within a capitalist framework and the prevention of another Cuba remained in force.

Nevertheless, there were some important differences in the style, if not the basic substance, of the two policies. Johnson began where Kennedy left off and could operate on the basis of the experience of his predecessor. By 1964 the Castro threat had diminished considerably. Vietnam was becoming a major issue and increasingly absorbed United States attention and resources. As a result, Latin America became less of a priority area than it had been under Kennedy: the rhetoric of basic social reform and political democracy dwindled; the focus on traditional capitalist economic development and on strengthening the military increased; and the apparent ambiguity of the first year of the Kennedy Administration disappeared completely.

One of the key architects of Johnson's Latin American policy was Thomas Mann, assistant secretary of state for Inter-American Affairs from December 1963 to February 1966. Mann had been assistant secretary of state for Economic Affairs during the latter years of the Eisenhower Administration and ambassador to Mexico under Kennedy. He was an ardent advocate of United States business interests and a strident anti-communist. In mid-March 1964 Mann brought the United States ambassadors in Latin America to Washington for a three-day briefing session on United States policy. His formulation of policy, the so-called Mann Doctrine, consisted of four basic points: foster economic growth and be neutral regarding social reform; protect the $9 billion United

States investment in the area; avoid intervention in the internal political affairs of the Latin American countries (i.e., show no preference for democratic over military and other authoritarian regimes); and actively oppose communism.[31]

Although these meetings were supposed to be confidential, *The New York Times* reported that Mann openly rejected the never fully supported policy of opposing rightists and military dictators in Latin America because the policy had not worked and it had involved the United States in the internal politics of the countries involved. Furthermore, he found it difficult to distinguish among the various dictators and rulers. He lumped Juan Perón of Argentina and Anastasio Somoza of Nicaragua together, and he was quoted as having said that he found it difficult to distinguish politically between Alfonso López Mateos of Mexico, Víctor Paz Estenssoro of Bolivia, and the traditional, conservative dictator of Paraguay, Alfredo Stroessner.[32] This inability to distinguish among five such ideologically different Latin American leaders produced a less ambiguous, but rather simplistic, policy.

In a commencement address delivered at Notre Dame University on June 7, 1964, Mann publicly elaborated on his doctrine. He focused on what the United States would do "to bring about a more effective exercise of representative democracy in the Western Hemisphere," but at the same time justified support for military dictatorships.[33] United States policy, he explained, is to discourage any who "conspire to overthrow constitutionally elected governments." But, once a constitutional government is overthrown, the United States will concentrate on bringing about free elections and a return to full constitutional procedures, not on opposition to the dictatorship. If communism is involved in any way, Mann continued, the issue is different. "The question of our relations with Communist regimes in this hemisphere is, of course, a separate subject. . . . It raises separate questions, such as our inherent right of self-defense and measures, under existing treaties, to deal with situations which threaten the peace and security of the hemisphere."

He went on to discuss how to judge the rate of progress toward democracy, and what could be done to work toward the democratic ideal, carefully avoiding any suggestion of incompatibility between military and democratic government. One should judge progress toward democracy, he said, not solely in terms of the number of military coups, but also in terms of the degree of individual freedom, the life-span of *de facto* governments, the extent of political repression, the degree of freedom of the press and peaceful assembly, and the number of people supporting free and periodic elections. Regarding what could be done to help realize the democratic ideal, Mann said the United States should:

> . . . encourage democracy in a quiet, unpublicized way and on . . . [a] day-to-day basis; broaden the scope of collective action in the hemisphere; [make] a careful evaluation of each case of the use of force to overthrow a government; if as a result of this evaluation it is decided not to recognize a regime, it should be made clear that nonrecognition is tied to a breach in established international conduct; and if it is decided to recognize a government, it should be made clear that recognition in no way constitutes approval.

In 1965, as a result of the situation in the Dominican Republic, the meaning of the Mann Doctrine was operationally spelled out. Since May 30, 1961, when pro-United States dictator Rafael Trujillo had been assassinated, the Dominican Republic had suffered a series of political upheavals. After a year and a half of turmoil, democratic reformer Juan Bosch had been elected president. Seven months later he had been ousted by the military. The Kennedy Administration had broken economic and diplomatic relations with the military government, but Johnson, fearing that such United States-imposed isolation might facilitate a Castro-type revolution, had recognized the military government and had restored economic and military aid.[34]

In April 1965 a rebellion broke out against the military government, and the United States landed troops to prevent its success. A belated OAS meeting endorsed the United States action and established an Inter-American Peace Force to keep order in the Dominican Republic: Chile, Mexico, Peru, Ecuador, and Uruguay opposed the United States action and Venezuela abstained. The delegate of the nearly toppled military government of the Dominican Republic was allowed to vote and provided the fourteenth vote to make up the two-thirds majority necessary for action. The troops (9,100 from the United States and 2,000 from Latin America, mostly from Brazil) remained in the Dominican Republic for more than a year, until the United States was satisfied that neither former President Bosch, the rebel leader, nor any pro-communist leader would come to power. This action established what has become known as the Johnson Doctrine, that is, the United States can and will intervene unilaterally anywhere in Latin America to prevent the possibility of a communist regime from seizing power.

The most important examples of the Johnson Administration's policy toward the South American military concern Brazil and Argentina. As a result of the deterioration of relations following the Bell-Dantas Agreement (March 1963), the United States cut its aid to Brazil to a bare minimum. In addition, in late 1963 and early 1964, it adopted a policy of granting aid to state governments in Brazil whose leaders were friendly to the United States. Furthermore, United States business and labor interests openly sided with the growing domestic opposition. On April 1, 1964, the military overthrew the constitutional government of Goulart and established a repressive dictatorship. The United States immediately recognized the new military government and promised it aid. Within twelve hours, something of a record, Johnson telegrammed his congratulations and support to the new regime. Brazil quickly became the United States "model" for development in South America and between 1964 and 1968 received more than $1.5 billion in economic and military aid from the United States, nearly 25 percent of the Latin American total (Table 3–2).

The United States' enthusiastic and financially lavish support of the Brazilian military regime had repercussions in Argentina. The Argentine military, impatient with the faltering, democratically elected regime of Arturo Illia, decided to pursue the Brazilian solution. Although State Department officials tried to persuade the Argentine military that the United States was opposed to a coup, the effort was obviously unconvincing and the attraction of the Brazilian solution strong. In June 1966 the military overthrew the government, placed a general in the presidency, abolished all elected legislative bodies, outlawed all political parties, and embarked on an economically conservative development program designed to attract foreign private capital. The United States warmly welcomed the Argentine military government and its development program and increased United States aid to Argentina from an annual average of $31 million in 1964–1965 to $45 million in 1966–1968 (Table 3–2).

The "success" of the pro-military policy in Brazil and Argentina encouraged Washington to become increasingly firm with democratic governments that in any way adversely affected or threatened United States economic interests. The United States reluctantly supported the Christian Democrats in Chile, who promised gradual nationalization of the United States-owned copper mines, because the only viable alternative to them was a radical Marxist coalition of parties (see Chapter 6).

In Peru, however, there was no leftist alternative to the progressive center-of-the-road government of Fernando Belaunde, so the United States proceeded to undermine it in the name of defending United States economic interests. In 1924 Standard Oil of New Jersey, through its subsidiary the International Petroleum Company (IPC), had acquired the questionable rights of a British oil company to extensive oil lands in Peru. Over the next forty years IPC had grown tremendously and had come to dominate the Peruvian oil industry. In 1963, when Belaunde was elected president, he promised to investigate IPC's claim to the oil fields. Shortly thereafter the Peruvian Congress demanded the reassertion of Peruvian sovereignty over the oil fields and instructed Belaunde to negotiate a settlement with IPC. The United States government took the side of the oil company; it froze loan authorizations pending the outcome of the negotiations and United States aid declined drastically. The cut in aid hurt Belaunde's reform programs, increased internal pressure, and contributed to his removal by the military in October 1968.[35]

The Alliance for Progress and the Development of South America

The Kennedy and Johnson administrations poured unprecedented sums of aid into South America because Washington officials assumed that controlled development within a capitalist framework was the best way to insulate the area from Castroism and to protect United States economic interests. Under these Democratic presidents, United States Latin American policy evolved from support for democratic development to support for authoritarian development, but the goal remained to develop the area in order to immunize it from communism. The critical question is how much did South America develop during the first eight years of the Alliance for Progress? Was the quality of life of the average South American any better in 1968 that it had been in

1960? Was he better fed, clothed, housed, educated, and employed? Did he enjoy greater personal freedom, liberty, and security? Did he exercise greater control over his working and living situations?

It is impossible to argue that political life in South America was more democratic in 1968 than it had been in 1960. When Kennedy assumed the presidency, there was only one dictator ruling in South America, Alfredo Stroessner of Paraguay. Between 1960 and 1968 there were nine coup d'etats in South America: two in Argentina (1962, 1966), one in Bolivia (1964), two in Brazil (1961, 1964), two in Ecuador (1961, 1963), and two in Peru (1962, 1968). By the end of 1968, military dictators ruled in Argentina (Ongania), Brazil (Costa y Silva), and Peru (Velasco), and Stroessner continued to rule Paraguay. Bolivia and Ecuador, although at the time ruled by constitutionally elected presidents, were both controlled by the military. Furthermore, military expenditures increased substantially in Brazil, Peru, Venezuela, Uruguay, and Colombia. During the 1960s the military increased its influence throughout South America and government became correspondingly more authoritarian.

Granting the fact that there was no increase in the exercise of democratic rights in South America during the 1960s, is there nevertheless evidence to suggest that there was economic development that significantly improved the quality of life of the people of the area? The answer is negative. There was some economic growth, some structural reform, and some improvement in the living conditions, but it was so limited that it was almost meaningless. Certainly the accomplishments of the Alliance for Progress did not approximate the stated developmental goals.

In March 1969 AID presented an informative report entitled *A Review of Alliance for Progress Goals* to the House committee on Foreign Affairs.[36] The report was cautiously optimistic in its evaluation of the Alliance for Progress. It mentioned some problems (slow economic growth, lack of investment capital, ineffective agrarian reform, and unequal distribution of wealth) and acknowledged that the program had been too ambitious and had "attempted too much too soon," but it nevertheless emphasized the "substantial achievements." Among those cited were: a "new commitment, competence, and confidence throughout governments in Latin America"; "adroit management of complex stabilization programs in Brazil, Chile, and Colombia"; increased tax collection; improved organization in the Ministries of Health, Education, Agriculture, Transportation, and Finance; increased monetary and fiscal stability; economic integration; and export diversification.[37]

This emphasis on the accomplishments of the Alliance for Progress only served to obscure its overall impact on South America. Although, between 1960 and 1968, the United States provided Latin America with $10 billion in aid, and private United States investment increased from $8.4 billion to $11 billion, the net flow of resources was at best negligible and very likely negative. With the increased gross flow of aid came restrictions brought about by special interest groups seeking to make aid serve their private interests. Whatever benefits that might have been brought about in the areas of economic growth, planning, education, and public health were for the most part offset by the outflow of resources and the failure to produce such structural reforms as the redistribution of land and income. Furthermore, in 1968 the South American governments had even less control over the critical economic and political decisions affecting their societies.

The Foreign Assistance Act of 1961, and subsequent amendments to it, established the rules for granting aid to Latin America. It created the Development Loan Committee (DLC) to coordinate the frequently divergent interests of the Treasury, Commerce, Agriculture, and State departments and to advise AID. The Treasury Department was concerned about the loss of foreign exchange through aid programs and increasingly sought to use aid to counteract the financial drain caused by Vietnam expenditures and the deterioration in the balance of payments. The Commerce Department saw aid as a way of increasing United States exports and supporting United States business interests abroad. The Agriculture Department was concerned that aid not assist in the production of products competitive with those grown in the United States.

Not surprisingly, these various pressures on the nature of aid resulted in the restriction of its use. Purchases financed by United States aid had to be made in the United States—even if they were more costly than from other sources—unless the President made a special ruling that such a restriction was not consistent with United States interests. At least 50 percent of the goods financed by United States aid had to be transported in United States ships even though United States shipping companies charged considerably more than others to carry the goods. The President had to suspend all economic aid to any country that expropriated United States property without prompt and adequate compensation, that canceled a contract with a United States company, or that subjected a United States company to any form of discrimination. Increasingly, the United States made loans that would produce "additional" imports from the United States. And the United States refused to give Latin America any say in determining the criteria for or conditions of loans. More money was available, but if South America wanted the aid, it had to submit to increasing controls that favored United States special interests.

The results of such a policy were of doubtful benefit to South America. Latin America's balance of trade with the United States was unfavorable in 1960 and continued to deteriorate during the 1960s. In every South American country one or two items continued to account for from 49 to 98 percent of total exports. Remittance of profits exceeded new private investment. Debt service on previous and on new loans was high and increased. Thus it is not surprising that from 1960 to 1968 the net flow of resources to Latin America was probably negative.[38]

William T. Dentzer, Jr., deputy United States ambassador to the OAS, explained the situation to the House committee on Foreign Affairs in March 1969. To determine the net flow of resources into Latin America, he noted, one had to subtract what Latin America pays back to the United States from the flow of resources into the area:

When one starts to consider, however, what Latin America pays back to the United States and other lenders, that total amount of resource transfer diminishes very substantially. If one deducts debt payments, amortization and interest, from Latin America to the United States Government, the official flow of capital diminishes . . . and if one further deducts the net flow of capital income payments to United States private investors in the United States, that is to say, gross remittance less new investment and reinvested earnings, that flow is about nil. . . . I am placing to one side, of course, the increased export earnings which come to Latin America thanks to private United States investment and the many other advantages of such investment. . . . I am pointing out, however, that high gross official capital flows to Latin America under the Alliance have been necessary to help Latin America deal with the problems she had accumulated previously. *When you look at net capital flows and their economic effect, and after all due credit is given to the U.S. effort to step up support to Latin America, one sees that not that much money has been put into Latin America after all.*[39]

The AID report did not devote much more space to economic growth than it had to the net flow of resources to Latin America. It set forth various figures to demonstrate the increase in GDP, but quickly passed over the low per capita increase as the inevitable result of the population explosion. Of the ten major South American countries, only Brazil and Bolivia exceeded the Alliance goal of 2.5 percent per capita growth per year during the 1960s. The average per capita growth of all ten countries was 1.8 percent per year for the decade. Most of the growth occurred during the the late 1960s and was concentrated in a few countries.[40] Furthermore, the report did not mention that although per capita GDP in South America increased somewhat, it had fallen farther behind that of the United States and the other developed countries. The 1969 *Survey* of the Economic Commission for Latin America (ECLA) summed up as follows:

Average per capita income in the region [Latin America] as a whole is one seventh of that of the United States, one fifth that of Western Europe and probably less than half that of the Soviet Union. . . . Economically and technologically, Latin America is lagging further and further behind. The region is to all intents and purposes excluded from the development that is taking place in the great centers. . . . And Latin America is thus in the position of becoming increasingly dependent, financially and politically, in the international context, while at the same time declining in economic importance.[41]

The AID report did acknowledge the critical importance of the distribution of income, but then rather lamely said nothing much had been done about it. "If the purpose of development is broadly viewed as being the attainment of a more adequate and ample income distribution," the report noted, "this goal can be viewed as the paramount Alliance objective. In this sense the other charter objectives are means to this end." [42] It cited an ECLA study which showed that the top 10 percent in Argentina, Brazil, and Mexico received 40 percent of total income, while the bottom 40 percent received between 10 and 14 percent, but said no more.

Since the ECLA study cited by the AID report was considerably more blunt and informative, it is worth examining in greater detail. Table 4-1, which is based on the ECLA study, shows even greater inequality than the figures cited by AID. The bottom 80 percent of the population in Latin America received only 37.5 percent of the area's income and its average per capita income was less than $200 per year. At the same time the top 5 percent of the population received 33.4 percent of the area's income and its average per capita income was $2,600 per year! The ECLA study also showed that there was a wide discrepancy between urban and rural income and between the income of different regions within the respective Latin American countries.

Furthermore, the nature of income distribution in Latin America differed significantly from the United States and other industrialized countries. The ECLA study pointed out that: (1) in Latin America low income is generally permanent, while low income in the industrialized countries is not; (2) low incomes in industrialized countries are generally specialized cases (unemployment, sickness, retirement, and so on) and can therefore be taken care of by special means such as pensions, unemployment, sickness and dental benefits, allowances for women with dependents, and so on, whereas in Latin America most low incomes are not special cases but are active members of the labor force and therefore not eligible for such benefits; (3) middle-income groups see their incomes rise slowly and receive a much smaller percent of the total sum than the same groups in industrialized countries, thus reducing the potential for mass markets associated with high levels of development; and (4) income rises rapidly at the top of the scale and the top has a much higher percent of the total income than in the industrialized countries.[43]

A final critical problem, which the AID report minimized and which is closely related to unequal income distribution, is agrarian reform. Latin America is still a heavily agricultural area. As James Petras and Robert LaPorte explained in their excellent study of the subject, "the agricultural sector in Latin America is a strategic sector: it employs a majority of the economically active

TABLE **4–1**

Distribution of Wealth in Latin America: 1960

	Lowest 20% of population	30% below median	30% above median	15% below top	Top 5% of population
United States					
percent total income received	4.6	18.8	31.1	25.5	20.0
Latin America					
percent total income received	3.1	10.3	24.1	29.2	33.4
Latin America					
per capita income in U.S.$	60	130	310	750	2,600
Argentina					
per capita income in U.S.$	203	398	661	1,190	4,867
Brazil					
per capita income in U.S.$	40	88	181	338	1,820
Colombia					
per capita income in U.S.$	77	124	200	455	1,590
Venezuela					
per capita income in U.S.$	77	194	475	1,081	2,730

Source: United Nations, Economic Commission for Latin America, *Economic Survey of Latin America, 1969* (New York, 1970), pp. 65, 364–415. Although the data is from 1960, there is no evidence of significant change the past fifteen years.

population, land is an important economic resource, the distribution of economic resources has a profound effect on national as well as sectional politics, the performance of the agricultural sector has a decisive impact on the capacity and output of other sectors.[44] The AID report recognized the importance of agrarian reform but stressed the difficulty of bringing it about. Furthermore the report noted that the main focus has been on productivity rather than on the distribution of land, on what Petras and LaPorte would call technical modification from above rather than structural reform. Thus, the AID report included four tables on agricultural productivity and none on land concentration or distribution.

Table 4–2 suggests the dimensions of the problem. In the six major South American countries, 45 percent of all agricultural holdings were under 10 hectares and in no case did the area of these holdings account for more than 9 percent of the total land. At the other end of the spectrum, no more than 6 percent of all holdings were over 1,000 hectares and, with the exception of Colombia, they accounted for 45 percent or more of the total area. The data on some of the individual countries is even more extreme.

TABLE **4–2**

Agricultural Landholdings in South America: 1960
(in percent)

	Less than 10 hectares	10 to 100 hectares	100 to 1,000 hectares	Over 1,000 hectares
Argentina				
No. of holdings	—	67.6 —	26.7	5.8
Area of holdings	—	5.4 —	20.1	74.4
Brazil				
No. of holdings	44.8	44.7	9.4	.9
Area of holdings	2.4	19.0	34.4	44.2
Chile				
No. of holdings	61.8	29.2	7.6	1.3
Area of holdings	1.5	7.7	18.2	72.7
Colombia				
No. of holdings	76.5	19.9	3.2	.3
Area of holdings	8.8	25.3	35.6	30.4
Peru				
No. of holdings	92.3	6.5	1.1	.2
Area of holdings	8.5	7.6	14.6	69.2
Venezuela				
No. of holdings	66.8	25.5	5.1	1.3
Area of holdings	2.9	7.8	18.5	81.7

Source: Statistical Abstract of Latin America, 1971 (Los Angeles, 1973), pp. 196–199. Although the data is from 1960, there is no evidence of significant change in the past fifteen years.

Increased agricultural productivity is essential to the development of South America, but so is a more equitable distribution of wealth and power. And there will be no distribution of economic and political power in the rural areas of Latin America unless there is distribution of land. To increase the productivity of the small number who already control most of the land also increases their power. From a purely economic point of view one might argue that concentration of land ownership increases productivity more, but even this is not necessarily the case. What is certain is that the concentration of land ownership will not lead to the distribution of wealth and political power.

Since 1960 little effective progress has been made on land distribution in most of the South American countries and thus it remains a critical bottleneck to the kind of social and economic reform necessary for development. The United States has focused on productivity, and while talking about land distribution, has done little about it; it has constantly refused to grant aid or permit aid to be used to help pay for such a program and it has never made land distribution a condition for aid.

During its first eight years the Alliance for Progress had little success in stimulating the development of South America. As ECLA summed up, the gap between the rich and the poor increased during the 1960s and "the developed countries have not evinced the necessary willingness to make political changes and adopt decisions which will satisfy the legitimate intentions and aspirations of the developing countries. This reluctance to do so is in sharp contrast to the speed with which the industrialized countries reach agreement to promote their own economic expansion." [45]

Nixon-Ford and the Suzerainty of Business and the Military in South America: 1969–1975

Although the Nixon Administration's primary concerns in foreign policy were Vietnam and Southeast Asia, detente with Russia and China, the Middle East, balance of payments, and energy, the evolving situation in South America nevertheless forced the United States to pay some attention to that area. The failure of the Alliance for Progress, the growth of popular nationalist movements, and economic competition from European and Asian countries, combined with primary concern about other areas of the world, led to a South American policy that was designed to maintain the United States sphere of influence, to protect United States economic and security interests, and, at the same time, to cost less in terms of time and money. The Nixon policy was to support, more fully and exclusively than before, United States corporations and the South American military establishments, and to rely on them to carry out and control the process of development and maintain and protect United States interests.

The initial formulation of Latin American policy was based on the *Rockefeller Report,* the Latin American *Consensus of Viña del Mar,* and Nixon's personal experiences and convictions. In the spring of 1969 New York Governor Nelson Rockefeller made a series of fact-finding trips to Latin America and on August 30, 1969, presented his policy recommendations to the President. In this *Report* Rockefeller stressed the importance of the special relationship between the United States and Latin America and insisted that the most important common goal of the two areas must be "the creation of a community of self-reliant, independent nations linked in a mutually beneficial regional system, and seeking to improve the efficiency of their societies and the quality of life of their peoples." [46]

Rockefeller then noted in an extraordinary passage that Washington had allowed the special relationship to deteriorate badly and candidly set forth some of the United States-created obstacles to better inter-American relations. United States

> . . . assistance and trade policies, so critical to the development process of other nations, have been distorted to serve a variety of purposes in the United States having nothing to do with the aspirations and interests of its neighbors; in fact, all too often these purposes have been in sharp conflict with the goals of development. Moreover, in its relations, the United States has all too often demonstrated, at least subconsciously, a paternalistic attitude toward the other nations of the hemisphere. It has tried to direct the internal affairs of other nations to an unseemly degree, thinking, perhaps arrogantly, that it knew what was best for them. It has underestimated the capacities of these nations and their willingness to assume responsibility for the course of future developments. The United States has talked about partnership, but it has not truly practiced it.[47]

Rockefeller supported freer Latin American access to the United States market, tariff preference for the developing world, commodity agreements to stabilize prices on raw materials, more low-interest development loans, and flexibility in rescheduling debts.[48] He also recognized and apparently lamented the paternalism and arrogance of the United States and the negative effect of its policy on development. Nevertheless, he urged increased support for the two groups that had become the mainstays of that policy—United States business and the Latin American military.

Regarding United States business interests in Latin America, Rockefeller began by noting that many in the hemisphere were suspicious of foreign investment, regarded it as a form of economic colonialism, and believed that it took more out of the area than it put into it. "The central problem," he continued, "is the failure of governments throughout the hemisphere to recognize fully the importance of private investment. Thus realistic steps have not been taken to encourage private investment, to create a framework within which it can operate and which assures that it will serve the best interests of the entire community. Yet history shows that democratic societies which have provided such encouragement and such a framework have been the most successful in attaining their broad objectives." He then recommended that the United States "provide maximum encouragement for private investment throughout the hemisphere." [49]

Rockefeller also recommended increased support for the Latin American military. He noted that the "commitment to representative, responsive democratic government is deeply imbedded in the collective political consciousness of the American people," and that the United States must continue its commitment to democratic governments. But, he warned, "democracy is a very subtle and difficult problem for most of the other countries in the hemisphere"; their authoritarian traditions and inadequate economic and social development make it difficult for them to support a "consistently democratic system. For many of these societies, therefore, the question is less one of democracy or a lack of it than it is simply of orderly ways of getting along. . . . Forces of anarchy, terror, and subversion are loose in the Americas," Rockefeller proclaimed, and in order to keep "covert communist forces" from exploiting inflation, racial strife, and poverty, the United States must support those capable of maintaining internal security. Without order, he believed, these problems could not be overcome. Therefore, he recommended that Washington increase its aid to the military and police forces in Latin America and permit them to buy the equipment they needed from the United States.[50]

In May 1969 representatives of the Latin American countries met without the United States for three days in the Chilean resort town of Viña del Mar to discuss solutions to the problems of the area. On June 11, 1969, they presented their findings, the *Consensus of Viña del Mar,* to President Nixon. The emphasis of the report was on the Latin American view, the Latin American way, the Latin American identity, and on Latin America's efforts to solve its own problems. But the report also reflected a keen awareness of the international context of development. It stated that there was a "need for a fairer international division of labor that will favor the rapid economic and social development of the developing countries, instead of impeding it, as has been the case hitherto." It then listed a series of "external obstacles impeding the rapid economic growth of Latin America": (1) tariff and non-tariff restrictions that limit access on equitable terms of the manufactured and semi-manufactured goods of the developing nations to world markets; (2) progressive deterioration in volume, terms, and forms of international financial assistance; (3) restrictions on international shipping; (4) restrictions on the transfer of technology; and (5) the view that private foreign investment is aid.[51]

The *Consensus* then set forth ways of eliminating the external obstacles to development: (1) the recognition of the legal equality of states; (2) non-intervention in any form; (3) respect for existing treaties; (4) respect for the sovereign right of each country to use national resources as it sees fit; (5) no military or political strings of any kind to aid; and (6) no economic or political coercion of any kind.[52]

Nixon's "Action for Progress for the Americas" speech of October 31, 1969, in which he set forth his Latin American policy, incorporated many of the ideas of the *Rockefeller Report* and some from the *Consensus of Viña del Mar*.[53] The President listed five principles upon which his "new approach" to Latin America would be based and spelled out the steps he would take to implement policy. The United States, he said, was committed to the inter-American system; it would respect national identity and dignity; it would continue development assistance to the hemisphere; it would support Latin American initiatives on a multilateral basis within the inter-American system; and it was dedicated to improving the quality of life in the hemisphere.

To make the new partnership work, Nixon went on to say, requires some fundamental changes "in the way in which we manage development assistance in the Hemisphere." He proposed that a multilateral inter-American agency be given more responsibility for setting priorities, development programs, and evaluating performance. In terms of trade he promised to work to reduce nontariff barriers to trade (quotas), to provide technical and financial assistance to promote trade, to consult regularly with Latin America, and to press for a general tariff preference system for all developing nations. He then promised to untie aid and announced that as of the next day loan dollars to Latin America could be used to purchase goods anywhere in Latin America or the United States. He promised to work on the problems of external debt service, economic integration, and the sharing of technology. And he announced the upgrading of the United States government structure for dealing with Latin America by raising the rank of assistant secretary of state for Inter-American Affairs to under secretary of state.

Yet Nixon, like Rockefeller, seemed most interested in supporting United States business and the Latin American military. He emphasized the critical importance of private investment in the development process and warned that capital-importing countries could not attract the necessary foreign investment funds if they acted

> . . . against existing investments in a way which runs counter to commonly accepted norms of international law and behavior. . . . We will not encourage U.S. private investment where it is not wanted, or where local political conditions face it with unwarranted risks. But my own strong belief is that properly motivated private enterprise has a vital role to play in social as well as economic development. We have seen it work in our own country. We have seen it work in other countries, whether they are developing or developed, that lately have been recording the world's most spectacular rates of economic growth.[54]

He then explained that the United States was seeking ways to strengthen both foreign- and locally-owned private enterprise in Latin America.

Nixon concluded his speech by reaffirming his commitment to democratic government and his "preference for democratic procedures," yet he also warned that the United States would not tolerate "armed subversion" or the "export of revolution." The President did not dwell explicitly on internal security, covert communist subversion, the forces of anarchy and terror, or support for the military and police as Rockefeller had, but his final paragraphs implicitly referred to them. Most significantly, the actions of the United States government during the Nixon Administration clearly manifested the commitment to the military.

During his five and a half years in office Nixon did very little of what he had promised to do.[55] He revealed either no understanding of or genuine commitment to multilateral funding for development. What the Latin Americans had sought in multilateral funding was the removal of political strings to development assistance. But the United States continually delayed making its financial contributions to multilateral groups (Inter-American Bank, World Bank, and so on) and demanded concessions to protect private capital.[56] It also used its considerable influence within the multilateral lending organizations to block funds to governments, such as Allende's Chile, whose politics it opposed.

There was no substantial improvement regarding trade either. Import quotas and restrictions, pushed by special interest groups in the United States, remained in effect. Thus, for example, processed (instant) Brazilian coffee was not allowed into the United States; only the raw coffee beans could enter to be processed in the United States. The much talked about and frequently promised tariff preference for the developing countries did not materialize. Instead, a 10 percent surcharge was placed on all imports to the United States during the latter part of 1971. Latin Americans were particularly resentful of this because they had for a long time had an unfavorable balance of trade with the United States (one of the few areas of the world in this position) and the 10 percent surcharge accentuated their problems.

Untying aid, which Nixon had made so much of in his speech, was practically meaningless the way it was done. Nixon did not untie aid. He merely loosened the strings a little. Previous policy restricted all purchases financed by United States aid. Nixon's policy permitted Latin America to use aid to purchase goods anywhere in Latin America and the United States, which meant, for the most part, in the United States, because Latin America produced little heavy or sophisticated equipment. What Latin America wanted, and was not granted, was to be able to buy goods anywhere in the world. Japan and West Germany, for example, were producing machinery at a much lower cost than was the United States, but Nixon's "untying" of aid did not permit Latin America to buy Japanese and West German products. Furthermore, the Nixon Administration did little to ease the problem of increasing debt service, to further economic integration, or to speed the transfer of technology and to break the monopoly on technology held by companies in the United States and other developed countries. He did raise the position of assistant secretary of state for Inter-American Affairs to under secretary of state.

Although the Nixon Administration did little of what it had promised, it was, nevertheless, forced to take some steps regarding South America. The failure of the Kennedy and Johnson development programs to improve the political and/or socioeconomic quality of life in South America initiated a demand for change. Much of this pressure was absorbed into and articulated by a series of popular nationalist and leftist movements, which, to varying degrees, sought to free their countries from United States domination, to establish control over national resources, to nationalize banks and public services, to bring about social and economic reforms, and to create more egalitarian societies. In October 1968 General Juan José Velasco toppled the government of Fernando Belaunde and proclaimed himself president of Peru. One of Velasco's first acts was to expropriate the holdings of the United States-owned International Petroleum Company (IPC), to announce that IPC owed Peru $600 million in back taxes and excess profits, and to declare therefore that Peru owed IPC nothing in the way of compensation. Velasco then made some attempt to create a coalition of independent South American states, an effort that revived United States fears of a Perón-Quadros-Goulart type independent foreign policy.

The Peruvian coup of October 1968 initiated a wave of populist-nationalist movements in South America that the United States perceived as a growing threat to its interests in the area. In March

1969 the recently elected president of Venezuela, Rafael Caldera, legalized the Communist Party, granted amnesty to terrorists, and initiated new contacts with Cuba. In May 1969 large sectors of the Argentine middle and working classes, protesting the decline in real wages, foreign economic penetration, and the circumscription of traditional civil liberties, nearly toppled the dictatorship of pro-United States General Juan Carlos Ongania. In September 1969 General Alfredo Ovando seized control of Bolivia and proceeded to nationalize the holdings of Gulf Oil. A year later Ovando was replaced by left-wing Air Force General Juan José Torres, who gave power to a popular assembly, nationalized more United States-owned property, and took an independent stand in international affairs. In April 1970 former populist dictator Gustavo Rojas Pinilla nearly won the presidential election in Colombia, and his National Popular Alliance moved increasingly to the left. In September 1970 the Marxist Salvador Allende was elected president of Chile. He nationalized foreign-owned mines, banks, and businesses, distributed wealth more equally, and established a neutral foreign policy. Shortly thereafter the center-left formed a similar coalition in Uruguay. And in March 1973 the Peronists, after a forced absence of eighteen years, returned to power in Argentina, nationalized banks and foreign companies, restricted foreign investment, and pursued an independent foreign policy.

At the same time the United States faced the challenge of popular nationalist and leftist movements in South America, it also faced an increasing economic challenge from European and Asian countries. Japan and Germany increased already substantial investments in and trade with Brazil and other South American countries. The Soviet Union developed its small but important trade with Chile, Peru, and Bolivia. And Communist China won recognition from Chile, Peru, and Argentina and proceeded to initiate trade with them and with Brazil.[57]

Washington responded to these challenges by increasing its support for United States corporations in the area and for the local military establishments and by withholding support from the popular nationalists. The United States cut back or eliminated economic aid to Velasco's Peru, to Torres' Bolivia, and to Allende's Chile, and used its influence within the international lending organizations to establish a credit blockade of Chile and to a lesser degree of Peru. Washington restored aid to Bolivia and Chile when pro-United States military officers overthrew Torres and Allende. In addition, while the United States cut economic aid to Allende's Chile, it did not cut military aid (see Chapter 6). In June 1973 the United States reversed established policy and resumed the sale of airplanes and other heavy military equipment to friendly South American governments.[58] Most importantly, the United States firmly supported Brazil as its junior partner in the area and used it as a counterbalance to the populist nationalist movements (see Chapter 5).

Nixon's replacement by Gerald Ford in August 1974 had no significant impact on the nature of United States-South American relations. Washington continued to talk about the importance of its southern neighbors, the common heritage and interdependence of the hemispheric countries, and the effort to help the area overcome its problems. United States actions, however, demonstrated the continuing commitment to business and to the local military. In October 1973 Henry Kissinger had revived hope of a new Latin American policy. "If the technically advanced nations can ever cooperate with the developing nations," he told the Latin American representatives to the United Nations, "then it must start here in the Western Hemisphere." The "New Dialogue" Kissinger promised was supposedly initiated at meetings of the OAS in Mexico City (February 1974), Atlanta (April 1974), and Quito (November 1974), but it amounted to nothing more than new promises.[59]

The United States Trade Act of 1974, signed by President Gerald Ford on January 3, 1975, was presented by the United States as a major effort to help Latin America and other underdeveloped countries of the world. The act, the first major trade legislation since the Trade Expansion Act of 1962, proposed ways to reduce trade barriers, to increase trade with the communist countries, and, by authorizing the President to extend duty-free treatment on certain items for a ten-year period, to help the underdeveloped countries. Yet, as the *International Economic Report of the President* explained: "Expressly excluded [by the Trade Act] are most Communist countries, all OPEC [Organization of Petroleum Exporting Countries] countries, nations participating in other cartel-type arrangements, nations expropriating U.S. property without providing prompt and adequate compensation or accepting arbitrated awards in favor of U.S. companies. . . ."[60]

The South Americans reacted to the Trade Act with hostility rather than with gratefulness as the United States had hoped. They felt that the act was discriminatory and coercive. Only Venezuela and Ecuador were members of OPEC and thus automatically denied the proposed benefits. But almost all of the other South American countries were exploring involvement in commodity marketing organizations which, if formed, would exclude them from the preferential status. Furthermore, they all believed that national rather than international law provided the guidelines for the settlement of investment disputes.

In addition, the United States reacted strongly and negatively, from the South American point of view, to Latin efforts to protect their economic and political interests. In the 1970s the South Americans increasingly identified their interests with those of the Third World, sought new ties with other developed countries, and talked about the creation of several regional organizations that would exclude the United States. In April 1972, at the Santiago, Chile, meeting of the UNCTAD, President Luis Echeverria of Mexico proposed a *Charter of the Economic Rights and Duties of the States* for the United Nations. The *Charter,* which was strongly supported by most of the South American countries, affirmed the right of all states to choose whatever form of economic and political organization best suited their needs, to maintain absolute sovereignty over their natural resources, to expropriate foreign enterprises when it was in their national interest to do so, and to provide compensation for expropriated property only when "the pertinent conditions call for it." It further called for price stabilization agreements on primary commodities, access to the markets of the industrialized countries on equal terms, the free transfer of technology at reasonable cost, and more international resources for the development of the poorer countries. In December 1974 the *Charter* was approved by the United Nations with 120 votes in favor, 6 opposed, and 10 abstentions. The United States, England, Germany, Belgium, Denmark, and Luxemborg were the six opposing votes.[61]

The United States objected to the *Charter* mainly because it denied the applicability of international law to investment disputes. Already irritated by the efforts of some to expel Israel from the United Nations, it used this occasion to launch a "get tough" policy against the Latin Americans and the rest of the Third World.

John A. Scali, United States ambassador to the United Nations, sharply attacked the Third World countries for disregarding the views and interests of the United States. He warned that the majority was imposing its views on the minority, and that this "tyranny of the majority" would undermine support for the United Nations within the United States. The attack was continued throughout 1975 by Daniel P. Moynihan, Scali's replacement at the United Nations, by Kissinger, and by Ford.[62]

At the same time, the Latin Americans explored the possibility of establishing a Latin American Economic System (LAES) without the participation of the United States. The idea was first discussed when President Luis Echeverria of Mexico visited President Carlos Andres Pérez of Venezuela in August 1974. It gained considerable support during the early months of 1975 as a result of the general Latin American reaction to the United States Trade Act. Brazil opposed the idea because the proposed organization did not include the United States. Nevertheless, on October 12, 1975, twenty-three Latin American countries signed a charter establishing LAES.[63]

United States reaction to Latin America's growing assertiveness and identification with the Third World countries was summarized by Kissinger at Houston on March 1, 1975.[64] In a speech entitled "United States and Latin America: the New Opportunity" he reaffirmed the importance of the defunct "New Dialogue" and the interdependence of the Western Hemisphere countries. He insisted that such issues as the Panama Canal and Cuba could indeed be negotiated and again promised help for Latin American development, trade concessions, price stabilization, and more funds for the Inter-American Development Bank.

Kissinger then came to the heart of the message, in which he chided the Latin Americans on some of their recent actions. He acknowledged a "new sense of Latin American unity" and proclaimed: "We welcome the strength and self-confidence that this evolution implies." But he warned that the United States "is concerned by the growing tendency of some Latin American countries to participate in tactics of confrontation between the developing and developed worlds. . . . Such tactics are particularly inappropriate for the Western Hemisphere where they threaten to repudiate a long tradition of cooperative relations with the United States at the very moment when the United States has dedicated itself to common progress." He was particularly annoyed at the Latin American postponement of the Buenos Aires meeting of the foreign ministers to protest the United States Trade Act. "Some Latin American nations chose to read into this legislation a coercive intent which did not exist and asked for immediate remedies beyond the capacity of our constitutional process to provide. As a result, the next step in the New Dialogue was delayed just when it was most needed. The nations of America face too many challenges to permit their energies to be expended in such fruitless and artificial confrontations."

The Nixon and Ford Administrations were forced by the growth of popular nationalist movements and by a "new sense of Latin American unity" to devote some attention to South America. They continued, nevertheless, to rely on the traditional policy of support for Brazil, business, and the military, coupled with a new "get tough" stance in the United Nations, the OAS, and other international forums to maintain United States influence. They did repeatedly promise many reforms, but, to date, these promises have remained unfilled.

NOTES

1. Arthur M. Schlesinger, Jr., *A Thousand Days* (Boston, 1965), pp. 516, 716.

2. *Ibid.,* p. 769.

3. Jerome Levinson and Juan de Onis, *The Alliance That Lost its Way* (Chicago, 1970), p. 54.

4. Task Force on Immediate Latin American Problems, "Report to the President-Elect," January 4, 1961 (available at the Kennedy Library, Cambridge, Mass.), pp. 2, 4, 9–11.

5. *Ibid.,* pp. 28–30.

6. The best account of Operation Bootstrap is Gordon K. Lewis, *Puerto Rico* (New York, 1968), Chapter 6. See also Manuel Maldonado-Denis, *Puerto Rico* (New York, 1972), Chapter 7.

7. Roberto Campos, recorded interview by Dr. John E. Reilly, May 29, 1964, in the home of Mr. Campos in Rio de Janeiro, Brazil, John F. Ken-

nedy Library Oral History Program, p. 20. Hereafter cited as *Campos Interview.*

8. The following paragraphs are based on Delesseps S. Morrison, *Latin American Mission* (New York, 1965), pp. 34, 97–105, 199.

9. The following paragraphs are based on Schlesinger, *Thousand,* pp. 174, 200, 506–507, 760–763.

10. *Ibid.,* p. 473.

11. *Ibid.,* p. 783.

12. Barber and Ronning, *Internal Security,* pp. 31–32; David Halberstam, *The Best and the Brightest* (New York, 1972), pp. 94–96, 151–157; Schlesinger, *Thousand,* p. 774.

13. Schlesinger, *Thousand,* pp. 773–779.

14. *Ibid.,* p. 779.

15. *The New York Times,* February 22, 1967; Senate Foreign Relations Committee, *Hearings on the American Institute for Free Labor Development, August 1, 1969* (Washington, D.C., 1969); Serafino Romualdi, *Presidents and Peons* (New York, 1967), pp. 345–352; Ronald Radosh, *American Labor and United States Foreign Policy* (New York, 1969), pp. 393–405.

16. See Barber and Ronning, *Internal Security.*

17. *Ibid.,* pp. 53–90.

18. Quoted in *Ibid.,* p. 45. See also Robert S. McNamara, *The Essence of Security* (New York, 1968), pp. 28–31.

19. Morrison, *Mission,* p. 225.

20. Schlesinger, *Thousand,* p. 788; Barber and Ronning, *Internal Security,* pp. 218–219.

21. *Campos Interview,* pp. 2, 5–6.

22. *Ibid.,* pp. 6–7.

23. *Ibid.,* pp. 9–10.

24. *Ibid.,* pp. 12–14.

25. *Ibid.,* pp. 14–16.

26. *Ibid.,* pp. 40–42.

27. *Ibid.,* pp. 33–34.

28. *Ibid.,* pp. 47–49.

29. Ricardo H. Pueyrredon, interview with Samuel L. Baily, August 22, 23, 1969, at the business office of Mr. Pueyrredon in Buenos Aires, Argentina. In the files of Mr. Baily. The following account is based on this interview.

30. *The New York Times,* November 17, 1963.

31. *Ibid.,* March 19, 1964; Levinson and Onis, *Alliance,* p. 88.

32. *The New York Times,* March 19, 1964.

33. For the complete text, see Martin C. Needler, *The United States and the Latin American Revolution* (Boston, 1972), pp. 145–153.

34. Abraham F. Lowenthal, *The Dominican Intervention* (Cambridge, Mass., 1972); Tad Szulc, *Dominican Diary* (New York, 1965); Senate Committee on Foreign Relations, *Background Information Relating to the Dominican Republic* (Washington, D.C., 1965).

35. Fernando Fuenzalida, et al., *Peru hoy* (Mexico, 1971); Anibal Quijano, *Nationalism and Capitalism in Peru* (New York, 1972).

36. United States, House Committee on Foreign Affairs, *Hearings on New Directions for the 1970's: Toward a Strategy of Inter-American Development, February 25–May 8, 1969* (Washington, D.C., 1969), pp. 656–754. Hereafter cited as House, *New Directions for the 1970's*.

37. *Ibid.*, pp. 656–659.

38. Agency for International Development, *Latin America, Economic Growth Trends* (Washington, D.C., 1971), pp. 22–23; United Nations, Economic Commission for Latin America, *Economic Survey of Latin America, 1969* (New York, 1971), pp. 267, 269; Organization of American States, *External Financing for Latin American Development* (Baltimore, 1971), pp. 18–19; Prebisch, *Change and Development*, p. 263. This view is challenged in the study of the Council for Latin America, *The Effects of U.S. and other Foreign Investment in Latin America* (New York, 1970).

39. House, *New Directions for the 1970's*, p. 44. Emphasis added.

40. AID, *Economic Growth*, pp. 10, 14; OAS, *External Financing*, pp. 38–39.

41. ECLA, *Survey 1969*, p. 3.

42. House, *New Directions for the 1970's*, pp. 675, 660.

43. ECLA, *Survey 1969*, p. 371.

44. James Petras and Robert LaPorte, Jr., *Cultivating Revolution* (New York, 1971), p. 4.

45. ECLA, *Survey 1969*, p. 3.

46. *Rockefeller Report*, p. 39.

47. *Ibid.*, p. 21.

48. *Ibid.*, pp. 65–101.

49. *Ibid.*, pp. 89–98.

50. *Ibid.*, pp. 57–58.

51. *Consensus*, pp. 5–6.

52. *Ibid.*, p. 7.

53. For the complete text, see Gray, *Latin America*, pp. 262–269.

54. *Ibid.*, p. 267.

55. Information on the recent events in inter-American relations must be culled from a wide variety of government publications, newspapers, and magazines. An excellent place to start is the indexed clipping service Information Service on Latin America.

56. For example, see *The New York Times*, September 20, 26, 27, 1973, and January 25, 1974.

57. For example, see *Christian Science Monitor*, March 9, 1972; *Wall Street Journal*, March 13, 1972; *Journal of Commerce*, November 13, 1972; *The New York Times*, May 27, 1973.

58. *The New York Times*, June 6, 1973.

59. United States, Department of State, Bureau of Public Affairs, news release, "Secretary Kissinger Proposes New Program for the Americas" (2/21/74); Los Angeles *Times*, February 23, 1974; *Excelsior*, November 12–14, 1974.

60. United States, Office of the President, *International Economic Report of the President* (Washington, D.C., 1975), p. 35.

61. *Excelsior,* December 12, 1974, includes the full text.

62. *The New York Times,* December 7, 1974, November 21, 1975, January 9, 1976; *Excelsior,* December 7, 1974, February 14 and July 1, 1975.

63. *Excelsior,* December 9, 1974, February 15, 1975; *El Día,* February 16, 1975, May 29, 1975.

64. United States, Department of State, Bureau of Public Affairs, *The United States and Latin America: The New Opportunity* (Washington, D.C., 1975).

chapter
5

Brazil: Junior Partner of
the United States in
South America

Perhaps the most significant development in inter-American relations during recent years has been the emergence of Brazil as a
junior partner of the United States in South America. Since 1964
Brazil has increasingly assumed the role of defender of the interests of the United States in exchange for material aid and support
for its quest to become a major world power. For the United
States, such a relationship is an effective and efficient way to
maintain its South American sphere of influence, particularly since
balance of payments and other economic problems of recent years
have forced it to decrease its aid to the area.

Brazil is the logical choice for such a role. It has more than
half the population and land area of South America; it has common borders with all South American countries except Chile; its
natural resources are enormous; its government is stable, conservative, and anti-communist; and its rapid economic development
along orthodox lines is, from the perspective of Washington, an
acceptable model for the development of the other South American countries. Finally, Brazil has accepted so much United States
government aid and private investment that the present military
government is to a considerable degree dependent upon it. The

United States thus has substantial leverage with which to influence this or any future Brazilian government.

The post-1964 military governments of Brazil viewed this relationship as the best way to fight the international communist conspiracy, to obtain resources for development, to gain recognition of Brazil as a world power, and to maintain the military in power. They have sought and accepted "interdependence" with the United States because they see the United States as the economic and political leader of the "Free World," fighting to preserve Western civilization, the Christian tradition, and the free enterprise system from the threat of Marxist socialism.

Nevertheless, it is essential to keep in mind that Brazil's special role emerged in a particular set of historical circumstances and will not necessarily endure indefinitely. Those in power in the United States and Brazil since 1964 have shared a series of views and interests that have for the present made this relationship a reality. If at some time in the future circumstances in Brazil and/or the United States change, the relationship could also change, but for the immediate future this is unlikely. This chapter describes how the ideas necessary to produce the relationship germinated prior to 1964, how the relationship has worked since then, and how the relationship has affected the quality of life of the Brazilians.

The United States and Brazil: 1945–1964

The United States and Brazil had had a long tradition of friendship dating back to the nineteenth century, but during World War II the relationship was especially close.[1] Brazil established joint defense committees with the United States, provided the United States with air bases, cooperated fully in eliminating German influence, was host to the Latin American Defense Conference in January 1942, made available strategic natural resources, contributed a contingent to the Allied forces fighting in Italy, and played an important role in rounding up Latin American support for the war effort. The United States for its part supplied $366 million in Lend-Lease support during and immediately after the war, helped to minimize the impact of the economic dislocation caused by the war, and sent an economic mission (the Cooke Mission) to Brazil to stimulate and coordinate economic cooperation.

When the war was over, Brazil expected considerable United

States economic and technological aid in return for its wartime cooperation. It was anxious to continue the economic momentum generated by the war and to industrialize as rapidly as possible. To do this it needed investment capital, commodity price agreements, machinery, and technology. The United States, however, focused its attention on the reconstruction of Europe and was not prepared to provide the Brazilians with the kind or amount of aid to which they thought they were entitled. Even though General Eisenhower visited Brazil in August 1946 and President Truman visited the country in September 1947, these gestures of friendship, as pleasant as they may have been, were not what Brazil had in mind. Brazil became somewhat disillusioned with the United States.

As Brazil's foreign exchange reserves dwindled, the economy stagnated, real wages declined, inflation mounted, and anti-United States feelings became more pronounced, the United States belatedly decided to take some positive steps to improve relations. In 1949 the United States sent a technical mission to Brazil to formulate plans for resource development and to resume the lapsed economic cooperation that had been established in 1942 by the Cooke Mission. The new mission, the Abbink Mission, recommended measures similar to those recommended by its predecessor: primary focus on agriculture rather than industrial development, orthodox financial and fiscal policies, and predominant reliance on private enterprise to initiate and sustain development. The Abbink Mission also suggested limited state investment in transportation and energy.[2]

Although increased United States and international aid was not forthcoming for several years, the Abbink Report established the conditions upon which such aid would be forthcoming in the 1950s. Thus, although Brazilian Presidents Getulio Vargas (1950–1954) and Juscelino Kubitschek (1955–1960) attempted to break away from the neo-liberal development strategy of the late 1940s and to adopt a nationalist development strategy, they were only partially able to do so. The United States had the trump card—economic and technological resources—and Brazil had to accept certain policies to qualify for these resources. Vargas established a state petroleum company (Petrobras), laid the foundation for a state electric company (Electrobras), limited profit remittances abroad, and in general increased state control over the economy, but he had to adopt an anti-inflation economic program before he received major amounts of foreign economic aid. In mid-1953, with Europe well on the road to recovery, a new and more sympathetic administration in Washington, and Brazil's adoption of a tough anti-inflation program, international aid began to flow. The Export-Import Bank loaned Brazil $363 million and the World Bank $49 million. Bilateral United States aid jumped from a yearly average of $71.3 million during the Truman Administration to $139.1 million under Eisenhower, an increase of nearly 100 percent (Table 5–1).[3]

The suicide of Vargas in August 1954 temporarily stalled the fledgling development effort, but in 1956 the dynamic Juscelino Kubitschek took over as president of Brazil and, with United States support, initiated a program in which he promised, and nearly achieved, "fifty years of progress in five." Between 1955 and 1961 industrial production increased 80 percent, and from 1957 to 1961 GNP increased at an annual rate of 7 percent and per capita GNP grew at an annual rate of 4 percent. Furthermore, Kubitschek, convinced that the future of the country lay in the interior, built a new capital, Brasília, five hundred miles inland from Rio.

Kubitschek was able to produce such results because Brazil had a large domestic market and enormous natural resources, but these advantages were not unique to his administration. In addition, Kubitschek developed production capacity in key areas— iron and steel, for example, which formerly had held back development. He maintained political stability by providing something for nearly every group in society, and although he used government investment to overcome bottlenecks in areas where private investment would not go, he also sought increased domestic and foreign private investment.[4]

The program's success hinged ultimately on relatively high levels of foreign aid and investment, and Kubitschek was for the most part willing to give the United States and other foreign countries the necessary assurances to attract this aid and investment. First, Kubitschek was strongly anti-communist. Early in January 1956, before he had formally assumed the presidency, Kubitschek visited Washington and, in an address before Congress, assured the legislators that "The Brazilian nation rejects all forms of tyranny as you, too, reject them; tryanny and oppression, whether from right or left, are equally repulsive to us. . . . To combat extremist ideas in my country—ideas now defended by but a small minority—it is chiefly necessary to bring Brazil into line with her destiny, to work constantly toward a higher standard of living as you have done in this country."

TABLE 5–1

Foreign Aid to Brazil, Fiscal Years 1946–1974

Year	United States		International Organizations
	Total Aid	Military Aid	
1946–1948	73.9		⎫ 90.0
(per year)	(24.6)		⎬ (18.0)
1949	10.4		⎭
1950	15.3		
1951	27.2		15.0
1952	59.1		12.6
1953	384.2	3.0	3.5
1954	22.1	17.6	49.5
1955	69.0	12.7	.4
1956	103.4	7.7	.4
1957	342.8	18.4	2.0
1958	45.0	18.2	18.0
1959	155.7	20.2	90.6
1960	46.3	26.4	1.6
1961	328.3	23.9	17.4
1962	255.1	26.8	27.6
1963	159.3	17.5	23.1
1964	378.1	33.7	29.9
1965	288.0	11.2	159.9
1966	376.5	28.9	152.8
1967	302.6	30.6	242.0
1968	383.5	21.2	142.6
1969	57.9	.8	189.7
1970	218.0	.8	377.6
1971	204.7	10.2	298.9
1972	343.1	20.8	683.7
1973	217.2	17.7	368.6
1974	396.6	52.7	695.3

Source: Agency for International Development, U.S. Overseas Loans and Grants, 1961, 1971, 1972, 1974 (Washington, D.C.).

Nevertheless, at Kubitschek's inauguration in late January, Vice President Richard Nixon once more expressed the concerns of the United States and the conditions of United States support. After talking with Kubitschek and explaining that the United States public would object to substantial economic aid unless his administration took determined measures to control communism, Nixon told reporters: "I have been encouraged in talks here with government officials, with the keen understanding they displayed of the [Communist] problem, and from what I have seen of the people of Brazil I think the prospect for Red gains are not very bright." Nixon then proclaimed that the "United States must never get into the position of aiding countries economically for the purpose of controlling those countries and eventually have them as economic, political, or military satellites." The next day Nixon announced a $35 million loan from the United States Export-Import Bank to help expand Brazil's steel industry.[5]

The second assurance Kubitschek gave to investors was that foreign capital would be welcomed and protected in Brazil. Although he supported a nationalist strategy of development rather than the neo-liberal strategy of the early postwar years, he did so by using public investment in areas where private investment did not flow, and he at no time attacked private capital. Furthermore, he signed an investment guarantee agreement with the United States and provided tax incentives and other concessions to foreign investors. As a result, United States aid increased substantially in 1956 and 1957.

There was, nevertheless, a limit to Kubitschek's willingness to tailor his economic program to meet the demands of the United States and the international lending agencies. During the late 1950s the Brazilian economy suffered from a major drop in coffee prices (its chief export), a negative balance of trade, and a series of economic bottlenecks. The resulting disequilibrium led to chronic inflation, and inflation in turn stimulated popular protests. In 1959 Kubitschek was faced with a critical choice. The International Monetary Fund demanded that he pursue a tough anti-inflation policy if he were to receive $300 million in stabilization credit. He had to decide whether to continue the drive to reach his development targets and thus exacerbate inflation or constrict the domestic economy with an austerity program to curb inflation in order to get the $300 million in credits. He chose the former alternative and was praised by nationalists for his independent stand in the face of pressure from the international lending authorities.

Yet Kubitschek's significance was not his last-minute stand against the international lending agencies. The significance of Kubitschek, as was true of Eduardo Frei in Chile a few years later, was that in his effort to attract capital for development he saddled Brazil with an enormous foreign debt ($3 billion) that sharply limited the independence of all subsequent governments. In order to pay back the debt, Brazil had to increase production and exports, and in order to do this Brazil had to borrow more money. The increase in production did not, however, keep up with the growing debt, and thus Brazil, like Chile and others, became entangled in the spiraling debt cycle and became increasingly dependent on the United States.

In January 1961 Janio Quadros, an efficient, maverick populist politician from the industrial state of São Paulo, assumed the presidency of Brazil and introduced an important new dimension to United States-Brazilian relations. He pursued an anti-inflation austerity economic program, but he also developed an independent foreign policy. He visited Cuba during his campaign, favored debate on China's admission to the U.N., sought ties with Eastern Europe and Russia, decorated Cuba's Che Guevara, and sent a trade mission—headed by vice president Jango Goulart—to China. "Common ideals of life and organization," he explained, "draw us close to the major nations of the Western bloc . . . [but] we have other points in common with Latin America in particular, and with the recently emancipated peoples of Asia and Africa, which cannot be ignored. . . ." The basic point of Brazil's new foreign policy, he continued, "is the recognition of the legitimacy of the struggle for economic and political freedom. Development is an aim common to Brazil and to the nations with which we endeavor to have closer relations, and the rejection of colonialism is the inevitable and imperative corollary of that aim. . . . We cannot too often stress the extent to which poverty separates us from North America and the leading European countries of the Western World." Nevertheless, he insisted, Brazil is not opposed to foreign capital and indeed needs it. "The sole condition is that the gradual nationalization of profits be accepted. . . . The idea behind the foreign policy of Brazil . . . [is that it] has now become the instrument for a national development policy." [6]

Quadros, according to his ambassador to Washington, Roberto Campos, pursued such a foreign policy for a number of reasons. First, he believed it was something that flowed naturally out of Brazil's deep aspiration to become a world power. Second, he thought that it might prompt the United States to offer Brazil more assistance. And, third, he believed that he would have "a lot more authority to develop an austerity program at home if he took some bold moves used in international politics. . . . The provocative foreign policy was perhaps a passport to the adoption of conventional, conservative, stringent, austere, difficult financial policies at home." [7]

The United States did not fail to grasp the similarity between Quadros' independent foreign policy and Perón's Third Position and was concerned about its implications for continued United States influence in the area. Nevertheless, the new Kennedy Administration, anxious to recoup the loss of prestige it had suffered as a result of the Bay of Pigs fiasco and mindful of Brazil's essentially orthodox domestic economic policy, decided to support Quadros. In June 1961 the United States helped Brazil obtain a $2 billion package of loans, grants, and debt renegotiations. Given the specific circumstances in both countries, the United States supported a government whose foreign policy seemed to challenge U.S. influence in South America.

This situation endured only a few months. In August 1961 Quadros resigned. After a major political crisis, populist Vice President Jango Goulart assumed the presidency, but under a new parliamentary system that restricted presidential powers. The armed forces insisted on the parliamentary system because they feared that Goulart, a protégé of Vargas and a friend of Perón's, might, as president under the old system, attempt to strengthen the power of labor and use it to counterbalance military power.

The United States was concerned about left-wing influence within the Goulart administration, Brazil's "pro-Cuban" stand at Punta del Este II (January 1962), the expropriation of ITT holdings, and Goulart's continuation of an independent foreign policy. According to Campos, however, Goulart at first seemed anxious to cooperate with the United States. In April 1962 Goulart visited Washington, talked to Kennedy and his main advisers, and assured them he was opposed to Castroism and extremism, that his foreign policy was independent but not neutral, and that he was anxious to negotiate a just settlement of the ITT matter. Goulart asked for help in getting access to the United States domestic sugar market, in establishing an international coffee agreement, in getting the World Bank to resume operations in Brazil, and in getting more cooperation from the Export-Import Bank. Kennedy and his advisers promised to look into these matters and Goulart left Washington impressed by Kennedy and those around him.[8]

Yet relations between the two countries, not really based on shared goals, genuine understanding, and mutual respect, deteriorated thereafter. In September 1962 Goulart signed a law which, like that of Kubitschek some years earlier, limited the remittance abroad of profits to 10 percent of invested capital, but in addition provided that remaining profits could not be reinvested as new capital. As a result, foreign investment immediately declined. Furthermore, the issues of left-wing influence in the regime, nationalization of United States property, and inflation continued to strain relations.

The final break came as a result of the Bell-Dantas agreement of March 1963, as mentioned in the preceding chapter. Foreign Minister San Tiago Dantas went to Washington to negotiate an aid agreement. With such an agreement he planned to go to Europe to renegotiate Brazil's large foreign debt. The United States responded with considerable caution, and Brazil received $398.5 million of which only $84 million could be used immediately. Dantas was disappointed. Goulart believed this demonstrated that the United States was uninterested in helping Brazil.

As the Brazilian economic situation deteriorated, Goulart's opponents—business groups, women's organizations, the leaders of the military, and some labor unions—increased their attacks on the government and carried out a number of protest demonstrations. The United States—particularly after Johnson assumed the presidency in November 1963—sought to aggravate the deteriorating economic situation and to support the growing domestic opposition. It suspended all economic assistance to the federal government of Brazil and postponed debt renegotiation talks. At the same time it proceeded to negotiate loans with Brazilian state governments (Guanabara and Rio Grande do Norte) whose governors were opposed to Goulart and sympathetic to the United States and to a military coup.

Goulart in the meantime turned increasingly to the left for support, and Brazil, like Chile in 1973, became increasingly polarized along working-class and middle-upper-class lines. The showdown came in March 1964. In the midst of a series of pro- and anti-Goulart demonstrations, the president signed an agrarian reform law strongly opposed by the conservative landed-business elites, and he antagonized and threatened the military leadership by siding with the mutineers in a naval revolt. On March 31 the armed forces acted, replacing Goulart with the military government that has ruled Brazil ever since.[9]

Secretary of State Dean Rusk and United States Ambassador Lincoln Gordon denied that there had been any United States involvement in the coup. "The movement which overthrew President Goulart," Gordon proclaimed, "was a purely 100 percent—not 99.44—but 100 percent purely Brazilian movement." Yet there is considerable and persuasive evidence to suggest that the United States was at least indirectly very much involved in the coup.

First, the United States clearly opposed Goulart and was concerned about the general drift of his regime toward "extremism." Shortly after the coup, Assistant Secretaary of State for Inter-American Affairs Thomas Mann recalled that "We were aware in January [1964] by the time I got there, that the erosion toward Communism in Brazil was very rapid." William Ellis, former director of AID in Brazil, explained the situation in slightly different words to the Senate Subcommittee on Western Hemisphere Affairs. "I felt then [1964]," Ellis noted, "and I still do, sir, that this enormous country, which was shifting into a period of both economic and perhaps even political anarchy, was, I was about to say, ripe for political developments which might be antithetical to our interests, at least the possibility of such political developments was high enough to pose a serious risk to U.S. interests." [10]

The New York Times correspondent Tad Szulc suggested that the United States was concerned with more than extremism in Brazil. "Historically," he explained, "Latin American political movements develop in terms of patterns, some of which succeed in establishing themselves for longer or shorter periods, and some of which have become absorbed." The Cuban Revolution, he continued, might possibly have been the starting point of a new pattern, and "if Goulart had been successful in setting up his leftist state, it might have had an electrifying effect on Chile, Bolivia and Peru. . . . If the Brazilian situation now becomes reasonably stable . . . a measure of relative stability will have returned to South America. . . ." [11]

Second, the United States was favorably disposed toward the new military government. The United States recognized the new regime within twelve hours and promised its support. President Johnson at his weekly press conference praised the Brazilian Revolution, insisted that it was constitutional, and proclaimed that it had been a "good week in the hemisphere." The United States ambassador to Brazil, Lincoln Gordon, announced that the overthrow of Goulart "had brought conditions favorable for the Alliance for Progress in Brazil," and suggested that the coup "can indeed be included along with the Marshall Plan proposal, the Berlin Blockade, the defeat of Communist aggression in Korea, and the resolution of the missile crisis in Cuba as one of the major turning points in world history in the middle of the twentieth century."

Even *The New York Times,* which supported the new military government in Brazil, felt that the unabashed glee of the United States government was a bit too much. "It would be hard to figure out from the publications and official pronouncements," the *Times* editorialized, "who got more satisfaction in the overthrow of President Goulart, the Brazilians or the United States State Department. 'Diplomacy' that is so hasty, so exuberant and so openly partisan regarding the internal affairs of another nation belies the definition of the word." [12]

Third, the United States had prior knowledge of the coup. General Vernon Walters, United States military attaché to Brazil, and General Humberto Castello Branco, coordinator of the anti-Goulart coup, had been good friends since they had worked closely together in Italy in 1945. The conservative and pro-military government newspaper, *O Estado de São Paulo*, published a series of articles describing several pre-coup contacts between the military conspirators and Walters. Another sympathetic account noted that the conspirators "sent an emissary to ask United States Ambassador Lincoln Gordon what the United States position would be if civil war broke out, who reported back that Gordon was cautious and diplomatic, but he left the impression that if the Paulistas [people from the state of São Paulo] could hold out for 48 hours they would get United States recognition and help." [13]

And fourth, United States business and labor were involved to varying degrees in the coup. United States businesses in Brazil worked closely with the Brazilian businessmen who were so active in the overthrow of Goulart. Although there are no ITT documents to prove it conclusively, it seems unlikely that the United States business concerns were unaware of the planned coup or would avoid contributing money to their friends in the anti-Goulart forces. United States labor, on the other hand, openly boasted about its involvement. William C. Doherty, executive director of the American Institute of Free Labor Development (AIFLD), explained on television that graduates of the AIFLD school in Brazil "were so active that they became intimately involved in some of the clandestine operations of the revolution before it took place on April 1. What happened in Brazil on April 1 did not just happen—it was planned months in advance. Many of the trade union leaders—some of whom were actually trained in our institute— were involved in the revolution, and in the overthrow of the Goulart regime." [14]

This evidence does not suggest direct United States involvement, but there was no need for direct United States involvement to achieve the desired results. The United States operated along lines that it had followed in British Guiana in 1963, and would follow in Chile in 1964, 1970, and 1973, and in Bolivia in 1971. It increased pressure on Goulart by withholding aid, encouraged opposition politicians with selective aid to the states, and gave the "impression" of support if there were to be a coup.

There is little practical difference between this kind of "involvement" and the direct intervention in the Dominican Republic a year later. The United States clearly involved itself in the internal affairs of Brazil with the objective of producing the overthrow of Goulart. It is debatable whether the United States could have prevented the coup, but it is clear that if the United States had emphasized its commitment to constitutional government, had refused to support any government that came to power by force (i.e., cut off aid), and had made sure that United States private interests in Brazil (business and labor) had remained aloof, the

Brazilian military would have been much more reluctant to stage the coup and might possibly have worked out a constitutional solution.

The Interdependence of the United States and Brazil

Although the United States and Brazil had had a long tradition of friendship and cooperation, prior to 1964 this relationship did not include Brazil's assumption of a special role. During the later 1940s and the 1950s, the United States was not interested in Brazil's assuming such a role, and during the early 1960s the governments of Janio Quadros and Jango Goulart pursued an independent foreign policy. Nevertheless, the ideas necessary for Brazil's assumption of the special role developed during the two decades following World War II. Most important was the concept of interdependence.

Interdependence meant simply that Brazil's best chance to develop and become a world power lay in economic and international political integration with the United States. Genuine interdependence, however, necessitates equality among the countries involved. Since the United States was economically, technologically, and militarily superior to Brazil, interdependence meant in fact the subordination of Brazil to the United States. The junior partner relationship was the implementation of the concept of interdependence between the United States and Brazil given the disparity of their power.

The group most responsible for the development of the interdependence concept was the Brazilian military. The Brazilian military cooperated closely with the United States during World War II. Most importantly, Brazil sent a 25,000-man ground force (Força Expedicionaria Brasileira—FEB) and an air squadron to fight with the United States in Italy during the last ten months of the war. The Brazilian troops were integrated into the United States command in terms of equipment, organization, procedures, and tactics. This close working relationship with the leader of the Allies seemed to create and/or reinforce an ideology among the Brazilian officers that would support the special role.[15]

The Brazilian officers were impressed with the United States military and the political, economic, and ideological system it represented. This strengthened their belief that capitalism was the best form of economic organization to create a powerful Brazil, that democracy was the most civilized style of politics, that excessive nationalism stood in the way of Brazilian development, and that close cooperation with the United States was in the best interests of their country. Furthermore, the United States was the acknowledged leader of Western Christian civilization in the struggle against both fascism and totalitarian communism, and Brazil would therefore do well to develop an interdependent foreign policy with it.

Late in July 1945 United States Ambassador to Brazil Adolph Berle, Jr., sent home his evaluation of a series of conversations between the United States and the Brazilian armed forces:

> The United States officers proceeded on the theory that Brazil was willing and anxious to become a southern partner of the United States in a military sense . . . [and that] it is the desire of the United States that Brazil be able to play a strong and cooperative role in the maintenance of hemispherical defense. . . . The fact has to be faced that Brazil with roughly half the territory and roughly half the population of the entire continent is destined to have the major position in the continent, if she is able to develop powers of organization giving her capacity to use her manpower and her resources.[16]

Nevertheless, at that time the United States was unwilling to grant Brazil the resources and support necessary for it to become the junior partner of the United States in South America. Berle argued that the United States could best handle the major defense burden and that a large Brazilian army, navy, and air force, capable of defending the continent, should "be left as a possible ideal to be attained at some future date." Brazil's defense at present, the ambassador insisted, "should be her virtual alliance with the United States within the framework of the inter-American arrangements envisaged by the Act of Chapultepec. . . ."[17]

By the end of the year, the Brazilian military was expressing its unhappiness with the decision of the United States to provide Brazil with only limited amounts of equipment and support. On December 28, 1945, Colonel Bina Machado, who claimed to speak for President-elect Enrico Dutra and Minister of War General Goes Monteiro, called on Berle to discuss Brazilian-American cooperation. Berle reported that

Col. Bina said that as a true friend of the U.S. he viewed with the utmost alarm the recent growth of anti-American sentiment in high Brazilian Army circles, gravely threatening the future of Brazilian-American military cooperation. He said that the feeling was growing that the U.S. was inclined to treat Brazil as a small brother rather than an important nation pledged to full military cooperation. He said doubts existed that the U.S. even was sincerely desirous of following a wholehearted policy of cooperation with Brazil.[18]

Despite the doubts, close ties between the Brazilian and United States military establishments continued. United States General Mark Clark, who had directed Brazilian troops in Italy, visited Brazil in July 1945 to confer medals on its top officers. General Eisenhower visited Brazil in August 1946. And in August 1950 President Enrico Dutra made General Clark a general in the Brazilian army. In addition, large numbers of Brazilian officers visited the United States, the United States provided Brazil with considerable surplus military stock, and between 1953 and 1964 the United States granted Brazil more than $200 million in military aid.

Most importantly, the United States worked closely with the Brazilian military to create and develop the Escola Superior de Guerra (ESG), the Higher War College. In 1948 a United States advisory military mission went to Brazil and a year later the college was formally established. The United States mission remained in Brazil until 1960 and then was replaced by a permanent United States liason officer. The first two commanders of the ESG, Generals Cordeiro de Farias and Juarez Távora, and its leading theoretician, General Golbery do Couto e Silva, had worked closely with the United States military as officers of the FEB in Italy.

The ESG was modeled on the United States National War College but with two important differences: first, the curriculum sought to integrate all aspects of internal and external security—the armed forces, economic development, education, politics, agriculture, and industry; and second, the college included substantial numbers of civilians as well as military men (646, or 51 percent of the 1,276 graduates between 1950 and 1967 were civilians). [19]

Between 1949 and 1964 the ESG was an important center for the exchange of ideas among the Brazilian military, civilian Brazilians, and the United States military. Incorporating much of the ideology of the leaders of the FEB, the ESG imparted to its students the concept of interdependence with the United States; it emphasized development within the international capitalist framework, integration into the international anti-communist movement, and the dangers for Brazil of "excessive nationalism." As time passed, the ESG modified the FEB commitment to democracy. Instead, it stressed the importance of a strong executive to protect the country from internal subversion. In addition, it elaborated a more detailed theory of the relationship between security and development. Development was essential to national security because underdeveloped countries were subjected to severe internal pressures, not only as a result of their underdevelopment, but also of the global ideological conflict. Brazil was a key arena of the cold war and therefore had to develop rapidly if it were to be able to maintain its security.[20]

The staff and the graduates of the ESG proved to be the most important supporters of interdependence and therefore of the junior partner role Brazil was to assume after 1964. But in the period 1960 to 1964 a number of other groups, all of whom had ties with the ESG, supported the idea. Each of them was committed to capitalist development, believed that Brazil was a critical battleground in the global struggle between capitalism and communism, feared the growing strength of socialism and communism under Goulart, supported the military as the ultimate guarantor of Brazilian capitalism, and favored the creation of an interdependent foreign policy with the United States.

In 1961 a small group of leading business executives from São Paulo and Rio (Gilbert Huber, Jr., João Baptista Figueiredo, and Paulo Ayres, Jr., among others) established the Instituto de Pesquisas e Estudos Sociais (IPES) to fight what they perceived as the leftward drift of the government.[21] They believed that since the early 1950s the communists had increasingly infiltrated the larger and more vital labor unions, the universities and schools, and the newspapers and TV, and that "one of the most important cold war battles was going on in Latin America and specifically in Brazil." Inspired by such church pronouncements as *Mater et Magistra* and by such programs as the Alliance for Progress, the members of IPES sought to defend the free enterprise system, democratic institutions, and the Christian tradition. Through research, publications, and special conferences, they spread their message widely. Whenever possible they worked closely with universities and schools, labor unions, women's organizations, and the armed forces. Thus, members of IPES frequently invited military officers to visit their factories, and while they were there explained to the officers their concern about communism. IPES also established close associations with United States business interests in Brazil. At the height of its influence in early 1964, the organization represented some four hundred enterprises, which provided $500,000 a year for its work, and it became the major focus of the civilian opposition to Goulart.

In early 1963, just after the plebiscite that restored full presidential powers to Goulart, several members of IPES (Flavio Galvão, Luiz Werneck, and João-Adelino Prado Neto) initiated an action group to bring down Goulart by whatever methods necessary. They won the support of the owner of the influential paper *O Estado de São Paulo* and of the governor of the State of São Paulo among others. Most importantly, they established contact with military officers who shared their views. As a result, Lieutenant Colonel Rubens Resstel, who had fought with the FEB in Italy and had graduated from the ESG, traveled about Brazil sounding out military men regarding the possibility of a coup. The group also contacted United States Ambassador Lincoln Gordon regarding possible United States support for a coup, but Gordon was circumspect. As Paulo Ayres, Jr., summed up:

> A national movement thus developed to repulse, by force if necessary, the attempts to lead the country into a leftist dictatorship. . . . The Brazilian people and the Armed Forces did just what was to be done to prevent Brazil from turning Communist. And this minimum represents so much for the security of this hemisphere and for the defense of freedom all over the world that we, Brazilians, have now the right of demanding, from other nations, a more sympathetic attitude to our problems, our intentions, and our democratic Revolution—the greatest victory ever won by the free world in the cold war.[22]

Another pro-interdependence groups, the Instituto Brasileiro de Ação Democrática (IBAD), was established in 1959 to support the development of free enterprise in Brazil.[23] While IPES was initially more intellectually oriented, IBAD was from the start an action group. It operated in a wide variety of ways: It sponsored radio and TV programs, issued press releases, published the magazine *Açáo Democrática* (circulation: 250,000), which it distributed free, gave courses, held conferences, conducted research, and even provided direct social assistance to the poor in critical areas. For example, IBAD sponsored seventeen permanent and twenty mobile medical and dental clinics in the poverty-struck northeast, it studied agrarian reform through a series of conferences, which included such people as General Juarez Távora, second commander of the ESG, and it produced two weekly TV programs. The source of funds to support this extensive program is unknown, but in 1963 a Brazilian Congressional Investigating Committee accused IBAD of being a conduit for foreign funds to Brazilian anti-communist organizations. As a result, the Brazilian National Security Agency closed IBAD and its director, the North American Ivan Hasslocker, was declared *persona non grata*.[24]

Other groups were also active in support of the idea. Ação Democrática Parlamentar provided funds for anti-communist candidates in the 1962 elections. The Movimento Estudantil Democrática attempted unsuccessfully to gain a foothold among the predominantly left university students. The Movimento Sindical Democrático and the Instituto Cultural do Trabalho attempted to gain influence in the pro-Goulart labor movement. And a number of women's groups actively protested in the streets. All of these groups, with the exception of the Instituto Cultural do Trabalho, were allegedly funded in part through IBAD by the CIA. The Instituto Cultural do Trabalho, established in January 1964, was funded openly by the AIFLD.[25]

Finally, the conservative brand of Brazilian nationalism contributed to the idea of interdependence. During the eight years preceding the 1964 coup, the left-wing and populist varieties of nationalism were clearly in evidence with their spokesmen attacking foreign domination (the United States) and supporting rapid and more egalitarian economic development under state control.[26] Less in evidence, yet just as intense and alive, were the right-wing conservative varieties of nationalism, whose spokesmen included the staff of the ESG, the conservative politician Carlos Lacerda and other leaders of the União Democrática Nacional (UDN), and the scholar Gilberto Freyre.[27] They stressed a variety of points, but they all had several ideas in common that supported the concept of interdependence. First, they believed that Brazil was destined to be the great future power in Latin America and a major world power. Second, they believed that Brazil was an important outpost of Western Christian civilization. Third, they believed that economic development within a capitalist framework was an essential part of national security and prestige. And fourth, they believed that Brazil, in alliance with the United States and Western Europe, was engaged in a global struggle against communism.

In the two decades following World War II, Brazil did not assume the role of junior partner to the United States in South America, despite close and friendly relations between the two countries. The necessary economic and political circumstances were not yet in existence. But the period is important because a number of interrelated Brazilian groups, most importantly the ESG, developed the concept of interdependence with the United States, which, after 1964, was to become the basis of the new partnership.

Brazil as Junior Partner: 1964–1975

The coup that overthrew Goulart and brought the military to power made possible the realization of the new partnership with the United States. Since 1964 the rulers of Brazil have included General Humberto de Alencar Castello Branco (1964–1967), General Artur da Costa e Silva (1967–1969), General Emilio Garrastazu Médici (1969–1974), and General Ernesto Geisel (1974–). The rule of each has differed somewhat according to differing circumstances, but the similarity among them in terms of basic ideology, goals, and methods has been much greater than their differences and has provided a high degree of continuity to the past decade.

The continuity in Brazilian policy since 1964 stems in large part from the enormous influence of the ESG on all four presidents, but particularly on Castello Branco, whose administration established the basic pattern followed thereafter. Alfred Stepan, in his excellent study of the Brazilian military, documented the striking differences in background and training between the ten-man "core group" that ran the Castello Branco government and the twenty pro-Goulart officers purged by the Castello Branco administration. He showed that the overwhelming majority of Castello Branco's core group had close ties with the ESG (attended the

ESG and/or was on the permanent staff) and with the United States military (FEB and/or attended military school in the United States), while the pro-Goulart group ranked low on both accounts.[28] It is not surprising, then, that the Castello Branco government, faced with the task of running the country without a clearly defined program, turned to the ESG for ideas and programs.

Most importantly, the new administration subscribed to the ESG philosophy of interdependence; that given the global ideological conflict between communism and capitalism and Brazil's underdeveloped condition, Brazilian security depended on rapid development within a capitalist framework, the temporary tutelage of a strong executive, and integration with the United States in foreign policy. President Castello Branco explained in a speech at the Brazilian Foreign Ministry on July 31, 1964:

> In the present context of a bipolar power confrontation with a radical political and ideological divorce between the two respective centers, the preservation of independence presupposes the acceptance of a degree of interdependence, whether in the military, economic, or political fields.
>
> In the Brazilian case, in foreign policy [we] cannot forget that we have made a basic option which stems from cultural and political fidelity to the Western democratic system.
>
> The interests of Brazil coincide, in many cases, in concentric circles with Latin America, the American continent and the Western community.[29]

The military government moved quickly to eliminate what it considered to be the communist threat to Brazilian security. It promulgated Institutional Act I as a document with superior authority to that of the Constitution or the elected Congress. "The Revolution does not seek legitimacy itself through Congress," the act proclaimed. "It is the latter that receives its legitimacy from the Institutional Act, resulting from the exercise of the Constituent Power inherent in all revolutions." The act provided, among other things, that Congress take action within thirty days on bills submitted to it by the president or they were automatically approved, the president had exclusive authority to initiate financial bills, the president could declare a state of siege without congressional approval, the constitutional and legal rights of job tenure were suspended for six months, and the president could suspend the political rights of any citizen, including elected officials, for ten years.[30]

Armed with this act, Castello Branco suspended the political rights of three ex-presidents (Kubitschek, Quadros, and Goulart), six state governors, fifty-five congressmen, and hundreds of labor leaders, army officers, public officials, and intellectuals. He also broke diplomatic relations with Cuba, froze wages except for a 100 percent increase in military salaries, modified the Goulart profits remittance law so that profits in excess of 10 percent could be reinvested in Brazil, and worked out favorable agreements with ITT, the Hanna Mining Company, and other United States concerns.

In the elections of October 1965 the followers of former President Kubitschek won several important state governorships and the Labor Party of former President Goulart also did well. This led to a crisis within the military and the promulgation of Institutional Act II. The act abolished the traditional political parties and established in their place a government party (Aliança Renovadora Nacional (ARENA), and an official, and hopefully more docile, opposition party, Movimento Democrático Brasileiro (MDB). In addition, the government decreed a strict press control bill, providing fines and imprisonment for anyone who published news that was detrimental to the banking system or to national security.[31]

In March 1967, when Costa e Silva became president, it seemed possible that he might relax some of the more repressive measures of his predecessor. He had talked about democracy and social humanism and had said that he would not enforce the press control law. Yet growing student-labor opposition and the recalcitrance of the supposedly emasculated Congress led to the imposition of even harsher repression and increased government control.

The military was concerned about the strength of the opposition and by the fact that the courts were freeing many of the student and labor leaders. The incident that most concerned it, however, involved opposition deputy and journalist Mario Moreira Alves. Alves attacked the military regime in the Chamber of Deputies, and the military, in order to prosecute him, wanted the Chamber to lift his parliamentary immunity. When the government realized that the Justice Committee of the Chamber would not vote to lift Alves' immunity, it changed the composition of the committee and then was able to get a 19–12 vote in favor of its position. Early in December 1968 the measure went before the full Chamber of Deputies and, to the astonishment of the government, the Chamber voted 216–141–15 not to lift Alves' immunity. The vote was all the more remarkable since the government party (ARENA) had 249 deputies to only 123 for the official opposition (MDB). Thus, 93 government deputies broke rank in this critical case and supported the opposition.

The government responded swiftly with Draconian measures. Institutional Act V granted the president authority to recess all legislative bodies, intervene at will in the states, cancel elections, suspend the political rights of any citizen, and to set aside *habeas corpus* proceedings. Furthermore, all of this could be done without recourse to judicial review. The government then closed Congress and suspended the political rights of 77 of the 409 deputies, a number of senators, and several dozen justices. It also canceled the forthcoming elections of 1970.[32]

The December 1968 crisis and Institutional Act V also marked the increased use of torture and assassination against suspected opponents of the regime. Since that time the government has resorted to the systematic and widespread use of torture to intimidate students, workers, and Catholic priests who in various ways have questioned its policies. In some cases political prisoners simply disappear. A number of right-wing terrorist groups—most notably the Command for Communist Hunting (CCC) and the Anti-Communist Movement (MAC)—have engaged in assassination campaigns that have resulted in the deaths of hundreds of people, while the government conveniently looks the other way.[33]

In September 1969 Costa e Silva had a stroke and was replaced by General Emilio Garrastazu Médici. The purged Congress was temporarily called back into session to ratify the choice of the military. Médici, like Costa e Silva, at first talked of restoring political democracy but soon replaced this rhetoric with that of the indefinite tutelage of the military. Repression and torture continued apace. General Ernesto Geisel's assumption of power in March 1974 brought no significant change.

The Brazilian military, committed to interdependence with a much more powerful United States, served in fact as a junior

partner of the United States in South America. During the first
ten years of the military dictatorship, Brazil did a number of
things to fulfill this role. First of all, Brazil developed rapidly
within a capitalist framework, using large sums of private and
public foreign capital, and worked closely with the United States.
It thus provided a model of economic development for the other
South American countries which was completely acceptable to the
United States and the international lending agencies. Indeed, Brazil was so successful in economic terms that many United States
observers referred to its development program as "the Brazilian
miracle" and to the country as the "Japan of South America." [34]

A few statistics sum up the Brazilian miracle: Brazil's real economic growth averaged 10 percent per year from 1968 to 1973
with economic output reaching $60 billion in 1973; inflation,
which was 150 percent in 1964, dropped to less than 20 percent
in 1973; foreign trade grew enormously; exports were diversified,
ending the nearly complete reliance on coffee; and foreign exchange reserves reached $6.5 billion in 1972. Furthermore, the
value of foreign private and particularly United States investment
increased dramatically, more than doubling from 1966 to 1972. [35]

The economic success of Brazil, based on capitalism and close
cooperation with the United States, was important to Washington
since it provided a desirable developmental model. No other country in Latin America matched Brazil's record of economic growth.
Most importantly, the socialist governments—Castro's Cuba and
Allende's Chile—lagged far behind. The Brazilian example was,
for the United States, living proof of the superiority of the capitalist system and a refutation of socialism as the basis for rapid development.

Without minimizing the importance of obtaining and sustaining
high rates of economic growth, it is essential to note that there
was another side to the Brazilian miracle. The Brazilian model
was based on capital-intensive as opposed to labor-intensive industrialization and, as a result, led to increased unemployment
and to the marginalization of the urban poor. For those who had
jobs, real wages were low. Wealth was highly concentrated and
became increasingly so. The foreign debt, and therefore the potential leverage of foreigners to influence internal decisions, was
growing dramatically. [36]

Specifically, real wages in industry declined 10 to 15 percent between 1964 and 1971. World Bank figures show that during the 1960s the top 5 percent of the population increased its share of total income from 20 to 38 percent. During the same period, the bottom 40 percent of the population saw its share of total income drop from 10 to 8 percent. The *Wall Street Journal* noted that the boom had "practically no impact at all on well over half the country's 95 million citizens. In fact many are actually poorer now than they were five years ago. . . . Only 20 million people in the whole country can really be called consumers." Furthermore, there was a serious imbalance in distribution of wealth among regions as well as individuals. The average income in the south was 23 percent above the national average, while the average income in the north and the west-central sections—despite special efforts to develop these areas—was 13 percent below the national average. And in the northeast, the average income was an astonishing 53 percent below the national average. Finally, the foreign debt rose from approximately $3 billion in 1963 to $17 billion in 1975 and the service payments rose accordingly.[37]

While only a few benefited from the Brazilian miracle, the country became so deeply indebted to the United States and other foreign countries that it lost more control over internal decision making. The only way to pay off the debt is to continue to borrow. The more Brazil borrows, the more leverage the United States has to exert its influence. If a new government with a different policy should come to power in Brazil, it would have enormous difficulty in doing anything that the United States did not approve of. It could, of course, repudiate the debt, but as Allende found out in Chile, such a move would most certainly jeopardize continued development.

A second thing Brazil did to fulfill its role as junior partner of the United States in South America was to pursue a pro-United States and anti-communist foreign policy. During the early years of the military regime, Brazil gave priority to domestic rather than foreign policy, but even then it was the strongest supporter of the United States in South America. Increasingly, foreign policy became important, and Brazil sought to expand its influence in the area. In 1965 Brazil strongly supported the United States military intervention in the Dominican Republic and took a leading role in the Inter-American Peace Force sent to police that country. A Brazilian general was named commander of the force and Brazil contributed by far the largest number of Latin American troops.

In the United Nations, Brazil supported the United States on practically every issue, while other South American countries increasingly voted an independent line. For example, on the question of seating Communist China and expelling Nationalist China, the United States voted no from 1965 to 1971. Brazil voted the same way. Argentina abstained in 1971; Bolivia abstained in 1970; Chile abstained in 1969 and voted yes in 1970 and 1971; Ecuador abstained in 1969 and 1970 and voted yes in 1971; and Peru abstained in 1970 and voted yes in 1971. Late in 1971, the executive council of UNESCO followed the example of the General Assembly and voted 25–2–5 to declare Peking the representative of China. The two no votes were the United States and Brazil.[38]

Brazil played a similar role in the Organization of American States. At Tlatelolco in February 1974 Brazil worked with the United States to modify a statement attacking United States-owned multinational corporations. The original draft of the motion attacked the corporations for "intervention in the political affairs of the host countries with the support of U.S. diplomats." The final version simply referred to the need to examine the problem at a later date. Again at Quito in November 1974 Brazil joined the United States in abstaining on the vote to lift sanctions against Cuba, and thus contributed to frustrating the will of the majority of members of the organization. And in March 1975 Brazil did its best to undermine the efforts to create an independent Latin American Economic System by refusing to support any regional economic organization that did not include the United States.[39]

Perhaps most important, however, was Brazil's effort to increase its influence in and control over South America. This expansion served three functions for Brazil: first, it fulfilled its bargain with the United States to police the area, to oppose left-wing populist and Marxist influence, and to undermine any effort to create an independent or anti-United States bloc; second, it enabled Brazil to gain new markets and investment opportunities for its growing industry; and third, it gave Brazil a claim to world power status. The expansion of Brazilian influence in South America was thus mutually satisfactory for Brazil and the United States.

Brazilian expansion was both economic and political. It involved such things as the establishment of new branches of the Bank of Brazil, the extension of the Brazilian national airline (Varig), and the development of the Brazilian merchant marine. It also meant the construction of international hydroelectric dams and the building of roads that linked Brazil with its neighbors. The first section of the Trans-Amazonian Highway was opened in September 1972 and successive sections are in progress.

Brazil expanded trade with its neighbors and had a positive balance of trade with every South American country except Venezuela, from which it imported huge quantities of oil. Brazil was involved increasingly in the internal politics of its neighbors and talked of occupying that part of Antarctica traditionally claimed by Argentina. And finally, Brazil, itself a recipient of enormous quantities of foreign aid, initiated a program of aid to the other South American countries. By the end of 1972 Brazil had distributed approximately $80 million in foreign aid to South America and the amount has grown since; Brazil had given Bolivia $22.5 million in foreign aid; Peru, Ecuador, Uruguay, and Colombia $10 million each; Chile $6 million (contracted before Allende came to power); and Guyana $3 million.[40]

Brazil increased its economic and political influence in other parts of the world as well. It has for many years been especially interested in establishing close ties with the countries of Africa and has been sending trade and technical missions to visit that continent.[41] Closer to home, Brazil, along with the United States, was particularly concerned with Allende's rise to power in Chile. Both countries viewed Allende's Chile as an alternate socialist model of development with potential appeal for the rest of South America and, therefore, were anxious that it fail. There is no evidence at present that the Brazilian government played a direct role in the anti-Allende effort, although it did know about the coup ahead of time and it was the first government to recognize the new Chilean military junta. Nevertheless, members of Brazil's anti-communist business organization, IPES, worked closely with Chilean business and professional associations and provided them with advice and financial support. In addition, Brazil's right-wing paramilitary group, the Anti-Communist Movement (MAC), provided weapons and money for similar groups in Chile. The Chileans who received support from IPES and MAC were critical to the success of the economic chaos formula that brought down the socialist government. Although the Brazilian government apparently played no direct part in the overthrow of Allende, its highly efficient intelligence agency certainly was aware of the activity of IPES, MAC, and others and did nothing to stop it.[42]

Yet Brazil's expansion was most visible in the Rio de la Plata basin. This area (Cuenca del Plata) is the 3.1 million square kilometers of Argentina, Bolivia, Paraguay, Uruguay, and Brazil through which flow three great rivers—the Paraná, the Paraguay, and the Uruguay. Approximately 80 million people live in the area, nearly one-third of the inhabitants of all of Latin America. It is an enormously rich basin with fertile soil, water, forests, minerals, natural transportation, and potential hydroelectric energy. Brazil's concern here was to gain control of the area and its resources for itself and to undermine Argentine influence.

Brazil's major efforts were in Bolivia. Its chief interests in establishing and maintaining control over Bolivia were (1) from 1970 to 1973 to provide a friendly buffer state between Brazil and Allende's Chile; (2) eventually to gain access to a port on the Pacific; (3) to gain control of the rich resources (iron and oil deposits, rice, sugar, cotton, cattle) of Bolivia and particularly of the trans-Andean province, Santa Cruz, which borders on Brazil's western flank; and (4) to eliminate Argentina's traditional influence.

While the populist-nationalist regimes of General Alfredo Ovando (1969–1970) and General Juan José Torres (1970–1971) were in power, Brazil's efforts to expand its influence in Bolivia were blocked. In August 1971, however, General Hugo Banzer, with Brazil's knowledge and help, overthrew the Torres government and Brazilian influence increased dramatically.[43] During the first year and a half of his administration (August 1971 to December 1972) Banzer received more than $22 million in aid from Brazil, which represented an estimated 20 to 25 percent of all foreign aid to Bolivia. Since then Brazilian aid has increased. Most of the money has gone into road and railroad construction.

Brazil's particular interest in the province of Santa Cruz stems from a number of things. Santa Cruz is rich in resources, borders on Brazil, and is isolated from the rest of Bolivia. The first highway connecting highland Bolivia with lowland Santa Cruz was inaugurated in 1956. Furthermore, the elites of Santa Cruz have long held separatist sentiments and have favored some form of Brazilian tutelage. Banzer and many of those in his government came from Santa Cruz, and the Banzer revolt began in Santa Cruz. Thus, Brazil channeled much of its aid into such things as a regional development plan for Santa Cruz, purchased large quantities of crude oil from the fields of Santa Cruz, and financed and helped develop the iron ore of El Mutún.

The Mutún deposits deserve special comment because of the competition and controversy regarding their exploitation. El Mutún, located about seventy miles from the Paraguay River near the Brazil-Paraguay-Bolivia border, is one of the largest high-grade iron ore deposits in the world. It was first discovered in 1845 but, because of its remoteness, was not exploited until recently. Former Bolivian President Ovando decreed that El Mutún would be exploited exclusively by the Bolivian state, and the Ovando-Torres governments constructed the seventy-mile road linking El Mutún with the Paraguay River.[44]

Argentina, which depends almost exclusively on Brazil for iron ore to supply its San Nicolás Steel Mill, has been interested in El Mutún for several reasons. First, the ore is high grade and practically unlimited. Second, there is cheap available transportation to get the ore from the mine to Argentina's steel mill; the mine is linked to the Paraguay River by road, and the connecting Paraná River flows right past the San Nicolás Steel Mill some twelve hundred miles below. And third, El Mutún would provide an alternate source of iron ore and thus decrease Argentina's dependence on Brazil.

In June 1972 Argentina signed an agreement with Bolivia to explore the possibility of using El Mutún ore in the San Nicolás plant. According to the agreement, Argentina was to test the ore and initially to buy fifty thousand tons. A future contract to ship the ore in Argentine ships was to be worked out. Bolivia, according to Argentine sources, sent poor quality ore for testing, gave the shipping contract to Brazil, and accepted Brazilian capital to construct a steel mill in the Mutún area. Since Brazil did not need the iron ore for internal use, the Argentine government believed that Brazil was trying to block its access to the ore and to undermine its capacity to manufacture steel products.

Brazil succeeded in expanding its influence in Bolivia at the expense of Argentina. The Bolivian military was divided between pro- and anti-Brazilian factions, but the pro-Brazilian faction was clearly dominant. Thus, toward the end of 1973 President Banzer attempted to increase sales of oil and natural gas to Argentina and to cut back on sales to Brazil. This effort nearly toppled his government; the pro-Brazilian element of the Bolivian armed forces insisted on a reversal of policy and Banzer backed down. Early in November 1974, after a year of political unrest, Banzer suspended the activities of all political parties, canceled all elections, and vowed to rule by force of arms until 1980. Bolivia thus openly adopted the Brazilian system.[45]

Brazil also expanded its influence in Uruguay. In 1971 it became particularly alarmed about the possibility of a victory for the left-wing Uruguayan coalition, the Frente Amplio, in the November presidential election. From the Brazilian point of view, the Frente Amplio was a carbon copy of Chile's Marxist Unidad Popular. The Brazilian military, therefore, developed a plan to invade Uruguay if the Frente won. Brazilian troops were stationed along the border, and Brazil supported the right-wing paramilitary groups harassing the Frente. In the election the Frente lost to conservative Juan M. Bordaberry, and Uruguay gradually adopted the Brazilian model. As president, Bordaberry increasingly attacked the left and restricted civil liberties. In June 1973 he dissolved Congress and began to rule by decree.

It is difficult to document the extent of Brazilian influence in Uruguay, but it is clear that Brazilian influence increased considerably under Bordaberry, that Brazil would not tolerate a Marxist government in that country, and that the growing strength of the pro-Brazilian military suggested that Uruguay might be moving toward the adoption of the Brazilian model of government and development.

Brazil also granted considerable aid to Paraguay and financed major cooperative projects with the Paraguayan government. Most importantly, Brazil and Paraguay joined to construct hydroelectric dams at Sete Quedas and Itaipu across the Uruguay and Paraguay rivers. Argentina objected, to little avail, because of the impact the dams would have on the waters of the two rivers, which also flow through Argentine territory.[46]

President Banzer of Bolivia, President Bordaberry of Uruguay, and President Pinochet Ugarte of Chile were among the honored guests at the March 15, 1974, inauguration of Brazil's new president, General Ernesto Geisel. The day after the inauguration the four South American leaders met to consolidate their relations. They denied that they were forming an anti-communist alliance, but they all admitted that they hoped to create "more intimate relations in the future." [47]

Whether or not the relationship is formal, Brazil has succeeded in creating a *de facto* anti-communist bloc in South America whose member states (Bolivia, Chile, Paraguay, Uruguay) are ruled by dictators committed to a pro-United States foreign policy and to a conservative elitist policy of economic development within a capitalist framework. Brazil, by providing a successful model of economic development that is acceptable to the United States and by extending its political and economic influence and control throughout the continent, fulfilled its junior partner role beyond expectation.

The United States' Relationship with Its Junior Partner

The United States did many things to support and encourage its South American imperial partner. It provided enormous though decreasing amounts of financial and technical assistance to Brazil and used its influence in such international lending agencies as the World Bank and the Inter-American Development Bank to make sure that Brazil received even more aid. From 1964 to 1974 Brazil received more than $3 billion of bilateral aid from the United States and an additional $3.5 billion from the international lending agencies for a total of $6.5 billion. During the preceding ten years, Brazil had received only $1.5 billion from the United States and $.5 billion from the international lending organizations for a total of $2 billion (Table 5-1).

Except for 1969, Brazil received more United States aid (about 40 percent of the total) than any other Latin American country and more aid from the international lending organizations except in 1964, 1966, and 1968, when it was second only to Mexico. Per capita aid figures for the period 1964 to 1969 put Brazil well below such countries as Chile, Bolivia, and Colombia, but, because aid is not divided and distributed on a per capita basis, total aid is the more important figure. Also, since 1970, the contribution of the international lending agencies, to which the United States contributes the lion's share, has exceeded direct bilateral

contributions of the United States to Brazil. This has permitted
the United States government to continue its high levels of support for Brazil without the critical inspection of the United States
Congress.[48]

This money, among other things, provided for: general support
of the government, foreign reserves with which to buy United
States commodities, infrastructure development, the training of
police and the army to fight subversion, and the dissemination of
favorable information about the United States. To carry out this
extensive program, the United States developed one of the largest
"Embassy establishments" in the world in Brazil. In 1969, AID
had the largest number of employees, followed by the Department
of State, the Department of Defense, and the USIS.[49]

Government money and personnel were a critical United States
contribution to Brazil, but the United States also invested large
amounts of private capital in the country. From 1964, the value
of private United States investment increased annually to an unbe-
lievable $2.5 billion in 1972. The United States percent of total
foreign investment decreased over the years, but it was still by far
the largest of any foreign investor. Most United States investment
went into the critical areas of manufacturing of food products,
chemicals, and transportation equipment.[50]

In addition to supporting Brazil with financial and technological
resources, the United States also supported it in the international
political and economic arena. The United States quickly settled
disputes with Brazil that it was not willing to settle with other
South American countries, and it supported Brazil's aspiration to
be a world power. For example, the United States had a long-
standing dispute with Ecuador and Peru over control of coastal
water and particularly over fishing rights. Ecuador and Peru felt
that the fish in their coastal waters out to two hundred miles were
a national natural resource. The United States refused to accept
this position, arguing that there is freedom of the seas beyond the
twelve-mile limit, and permitted United States vessels to fish
within two hundred miles of Ecuador and Peru. Since the 1950s,
Ecuador and Peru have seized and fined these boats. In 1971 Ecuador seized fifty-one United States tuna boats and demanded
fines totaling $2.5 million. The United States Congress retaliated
by cutting aid to Ecuador, which provoked bitter feelings and
charges of Yankee imperialism. Although this dispute has been

going on for two decades, it has not been resolved and there is no prospect that it will be resolved in the near future.

In 1970 Brazil, Chile, Argentina, and Uruguay joined Ecuador and Peru in declaring control over two hundred miles of coastal waters. Then in March 1971 Brazil established specific rules for fishing in its territorial waters: Any foreign vessel that wished to fish in Brazilian territorial waters had to pay $500 for a license and $20 a ton on the catch. Furthermore, they could fish only between the one-hundred- and two-hundred-mile limit.

The United States became involved because most of the five hundred foreign-owned shrimp boats fishing off Brazil, which brought in an annual catch worth approximately $20 million, were United States-owned. It advised the United States fishermen that they were not obliged under international law to purchase licenses from Brazil. In June 1971 the Brazilian navy began patrolling the coastal waters out to the two-hundred-mile limit and drove United States fishermen away.

The situation was tense and a solution seemed remote, yet on May 9, 1972, the United States and Brazil signed an agreement settling, at least temporarily, the dispute. Washington agreed to impose a voluntary limit on the number of boats fishing off the Brazilian coast, and both countries agreed tactily to ignore Brazil's claim to sovereignty of two hundred miles of coastal waters. It was the first time that the United States government had ever sought to restrict the entry of the private fishing industry into the coastal waters of another country. Such a compromise, although temporary, was in marked contrast with the treatment accorded Ecuador and Peru. Agreement was reached quickly with Brazil on other similar disputes, i.e., the sharing of revenues from coffee shipments to the United States, which indicated the special relationship Brazil had with the United States.[51]

The United States also supported Brazil's aspiration to be a major world power. For example, a Brazilian general headed the OAS Peace Keeping Force in the Dominican Republic, and the United States supported Brazil's efforts to become a member of the twenty-man executive committee of the IMF.[52] Clearly, however, the most important recognition the United States accorded Brazil was the invitation to President Médici to visit Washington in December 1971. Médici's visit came at a time when most of Latin America, disturbed by the 10 percent surcharge on imports, the decrease in United States aid, and the rigidly anti-communist policy toward the area, had become increasingly critical of the Nixon Administration. Brazil, however, did not criticize the United States.

During the three days of discussions there were no major items on the agenda, a significant fact in itself. Nevertheless, the talks and the meetings were of the utmost importance. It was the first time in more than a decade (since the beginning of the Alliance for Progress) that the President of the United States had invited a chief of a Latin American military government to visit Washington. This further undermined the policy of supporting democratic governments and maintaining only formal, as opposed to special, relations with military regimes. In addition, the United States now included Brazil among its "closest friends," whom it consulted prior to Nixon's visits to China and Russia. Brazil joined the ranks of France, England, Germany, Japan, and Canada as one of the United States' major allies. General Alejandro Lanusse, president of Argentina, received only a brief token consultation phone call from Nixon. The other South American states did not even get this much recognition. Furthermore, Nixon described Brazil as the leader of Latin America. "We know that as Brazil goes," Nixon said, "so will go the rest of that Latin American continent." He praised Médici for his success in building the Brazilian economy and made no mention of the torture, the lack of civil liberties, or the critically uneven distribution of wealth. Also, the two presidents agreed that Brazil would assume a new intermediary role in the distribution of economic aid to other South American countries. And finally, the two pledged to work together to safeguard hemispheric security against outside interference. Presumably they were referring to Russian "interference" in Cuba and Chile.

Médici told Nixon that Brazil "accepts the challenge of history, which places on its shoulders an increasing share of responsibility in the concert of nations," and noted that although "our position cannot be the same vis-à-vis every international problem—nor is this expected from our frank and loyal friendship—let us, nevertheless, endeavor to make our policies converge without requiring that they coincide in every case." [53]

Most of the other South American countries watched the development of Brazil as the junior partner of the United States with considerable trepidation. Argentina always viewed Brazil with the wary eye of a close rival, but after 1970, and particularly after Médici's visit to Washington in December 1971, the other South American states increasingly expressed their concern about Brazilian expansion. Venezuela's former President Rafael Caldera vigorously protested against any United States-sponsored "leader" among the South American states. Peru's President Juan José Velasco and Argentina's former President Alejandro Lanusse also strongly rejected Brazil's claim to continental leadership. The criticism was so universal and so strong that Médici made a speech shortly after he returned from Washington in which he insisted that Brazil was concerned only with its own progress and not with the domination of its South American neighbors.[54]

Brazil's denial of the junior partner role was unconvincing. In 1972, a popular Brazilian magazine, *Manchete,* summarized what it considered to be the role of Brazil in South America. Focusing on the visit of former Argentine President Lanusse to Brazil, *Manchete* began its article with the Nixon quote: "As Brazil goes, so will go the rest of that Latin American continent," and followed it with the headline: "Brazil or Argentina, the Statistics Speak Loudly." In his conversations with Médici, Lanusse said that Argentines would never accept the hegemony of any other power. *Manchete* was furious and argued that Brazilians in general were furious too. It then proceeded to compare Brazil and Argentina, point by point: (1) Brazil has 8.5 million square kilometers and 100 million people. Argentina has 2.8 million square kilometers and 26 million people. (2) Five years ago Argentina produced three times as many cars as Brazil. Today Brazil produces twice as many cars as Argentina. (3) Brazil exported $3 billion in goods in 1971. Argentina exported $2 billion. (4) Brazil's financial reserves are $2 billion. Argentine reserves are $0. (5) The cruzeiro doubled its value in relationship to the Argentine peso during the last twelve months. (6) Brazil's GNP is $45 billion. Argentina's GNP is $20 billion. Brazil's per capita GNP is $450 compared to $750 in Argentina, but it is only a matter of time before this changes. The article concluded with the following challenge: "General Lanusse is living on words, trips, meetings, communications, theses, declarations, papers, accords, and phrases. General Médici lives on works, economic progress, social and political peace, petroleum, exports, industries, hydroelectric power, communication, transports and resources. Who will win? [55]

In early 1975 there was some evidence of a change in Brazilian policy that could undermine the junior partner relationship. In November 1974 the official party (ARENA) was decisively beaten by the opposition MDB in the national and state legislative elections. In addition, there were indications that the Brazilian economic miracle was coming to an end. President Geisel admitted publicly that the military governments had not solved the problems of development and implied that he was not completely committed to the pro-United States policies of his predecessors. Indeed, Francisco Julião, an opponent of the regime, said in Mexico that he believed Geisel was looking for a new formula for development. If this is so, the evidence is far from overwhelming. In March 1975 Brazil opposed the efforts of the other Latin American states to create the Latin American Economic System without the United States. And the regime still has done little to distribute wealth more equally or to end political repression. [56]

Thus, Brazil's assumption of the junior partner role is for the present the basic operational principle of United States South American policy and will continue as such in the foreseeable future. From the points of view of the Nixon-Ford Administration and the military governments of Brazil, this relationship has been very advantageous; Brazil has developed economically within a capitalist framework working closely with the United States, and the strength of populism and socialism in South America have decreased. From the perspective of the non-elites, the vast majority of peasants and workers in Brazil and South America, the benefits of such a relationship may seem less obvious. The United States committed its economic and political power to a repressive military dictatorship as an effective and desirable means of marshaling a country's resources for development and to a strategy of development that in the short run benefited only a tiny elite. The theory is that in the long run all will benefit, but the millions of presently starving, unemployed, and sick Brazilians and South Americans can hardly take comfort in such a thought. And there is little evidence that the lot of the non-elites will improve substantially in the long run; the gap between the standard of living of the "haves" and "have nots" in South America and in the world is increasing. Thus, the special partnership between Brazil and the United States seems to mean that the majority of the inhabitants of South America will not share in the fruits of development for decades, if at all.

NOTES

1. Some of the most useful works on the 1945 to 1964 period are: Miguel Arraes, *Brazil: The People and the Power* (London, 1972); Carlos Alberto Astiz (ed.), *Latin American International Politics* (Notre Dame, Ind., 1969), pp. 167–286; John W. F. Dulles, *Unrest in Brazil* (Austin, Texas, 1970); Furtado, *Obstacles,* pp. 113–199; Octavio Ianni, Paulo Singer, Gabriel Cohn, Francisco C. Weffort, *Política e revolução social no Brasil* (Rio de Janeiro, 1965); Octavio Ianni, *O colapso do Populismo no Brasil* (Rio de Janeiro, 1968); Thomas E. Skidmore, *Politics in Brazil, 1930–1964* (New York, 1967).

2. See: Morris Llewellyn Cooke, *Brazil on the March, A Study in International Cooperation* (New York, 1944); Werner Baer, *Industrialization and Economic Development in Brazil* (Homewood, Ill., 1965); Department of State, *Report of the Joint Brazilian-United States Technical Commission, Rio de Janeiro, February 7, 1949* (Washington, D.C., 1949).

3. *The New York Times,* July 23, 1953.

4. For an analysis of the Kubitschek period, see the relevant chapters in the books cited in note 1. Especially useful is Skidmore, *Politics,* pp. 163–186.

5. *The New York Times,* February 3 and 4, 1956; *Congressional Record,* January 5, 1956, pp. 111–112.

6. *Foreign Affairs* (October 1961). For an analysis of this policy, see Keith Larry Storrs, "Brazil's Independent Foreign Policy, 1961–1964" (unpublished doctoral dissertation, Cornell University, 1973).

7. *Campos Interview,* p. 14.

8. *Ibid.,* p. 30.

9. For accounts of the coup from different perspectives, see: Arraes, *Brazil;* Alberto Dines, et al., *Os idos de marco e a queda em abril* (Rio de Janeiro, 1964); Dulles, *Unrest;* Ronald M. Schneider, *The Political System of Brazil* (New York, 1971); James W. Rowe, "Revolution or Counterrevolution in Brazil," *American Universities Field Staff: Reports Service,* East Coast South America Series, XI, 4 and 5; Philip Siekman, "When Executives Turned Revolutionaries," *Fortune,* LXX, 3 (September 1964), pp.

147–149, 210–221; Skidmore, *Politics;* Jose Stacchini, *Marco 64: Mobilizacao da Audacia* (São Paulo, 1965).

10. Quoted in Alfred Stepan, *The Military in Politics* (Princeton, N.J., 1971), p. 125. Senate Committee on Foreign Relations, *Hearings on United States Policies and Programs in Brazil, May 4–11, 1971* (Washington, D.C., 1971), p. 165. Hereafter cited as *Brazil Hearings.*

11. *The New York Times,* April 5, 1964.

12. *Ibid.,* April 3–7, April 24, and May 6, 1964.

13. Skidmore, *Politics,* p. 326; Siekman, "Executives"; Stacchini, *Marco 64,* pp. 87–89.

14. Siekman, "Executives"; Senate Foreign Relations Committee, *Survey of the Alliance for Progress, Labor Policies and Programs* (July 15, 1968), p. 14.

15. Manoel Thomaz Castello Branco, *O Brasil na II Grande Guerra* (Rio de Janeiro, 1960); Marechal Mascarenhas de Moraes, *A.F.E.B. Pelo Seu Comandante* (São Paulo, 1947). Frank D. McCann, Jr., *The Brazilian-American Alliance, 1937–1945* (Princeton. 1973), pp. 343–371.

16. *Foreign Relations,* 1945, pp. 600–620.

17. *Ibid.,* pp. 603, 605.

18. *Ibid.,* pp. 621–622.

19. The best study in English on the ESG is Stepan, *Military.*

20. Umberto Peregrino, "O Pensamiento da Escola Superior de Guerra," *Cadernos Brasileiros,* VII, 38 (November-December 1966), pp. 29–38.

21. The information on IPES is based on: Paulo Ayres, "The Brazilian Revolution," (Lecture at the Center for Strategic Studies, Georgetown University, Washington, D.C., July 1964, mimeograph copy); Siekman, "Executives"; Paulo Ayres, interview with Samuel L. Baily, São Paulo, February 1968; and the serial publications of IPES such as *Noticias do IPES* and *Cadernos Nacionalistas.*

22. Ayres, "Brazilian Revolution," p. 17.

23. Information on IBAD can best be found in the Brazilian dailies from June through September 1963. For example, see: *O Estado de São Paulo,* June 13 and 20, July 24 and 26, August 21 and 30, September 27, 1963; *Correio da Manha,* September 9, 1963; *Jornal do Brasil,* September 9, 1963.

24. *O Estado de São Paulo,* September 27, 1963; *Correio da Manha,* September 12, 1963; *Jornal do Brasil,* September 12, 1963.

25. *Boletim de Noticias* (Instituto Cultural do Trabalho); Romualdi, *Presidents,* pp. 270–291; Senate Foreign Relations Committee, *Labor Policies,* pp. 13–14; *O Estado de São Paolo,* March 28, April 28, September 12, November 17, 1962, January 24, 1963; *Jornal do Brasil,* November 22, October 22, 1961.

26. E. Bradford Burns, *Nationalism in Brazil* (New York, 1968), pp. 90–92; Baily, *Nationalism;* José Honório Rodrigues, *The Brazilians* (Austin, Texas, 1967).

27. Arthur P. Whitaker and David C. Jordan, *Nationalism in Contemporary Latin America* (New York, 1966); Romualdi, *Presidents,* pp.

283–284; Gilberto Freyre, *New World in the Tropics* (New York, 1971). See also note 20.

28. See, for example, *The New York Times*, August 2, 1972; Stepan, *Military*, pp. 240–241.

29. Quoted in Stepan, *Military*, pp. 231–232.

30. For the complete text, see Dines et al., *Os idos*, pp. 401–403.

31. Schneider, *Political*, pp. 169–173.

32. *Ibid.*, pp. 273–274.

33. There is an abundance of evidence to document the widespread use of torture in Brazil since 1964. See, for example: American Committee for Information on Brazil, *Terror in Brazil, a Dossier* (New York, 1970); *The New York Times*, February 21, 1971, May 19, 1973, November 16, 1975; Los Angeles *Times*, November 1, 1973, November 18, 1974; *Time*, November 18, 1974.

34. *The New York Times*, January 28, 1973.

35. *Wall Street Journal*, April 14 and 21, 1972. For a discussion of some of the problems related to economic expansion, see *The New York Times*, January 20, April 7 and 14, 1974.

36. For an analysis of capital-intensive industrialization and its impact on Brazil and Latin America, see: Glaucio Ary Dillon Soares, "The New Industrialization and the Brazilian Political System," in James Petras and M. Zeitlan, *Latin America, Reform or Revolution* (Greenwich, 1968); Rodolfo Stavengagen, "The Future of Latin America," in *Latin American Perspectives* (Spring 1974); and O'Donnell, *Modernization*.

37. *La Opinión*, February 27, 1973. *Brazil Hearings*, p. 249, indicates that the decline in real wages was only 10 percent! See also: ECLA, *Survey 1969*, p. 85; *Wall Street Journal*, April 14 and 21, 1972.

38. I am indebted to Eugene Sharkey for compiling the Latin American voting record in the United Nations. See United Nations, General Assembly, *Official Records* (1965–1971); *The New York Times*, October 30, 1971.

39. See *Latin American Index*, February 16–28, 1974, and Chapter 4, note 59.

40. Miami *Herald*, May 22, 1972; Manchester *Guardian*, December 30, 1972; Los Angeles *Times*, October 16, 1972; Embassy of Brazil, *Brazil Today* (Washington, D.C. 1973–).

41. José Honório Rodrigues, *Brazil and Africa* (Berkeley, Calif., 1965).

42. *Brazilian Information Bulletin* (Winter 1974), pp. 7–9.

43. Jorge Gallardo Lozada, *De Torres a Banzer* (Buenos Aires, 1972), pp. 401–496. Gallardo was taken from his house by the Chilean police at the end of October 1973 and has not been heard from since. See *The New York Times*, November 6, 1973, November 8, 1974.

44. For background on El Mutún, see: *Panorama*, January 18, 1973; *La Opinión*, February 23, 1973; *The New York Times*, February 4, 1974.

45. *ATLAS*, October 1971; Miami *Herald*, May 22, 1974; *The New York Times*, February 4, November 8, 1974.

46. *The New York Times*, February 4, May 23, 1974.

47. *The New York Times*, March 17, 1974.

48. *AID Statistics, 1973; Brazil Hearings*, p. 167.

49. *Brazil Hearings*, p. 259.

50. United States, Department of Commerce, *Statistical Abstract of the United States; Brazil Today*, September 28, 1973. See also Carlos Osmar Bertero, "Drugs and Dependency in Brazil" (Ph.D. dissertation, Cornell University, 1972).

51. *Journal of Commerce*, December 5, 1972.

52. Miami *Herald*, June 9, 1972.

53. Miami *Herald*, December 8, 1971; *The New York Times*, December 8, 1971. There are many other examples of the United States' special treatment of Brazil. Thus, the designation of Jack B. Kubish as assistant secretary of state for Inter-American Affairs in March 1973 granted recognition to Brazil's new status. Kubish had been director of AID in Brazil from 1962 to 1965, and director of the Office of Brazilian Affairs in the State Department from 1965 to 1969. In addition, the recent United States policy of withholding aid from Third World countries that did not vote with it in the United Nations was not applied to Brazil when Brazil voted to condemn Zionism as a racist doctrine. See *The New York Times*, January 9, 1976.

54. *The New York Times*, December 31, 1971.

55. *Manchete*, April 1, 1972.

56. *Excelsior*, February 23, 1975; *El Día*, March 3, April 17 and 19, 1975.

chapter
6

The Containment of
Revolutionary Change:
The Case of Chile

Revolutionary changes that will significantly redistribute economic
and political power in favor of the working classes are essential if
South America is to improve the quality of life of its people and
develop stable representative governments. Most South American
countries are controlled by small, well-entrenched commercial-
industrial-landed elites, which use the existing political and socioeconomic structures to protect and further their particular interests. The interests of the rural and urban working classes are for
the most part ignored or subverted. Today, however, no government can be truly legitimate unless it effectively represents the
whole or the vast majority of a society, and without legitimacy
there can be no genuine long-term political stability.[1]

The United States government has from time to time given at
least verbal recognition to this fact—most notably during the early
1960s—but its actions have consistently demonstrated that it
fears and opposes revolutionary change. The issue is control. The
United States has accepted and even supported some change if it
can influence its nature. But Washington officials have associated
revolutionary change with disruption, disorder, and violence,
which will undermine the dominant position of the entrenched

anti-communist local elites, jeopardize United States economic interests, and strengthen the position of populists, nationalists, and socialists. Thus, when revolutionary change is in the offing, the United States backs those who are committed to the preservation of order—the elites who oppose social and economic transformation and favor the *status quo*.

When confronted with any government seeking to bring about revolutionary change, the United States has used all available means to co-opt or destroy it. In Guatemala (1954) and British Guiana (1962–1963), the United States resorted to subversive activity to topple leftist governments. In the Dominican Republic (1965) it resorted to direct military intervention. In Brazil (1964) it encouraged local opposition to overthrow the leftist Goulart government. In Bolivia (1971) it encouraged local opposition and Brazilian involvement to overthrow Torres.

The methods used by the United States to contain revolutionary change have depended on the particular situation: the strength of the support for and the opposition to the government, the viability of the economy, the commitment to a constitutional tradition, and the availability of alternate external support. Thus, in Bolivia in 1971, where constitutionalism was weak, coups had been frequent, the economy stagnating and dependent on United States aid, opposition to the government strong, and no practical alternate source of external support, the United States had only to cut back its aid and let Brazil and elements of the local military know that it would not oppose a coup. Whatever the methods, the United States objective has been the same: to contain and destroy those elements that seek a revolutionary social transformation in South America. This chapter is the story of the United States' successful effort to contain and destroy those who sought to bring about revolutionary social and economic change in Chile.

The Emergence of Mass-Based Politics in Chile: 1930–1964

Until the 1950s, politics in Chile was essentially an affair of the upper- and middle-class elites; the mass of urban and rural working-class people was for the most part excluded from effective participation in the political system. In 1920 and again in 1938 a middle- and working-class coalition succeeded in electing a president of the country. In both cases middle-class elements dominated the coalition and in neither case did more than 8 percent of the total population vote. During the two decades following World War II, the percentage of the population that voted increased dramatically; between 1946 and 1952 it doubled, and between 1952 and 1964 it doubled again (Table 6-1). This rapid expansion of voters signaled the emergence of mass-based politics in Chile.

TABLE 6-1

Voting Population in Chile, 1946–1970

Year	Total Population	% Population Registered	% Population Voting
1946	5,488,339	11.50	8.73
1952	6,001,275	18.41	15.95
1958	6,984,507	21.45	17.90
1964	8,391,000	41.70	30.14
1970	9,780,000	36.19	30.11

Source: Latin American Center, University of California at Los Angeles, *Latin American Political Statistics* (Los Angeles, 1972), p. 106.

The dramatic extension of the vote had profound consequences on Chile. Most importantly, it meant that the government increasingly had to be responsible to the demands of the formerly inarticulate segments of the population—the urban and rural working classes and the lower middle classes. Although the working classes remained only partially mobilized, particularly in the rural areas, and had to rely on political alliances with segments of the middle classes to achieve any of their objectives, by 1964 they were, nevertheless, a major force in Chilean politics. There were different interests among rural and urban, skilled and unskilled, industrial and craft, government and private, and unionized and non-unionized workers, but all were to a greater or lesser degree demanding a series of social and economic changes designed to develop the economy, distribute national income more equitably, provide security, and improve the quality of their lives. It was these demands, thrust into the arena of national politics, that the United States government perceived as a threat to its economic and security interests and therefore attempted to contain.

Mass-based politics and the consequent demand for fundamental social and economic change were the logical results of Chile's previous economic development. During the nineteenth and early twentieth centuries the tiny Chilean elite, in partnership with foreign investors, prospered by mining and exporting first silver and then nitrates and copper. But the invention of synthetic nitrates and the world depression of the early 1930s destroyed the market for these commodities and provoked a major crisis. In order to stave off economic disaster, the Chilean governments of the late 1930s and the 1940s gradually introduced import-substitution industrialization. In 1939 the Popular Front government of Pedro Aguirre Cerda created the Compañía de Fomento (Development Corporation) to coordinate its efforts to stimulate industry, mining, agriculture, and fisheries. The Development Corporation increased production in light industry (clothing, glass, soap, paper, food) and established the basis for heavy industry (steel).

The resulting economic growth had two major consequences. First, since import-substitution industrialization primarily benefited the consumer-oriented middle classes, it tended to increase the gap between the middle and working classes. And second, import-substitution industrialization led quickly to increased dependence on the United States. In order to industrialize, Chile needed technology, heavy equipment, and capital. During and immediately after World War II, the United States was the only source of these things. At the same time, the United States needed Chilean nitrates and cooper. Thus, the two countries exchanged resources, but the exchange was not even; the price of machinery was high, while the price of nitrates and particularly copper was low. To pay for the machinery, Chile therefore borrowed increasing sums from the Export-Import Bank; between 1946 and 1952, Chile received $104 million in such loans out of a total of $664 million disbursed to all of Latin America.[2]

The development of the Huachipato Steel Plant near Concepción illustrates how the system worked. This plant, which was completed in 1950, was long in coming. Although the Export-Import Bank did eventually provide $48 million in credits to construct the plant, it imposed a series of conditions on the Chilean government. The equipment had to be purchased in the United States, the size of the plant had to be reduced so that it would not produce any steel for export, and Chile had to work with United States companies and management experts. The plant was planned by Americans, managed by Americans, utilized iron ore from American-owned mines in Chile, and depended on some high-grade coal imported from the United States.[3]

Another condition on such loans was that Chile adopt Washington's rigid anti-communism. President Gabriel González Videla (1946–1952) was a successful businessman who believed in the capitalist system, but he also believed that a popular front government (including socialists and communists) was the best form of government for Chile. He won the election of 1946 with the support of the Communist Party and included three communists in his cabinet. The United States objected to the participation of communists and held up requests for Export-Import Bank funds until they were removed and the government took a clearly anti-communist stand. Claude Bowers, United States ambassador to Chile at the time, reported that the "President [González Videla] complained bitterly of what he terms fulfillment of [a] previous threat to cut off credits and assistance to Chile" because the Chilean government had not curbed the activities of the Communist Party.[4] Nevertheless, in 1947 Chile suspended relations with Russia, Czechoslovakia, and Yugoslavia, and in September 1948 outlawed the Communist Party. There were a number of reasons, including internal politics, for this action, but United States pressure to do so was among the most important.

Industrialization via import substitution did not work very long or very well in Chile. Basically it failed because the new industries could not produce enough foreign exchange to pay for the foreign machinery they needed. Furthermore, although industrialization and urbanization created new markets, they also created new demands (housing, schools, sewers, and so on) on the country's resources. These services absorbed resources that were necessary for capital formation and further industrialization. In addition, the government neglected the agricultural sector of the economy. When the price of copper, Chile's leading source of foreign exchange, dropped sharply following the Korean War, the structure of industrialization via import substitution collapsed. The economy stagnated, inflation and unemployment grew, real wages declined, and foreign exchange reserves shrank.

The immediate political result of the economic crisis (collapse of the import-substitution structure) was the election of the populist-nationalist Carlos Ibáñez del Campo as president of Chile in 1952. Ibáñez represented more of an informal movement than any cohesive political group or ideology. He attacked political parties as unrepresentative and claimed that he was above them. He also attacked dependence on the United States. His election was particularly important because it marked the beginning of what James Petras calls "mass mobilization politics." By supporting Ibáñez, the rural workers defied the conservative landowners. Furthermore, women were able to vote in a presidential election for the first time.[5]

As president, Ibáñez found it more difficult than he had anticipated to get along without the United States. He worked out several trade agreements with Argentina, but neither Argentina nor anyone else could provide the necessary economic assistance or machinery. Ibáñez succumbed to United States and International Monetary Fund pressure and invited a team of private United States economic advisers (the Klein-Saks Mission) to study the Chilean situation and to make recommendations for improving it.

The Klein-Saks Mission recommended orthodox stabilization: cut government spending, limit credit, free the exchange rate, lower tariffs, support a liberal import policy, and reduce taxes. Ibáñez implemented many of these recommendations and in so doing undermined the limited industrialization that had taken place over the previous two decades. A North American Congress on Latin America (NACLA) study summarized the impact of implementing the Klein-Saks recommendations: (1) a decline in GNP from 1956 to 1959, (2) an increase in unemployment and a decrease in real wages, (3) the creation of a negative exchange reserve, (4) a negative trade balance financed by a spiraling foreign debt, and (5) a dramatic increase in foreign investment.[6]

The presidential election of 1958 reflected the rapid growth of mass mobilization politics and the widespread discontent with the results of the Klein-Saks policies. Jorge Alessandri, the Conservative-Liberal candidate, won the election with 390,000 votes or 31 percent of the total. In second place was Salvadore Allende, candidate of the Socialist-Communist Alliance (FRAP), with 356,000 votes or 28.5 percent of the vote. In 1952 Allende had received only 5.4 percent of the vote. But with the deterioration of the living and working conditions of the lower classes and segments of the middle classes, the reorganization and unification of the labor movement in the Marxist-controlled Central Unica de Trabajadores in 1953, the legalization of the Communist Party, and the establishment of the left-wing electoral coalition FRAP in 1956, Allende's supporters became a major political force in the country. In addition, the middle-class Christian Democratic candidate, Eduardo Frei, received 20 percent of the vote.[7]

The election of 1958 marked the beginning of a serious popular (Marxist and Christian Democratic) challenge to the established order and a significant realignment of Chilean politics. After 1958 three major blocs—two of which were the product of mass-based politics—competed in the Chilean political process: (1) the right—representing the elites and some segments of the middle classes—made up of the traditional Liberals, Conservatives, and many Radicals, who in recent years combined to form the National Party; (2) the center—representing primarily the middle classes—composed of Christian Democrats and a few others; and (3) the left—representing most of the working classes—based in the Communist-Socialist Alliance.[8]

Alessandri pursued a program of orthodox economics along the lines recommended by the Klein-Saks Mission. He trimmed the government payroll and government services, held down wages, balanced the budget, and for three years stabilized the currency. Yet the trade deficit continued to grow and between 1958 and 1961 the foreign debt nearly doubled. Inflation also continued, with prices increasing nearly 400 percent between 1956 and 1962. Thus, in 1962 the government was forced to devalue the escudo. Most importantly, the economy stagnated; GNP rose less than one percent per year between 1958 and 1964 and per capita agricultural production declined.[9]

With the advent of the Kennedy Administration and the Alliance for Progress, the Alessandri government de-emphasized austerity and began to focus more on social issues and economic growth. The United States, mindful of the potential threat embodied in the strong Allende showing in 1958 and fearful of the spread of Castroism to other parts of Latin America, decided to make Chile a showplace for the Alliance. Before 1961 the largest amount of annual United States aid to Chile had been $46.4 million (1960). In 1961 this figure jumped more than 300 percent to $142.5 million and continued in this range until the costs of the Vietnam War and the Allende victory in 1970 combined to produce a drastic cutback (Table 6–2). During this period Chile received the highest per capita aid in all of Latin America. To receive this enormous amount of aid, Chile agreed to protect United States economic interests (it signed an investment guarantee with the United States) and it followed the anti-communist political line (it broke relations with Cuba).

There can be no doubt that one of the central motivating forces behind United States-Chilean policy from 1961 to 1964 was the fear of an Allende victory in 1964. The United States had a wary eye not only on Allende, but also on Goulart in Brazil and Jagan in British Guiana. As *The New York Times* reporter Tad Szulc wrote just after the 1964 elections, "United States government officials could not recall any election, outside of the Italian election of 1948, that caused so much anxiety in Washington." [10]

In order to prevent an Allende victory, the United States worked diligently on many fronts. As mentioned above, United States aid to Chile was massive. From 1962 to 1964 Chile received a yearly average of $127 million, contrasted with $43 million a year from 1954 to 1961. Military aid, which had never exceeded $6.7 million per year and which was only $2.7 million in 1960, jumped to $9 million in 1961, $17.8 million in 1962, and $30.6 million in 1963! Most of the military aid was in the form of grants. Washington also brought substantial numbers of Chilean officers to the Canal Zone, Puerto Rico, and the United States for training. [11]

This aid was designed to do two things. First, it was supposed to strengthen the Chilean economy and improve the quality of life of the working classes so that they would see that the radical program of Allende was not necessary to improve their lot. Second, it was designed to strengthen the Chilean military and guarantee its loyalty in the event that it might be called upon to intervene in the political situation.

The United States also resorted to covert activity to undermine Allende. It provided substantial financial support for the Frei campaign and for an extensive anti-FRAP propaganda campaign. Estimates of the amount of United States money devoted to defeating Allende vary considerably. Barnard Collier, an anti-Allende *New York Times* correspondent, reported: "By mysterious ways, not talked about and always officially denied, Frei's campaign was bolstered by Yankee dollars and piles of Chilean pesos. A reasonable estimate is that the Christian Democrats got about $1 million a month for many months from American sources, and

TABLE **6-2**

Foreign Aid to Chile, Fiscal Years 1946–1973
(millions of U.S. dollars)

Year	United States		International
	Economic Aid	Military Aid	Organizations
1946-1953	116.5		17.4
(per year)	(14.6)		
1954-1961	347.9	39.8	134.9
(per year)	(43.5)	(5.0)	(16.9)
1962	169.8	17.8	18.7
1963	85.3	30.6	31.2
1964	127.1	9.0	41.4
1965	130.4	9.9	12.4
1966	111.1	10.2	72.0
1967	238.1	4.2	93.8
1968	96.3	7.8	19.4
1969	80.3	11.7	49.0
1970	26.3	.8	76.4
1971	8.6	5.7	15.4
1972	9.0	12.3	8.2
1973	6.9	15.0	9.4
1974	107.9	15.9	111.2

Source: Agency for International Development, *U.S. Overseas Loans and Grants, 1961, 1971, 1972, 1974* (Washington, D.C.).

an estimated $18 to $20 million more from the Christian Democrats in West Germany, Italy, and Belgium. At the same time, of course, Allende and the FRAP were known to be getting cash from sources of their own, including Cuba and the Soviet Union." And more recently, Laurence Stern of the Washington *Post* reported that the CIA and the State Department had played a major role in Allende's 1964 defeat. Citing unnamed former CIA and State Department officials, including a former ambassador to Chile, Stern wrote that "up to $20 million in U.S. funds reportedly were involved, and as many as 100 U.S. personnel." And on April 22, 1974, CIA Director William E. Colby told the House Armed Services Subcommittee on Intelligence that the CIA had spent $3 million in Chile in 1964.[12]

Non-governmental United States interests were also involved in the effort to defeat Allende. Serafino Romualdi, AFL-CIO representative in Latin America from 1946 to 1965, told the story with pride.[13] Chilean labor had traditionally been dominated by the Communist and Socialist parties and they had competed with each other for control of the movement. In 1953 the two groups united to form the Central Unica de Trabajadores (CUT), which was the main force in Chilean labor until the overthrow of Allende in September 1973. The AFL-CIO strongly opposed the Communist-Socialist union movement on the grounds that it was enhancing the political objectives of the two Marxist parties, and therefore attempted to support and develop a competing anti-communist labor movement. A March 1956 memorandum from Romualdi to George Meany summed up these efforts:

> In order to understand my cautiousness in relation to Chile, I must remind you that the AFL, as early as 1946, contributed substantial amounts of money to the "anti-Communist" elements in Chile; that the CIT* kept its headquarters in that country for two years devoting a large share of its income and personnel to the support of the local "anti-Communists"; that later the ORIT* and the Cuban CTC sent organizers and spent many thousands of dollars in similar work; that the United Mine Workers contributed likewise thousands of dollars; and that finally the ICFTU,* after keeping its Latin American representative in Chile for several months, installed an office and allotted to its maintenance a considerable amount of money. All these efforts have produced nothing more than a series of uninterrupted failures, disappointments, bickerings, and resentment. . . . Nevertheless, if we find that this time there is really a will to fight I am in favor of giving all the support we can muster.[14]

Meany and Romualdi decided that there was "a will to fight" in Chile and thus opened an ORIT-ICFTU* office in Santiago to "rally the independents around a program of nonpolitical, nonsectarian trade unionism, strongly opposed to the Communist-dominated left alliance." They took this step in 1956 because that was the year FRAP was established, and they were particularly anxious to undermine its power. They succeeded in persuading a few

---

* Regional and international anti-communist labor organizations strongly influenced by the United States.

small unions to abandon the CUT in 1957, but this effort never amounted to much.

After FRAP's impressive showing at the polls in 1958, Romualdi and the ORIT stepped up their efforts to divide the CUT. They believed that the "increasing Socialist-Communist use of CUT to enhance the political objectives of FRAP was resented by rank-and-file trade unionists of the Christian Democratic Party" and others, and mindful of the presidential elections of 1964 decided to make their stand. ORIT officials resumed talks with Christian Democratic trade union leaders "with the view of breaking the Christian Democratic unions away from CUT" at its Third Convention scheduled to meet in Santiago from August 1–5, 1962. An AFL-CIO representative (Morris Paladino) met with José Goldsack of the Christian Democrats and secretly agreed to the following:

> 1) In the event the Communists . . . refused to accept the credentials of about four hundred delegates representing agriculture workers' unions that were bitterly opposed to the Communists, the democratic forces would leave the Convention en masse. . . . 2) To strengthen the democratic forces inside the Convention, it was agreed that . . . [all] democratic unions would take part in the Convention with voice and vote. To make this possible, the ORIT representative agreed to pay the arrears in dues owed CUT by these organizations. . . . 3) If they abandoned the site of the CUT Convention . . . the democratic delegates would assemble in another hall . . . whose rent would be paid by ORIT. 4) A new National Democratic Labor Confederation would be launched. The convention itself would decide whether it should join the ORIT or CLASC.* It was agreed . . . that they would recommend, for the time being, independence from both. . . .[15]

The plan fell through, however, because the Christian Democrats backed out at the last minute. The party leaders apparently were afraid that such a close identification with United States labor would hurt their chances in the 1964 elections.[16]

In the election, Frei won 56 percent of the vote and Allende 39 percent. On the one hand, the politics of mass mobilization seemed to have come into its own; 95 percent of the voters sup-

---

* The Catholic international labor confederation.

ported the parties seeking one form or another of fundamental change. On the other hand, more than half of the voters supported the milder and non-Marxist alternative. The United States was overjoyed. President Johnson, already bolstered by the recent overthrow of Goulart in Brazil and the undermining of Jagan's strength in British Guiana, suggested that Frei's triumph "reminds us once more of the strength of democracy in Chile and in the Western Hemisphere." The last six months, he continued, "have been good for democracy and progress in the Americas." [17]

The Frei Administration, 1964–1970

Eduardo Frei Montalvo came to power in Chile under highly favorable circumstances. He had won 56 percent of the vote in an election in which twice the percent of the population had voted than in any previous election; the army was apparently loyal and apolitical; and there were more funds available for development (mainly from the United States) than ever before. There were the critical problems of economic stagnation and widespread poverty, but they were no worse in 1964 than they had been in the past. Frei thus initiated his "Revolution in Liberty" with great hope. By 1970, however, it was clear that he had failed to make much headway in resolving the country's problems, a fact that contributed to Allende's victory. There were many causes for this failure but United States intervention was one of the most important.[18]

Frei's Christian Democratic Party had been established in the late 1930s when a group of young socially minded Catholic intellectuals broke away from the Catholic Conservative Party to form the Falange. The Falange later changed its name to the Christian Democratic Party. During the 1940s and 1950s the party refused to affiliate with other political groups and remained small. With the fragmentation of parties in the 1950s and the failure of the populist-nationalist Ibáñez to solve the major problems confronting the country, however, the Christian Democrats began to seek mass support. Although they had never previously received more than 4 percent of the vote, in 1957 they received 9.4 percent, in 1958 20.46 percent, in 1961 16 percent, and in 1963 20 percent. In 1964, of course, they won 56 percent of the vote. The number of Christian Democratic deputies in the 150-member National Congress grew from 2 in 1941, to 14 in 1957, and to 82 in 1961. Their support came mainly from women who had gained the right to vote in 1958, the urban middle class, low paid urban workers in the service sector, isolated tenant farmers, and from middle-sized farmers.[19]

The Christian Democratic ideology was vague.[20] For the most part a middle-of-the-road reformist party, it rejected both Marxism and classical capitalism and sought instead to create an organic multi-class communitarian society based on Christian principles. James Petras explained: "The ideal of community replaces that of the competitive individual. Mass participation is emphasized instead of party competition. Technological and industrial expansion promoted by government planners and engineers is stressed, rather than dependence on the market mechanism." [21] The Christian Democrats competed with the left in their appeal to populism and reform and in their rejection of the right. But they rejected Marxism and accepted ties with domestic and foreign business.[22]

The program of the Frei administration was ambitious. Its objectives were to reduce inflation, increase the rate of economic growth, and redistribute income simultaneously, although both the international lending agencies (IMF, WB, USAID) and the FRAP believed this impossible.[23] The program included more housing, new but more equitable taxes, and increased real wages coupled with price controls and government subsidies on articles of primary necessity. The key issues, however, were agrarian reform and the Chileanization of copper.

The purpose of agrarian reform was to end the stagnation of the agrarian sector and to improve the conditions of the rural workers. The government approached this in a number of ways. It originally sought to settle 100,000 families (about 40 percent of the landless population) on expropriated land and to provide them with enough credit and technical help to make them productive. In addition the government made unionization of rural workers legal, established a minimum wage for all workers, set up sanctions to be applied to owners who did not comply with the laws, and constructed a tax program to stimulate the use of unproductive and unused land. Yet the success of the government was limited. The program was blocked in Congress for two years, and then it suffered as general economic problems diverted resources from agrarian reform and forced a major cutback in the original program.[24]

As it was with agrarian reform, the primary focus of mining reforms was to increase productivity. The government rejected outright nationalization for fear of losing essential United States economic support, and instead devised a plan in which it bought shares in the foreign-owned mining companies. Under this program, known as the Chileanization of copper, the government purchased 51 percent of Kennecott's large El Teniente mine and 49 percent of Anaconda's Rio Blanco and Cerro mines, and established jointly-owned mixed companies to run them. Chile would acquire complete ownership in fifteen years. The United States concerns promised to reinvest in Chile the money they received from the government for its shares in the mines and to double production by 1970. To persuade the companies to go along, the government granted them tax concessions, which served to increase their profits; between 1964 and 1970 the copper companies earned $728.9 million in profits. "The beauty of the deal," as *Newsweek* reported, "is that Kennecott is getting a bigger share of a bigger pie without any outlay of money from the United States." [25]

Chileanization was supposed to double copper production but at the cost of leaving effective control of the mines in the hands of foreign companies for the time being and of increased profits going abroad. As Albert Michaels explained:

> Having virtually no options, Frei pursued a strategy which seemed economically viable but was to prove politically dangerous. The government negotiated a "Chileanization" plan whereby Chile would buy into the companies and share management but leave the control and high profits with the foreign owners. In return, the companies would expand production and increase investments in Chile. Frei hoped this compromise would meet the political necessity of satisfying his own left, provide greater future state revenues to finance reforms, and encourage the United States government and foreign investors to continue their support. [26]

The success of all of these programs depended on large injections of foreign investment capital and aid, both of which were forthcoming on an unprecedented scale. Between 1964 and 1970, total foreign aid to Chile was $1.2 billion with the United States contributing more than 69 percent of the amount (Table 6–2). Frei encouraged United States and other foreign companies (particularly manufacturing concerns) to establish plants in Chile. Earlier in his career, Frei had attacked capitalism as incapable of achieving social justice since its sole objective was personal profit, but by 1964 he had changed his views and was anxious to encourage private foreign capitalists to invest in Chile. The results of Frei's efforts were dramatic. Foreign investment was not new in Chile, but previously it had concentrated in the extractive industries and in public services. During the 1960s, and especially under Frei, it came to dominate much of the manufacturing sector of the economy.[27]

During the first two years of his term, Frei had some success in achieving his objectives of simultaneously reducing inflation, increasing growth, and redistributing income. Rising taxes, high copper prices, record copper sales, and substantial foreign aid increased public investment and stimulated general economic expansion. Per capita GNP rose from 1.6 percent in 1964 to 4.6 percent in 1966, the rise in the cost of living decreased from 46 percent in 1964 to 18.1 percent in 1967, and unemployment held constant.

In 1967, however, the Chilean economy experienced a serious reversal. Drought struck, copper prices fell, tax increases had reached their limit, and foreign aid began to decline. Furthermore, investment declined and wages continued to rise, resulting in inflation and stagnation. As Sergio Molina, Frei's minister of finance from 1964 to 1968, summed up:

> From 1967 onwards it was an economic policy on the defensive. It was impossible to construct a new policy, for the party did not have the necessary social support; political opposition sharpened, and internal conflicts within the CD [Christian Democratic Party] weakened the government. The CD lacked a social and a political base.[28]

As the economy contracted, the IMF, the World Bank, and AID urged Frei to adopt an austerity program, to cut back on developmental and redistributive programs, and particularly to cut back on the housing and agrarian reform programs designed to improve the lot of the working class. In the name of economic necessity, the international lending agencies pressured Frei to discard the basic reforms that seemed so essential. As Teresa Hayter pointed out: "When the crunch came Chile seems to have abandoned many of its expansionist and reformist goals, and to have come down on the side of the international agencies." [29] The international agencies had considerable power and Frei apparently saw no alternative to accepting their views.

In addition to abandoning its objectives after 1967, the Frei government was saddled with a large and increasing foreign debt. As Table 6-3 shows, from 1966 to 1968 the net inflow of financial resources was negative and the ratio of debt service payments to income earned from exports increased. In 1968 Chile was forced to commit 61.3 percent of its income from exports to pay off debt services and principal, the highest percent of any South American country.

Frei initiated an ambitious program of economic and social development, which, if it were to have any chance of success, had to be accompanied by high copper prices and sales and by massive United States aid and investment. One obvious weakness of this approach was that Frei became dependent on financing that was beyond his direct control. If he were to continue to obtain the funds necessary to carry on his reform program, he had to accept many of the ideas of those giving the funds. When the initially responsive Chilean economy began to stagnate in 1967, Frei had no option but to accept the dictates of the United States. Aid was a critical means of exerting pressure, and the United States used its strength to alter and undermine Frei's original program. This is not to say that Frei's reform program necessarily would have been successful if the United States had not exerted any pressure. The point is that, as with Bolivia, Chilean debt dependency proved to be a critical mechanism for the United States in its efforts to minimize fundamental change and make it "acceptable."

The United States and the Election of 1970

Ironically, given the role of the United States in bringing it about, the failure of the Frei program improved the chances of an Allende victory in the 1970 presidential elections. As it had been in 1964, the United States was concerned by such a possibility and did many of the things it had done six years before to defeat Allende. At its meeting on June 27, 1970, the Committee of Forty of the National Security Council approved the spending of $500 million to support the anti-Allende forces. Chairman Henry Kissinger noted: "I don't see why we must sit with our arms

TABLE **6-3**

Inflow of Financial Resources to Chile, 1950–1968
(percentage of product)

Year	Gross Inflow of Capital	Total Service Payments	Net Inflow of Financial Resources
1950	1.79	3.60	−1.81
1951–1953	2.77	3.10	−.33
1954–1956	2.18	4.28	−2.10
1957–1959	5.04	3.89	1.15
1960–1962	8.37	4.78	3.59
1963–1965	7.80	7.63	.17
1966–1968	7.08	7.90	−.82

Source: Raul Prebisch, *Change and Development—Latin America's Great Task* (New York, 1971), p. 267.

	(A) Income from Exports of Goods & Services	(B) Service Payments on Foreign Capital	Ratio of (B) to (A)
1963	568.0	362.0	63.7
1964	691.0	382.0	55.3
1965	798.0	405.0	50.7
1966	987.0	430.0	43.6
1967	994.0	401.0	40.3
1968	1,035.0	634.0	61.3

Source: United Nations, Economic Commission for Latin America, *Economic Survey of Latin America, 1969* (New York, 1970), pp. 84–85.

folded when a country is slipping toward communism because of the irresponsibility of its own people." [30] Because of the high cost of the Vietnam War and the balance of payments deficit, however, United States aid to Chile decreased during the years preceding the 1970 election. Military aid went up dramatically in 1968 and 1969, just as it had in 1962 and 1963 (Table 6-2).

Despite United States efforts to forestall such a possibility, on September 4, 1970, Allende, the candidate of the left coalition, the Unidad Popular (UP), won with 36.5 percent of the vote. Jorge Alessandri, the candidate of the conservative coalition, received 35 percent of the vote, and the leftist Christian Democrat Radomiro Tomic gained 28 percent of the vote. Since no one obtained an absolute majority, the Chilean Congress had to meet on October 24 to decide who would be declared the winner. In previous cases, the candidate with the highest number of votes had been declared president, but the fact that this candidate was a Marxist opened the possibility of manipulation to deny him the office. United States efforts to influence the outcome of the election took place primarily during the month and a half from September 4 to October 24, 1970.

What makes the 1970 election unique for the scholar is the publication, through the efforts of newspaperman Jack Anderson, of the secret International Telephone and Telegraph Company documents. These documents, the record of subsequent United States Senate hearings, and the revelations of CIA Director William E. Colby, provide specific evidence and a rare internal view of how one United States company and the United States government attempted to block a democratically elected candidate's assumption of power.[31]

ITT began operations in Chile in 1927 and by 1970 had a variety of interests whose combined worth, about $160 million, was second only to that of the holdings of the United States copper companies, Anaconda and Kennecott. In addition to owning 70 percent of the Chilean Telephone Company, ITT had major investments in the telegraph system, the manufacture of radios and TV, and two large hotels. It believed, therefore, that it had a great deal to lose if the Marxist Allende became president.

Shortly after Allende's September 4, 1970, electoral victory, ITT set in motion two lines of operation designed to keep Allende out of power. The first, the "Alessandri formula," involved persuading enough Christian Democratic congressmen to support runner-up Jorge Alessandri so that he, rather than Allende, would be declared president on October 24. After Alessandri was declared president, he would resign, new elections would be called, and Frei—who under the constitution could not succeed himself —would then be eligible to be the candidate of a united anti-Allende coalition. The second line of operation was the "economic chaos-military coup formula." This involved creating economic chaos and provoking incidents that would lead the military to intervene and thus block Allende from ruling. ITT sought the support of various branches of the United States government and of other United States corporations operating in Chile as well as that of the Christian Democrats and the Chilean right.

On September 9 Alessandri announced that if he were elected by Congress on October 24 he would immediately resign. This announcement enabled ITT to pursue the Alessandri formula. The same day the ITT board of directors met in New York for its monthly meeting. Harold Geneen, president and chairman of the board of ITT, told John McCone, an ITT director and a former director of the CIA, that "he was prepared to put as much as a million dollars in support of any plan that was adopted by the government for the purpose of bringing about a coalition of the opposition to Allende so that when confirmation was up . . . this coalition would be united and deprive Allende of his position." McCone supported the proposal, went to Washington a few days later on behalf of Geneen, and informed presidential adviser Henry Kissinger and CIA Director Richard Helms of the offer.[32]

On September 11 Jack Neal, the international relations director in the ITT Washington office, spoke with Viron Vaky, the Latin American specialist on Henry Kissinger's National Security staff, and discussed the Chilean situation. "I told Mr. Vaky to tell Mr. Kissinger," Neal reported, "Mr. Geneen is willing to come to Washington to discuss ITT's interest and that we are prepared to assist financially in sums up to seven figures. I said Mr. Geneen's concern is not one of 'after the barn door has been locked,' but that all along we have feared the Allende victory and have been trying unsuccessfully to get other American companies aroused over the fate of their investments, and join us in pre-election efforts." Neal also communicated the message to Assistant Secretary of State Charles Meyer and to Attorney General John Mitchell.[33]

The United States government reacted to the Chilean situation and to the ITT offer with caution, but some high officials were receptive to certain types of anti-Allende activity. Assistant Secretary of State Meyer testified before the Senate Subcommittee on Multinational Corporations that shortly after the September 4 election the Forty Committee, the coordinating committee of the National Security Council, had discussed the Chilean situation, but he refused to divulge what was said or decided. Ambassador Edward Korry testified that immediately after the election he had advised the State Department that an Allende government would not be in the best interests of the United States. He further stated that he had supported the Alessandri formula and had met with a number of Chilean politicians and United States businessmen between September 4 and October 24. But both men insisted that the State Department had not been involved in Chilean politics in any way.[34]

Hal Hendrix, the ITT public relations director for Latin America, reported that on September 15 Ambassador Korry had received a message from the State Department "giving him the green light to move in the name of President Nixon. The message gave him maximum authority to do all possible—short of a Dominican Republic type action—to keep Allende from taking power." Hendrix also reported that the Alessandri formula had the Chilean government's and Frei's personal approval, and that although the armed forces understood "the extreme danger to democracy that Allende's assumption of power involves," both they and Frei preferred a constitutional solution. Hendrix concluded: "The leader we thought was missing is right there in the saddle [Frei], but he won't move unless he is provided with a constitutional threat. That threat must be provided one way or another through provocation."[35]

In his testimony before the Senate committee, Hendrix explained that the source of his information regarding the "green light" message from the State Department to Ambassador Korry had been a highly placed man in the Christian Democratic Party and not a United States government official. He also acknowledged that his source had not specifically mentioned President Nixon. But he insisted that he had considered the information reliable. Korry denied that he had ever received a "green light or anything approximating it," but he refused to discuss the content of official State Department communications. Assistant Secretary of State Meyer also refused to discuss such communications.[36]

On September 16 Kissinger held an off-the-record news briefing on Chile in which he postulated a Latin American domino theory: "It was fairly easy to predict that if Dr. Salvador Allende was elected president of Chile by Congress on October 24, a Communist government would emerge in Chile. Argentina, Bolivia, and Peru might follow Chile in forming Communist governments." At the same time the White House highlighted the September 9 visit of a Russian naval squadron to Cuba and the alleged efforts of the Russians to build a submarine base on the island. A Russian naval squadron had visited Cuba the preceding May and the information on the alleged submarine base had been available since the beginning of the year. The question then is why the particular concern at this moment? Reporter Tad Szulc suggested that the real purpose behind the submarine base issue was "to signal dangers that might develop if Dr. Salvador Allende, a Marxist, became Chile's President in November as expected." A few weeks later the Pentagon announced that "new evidence" made it less likely that the Soviet was planning to build a submarine base, but that was after the critical decision of the Christian Democrats (October 5) to support Allende.[37]

By the end of September, ITT and the United States government realized that despite the use of $350 million to persuade Chilean legislators to oppose Allende, the prevailing sentiment among the Christian Democrats was to support him, and thus Allende would be confirmed as president on October 24. They therefore abandoned the Alessandri formula and began to pursue the "economic chaos-military coup" formula. Robert Berrellez, ITT director of inter-American relations, noted this fact and suggested: "A more realistic hope among those who want to block Allende is that a swiftly deteriorating economy (bank runs, plant bankruptcies, etc.) will touch off a wave of violence, resulting in a military coup." Summing up, Berrellez said: "Despite some pessimism, a high level effort continues toward getting Frei and/or the military to stop Allende. Although its chances of success seem slender, we cannot ignore that a roadblock to Allende's assumption of power through an economic collapse has the brightest possibilities."[38]

Most significantly, on September 29, an agency of the United States government initiated contact with ITT for the first time. On orders from CIA Director Helms, William Broe, director of the CIA's Latin American Division of Clandestine Services, called ITT Vice President Edward Gerrity and arranged to meet him. According to Gerrity, Broe "indicated that certain steps were being taken but that he was looking for additional help aimed at inducing economic collapse." Broe also made the following specific suggestions: "(1) Banks should not renew credits or should delay in doing so; (2) Companies should drag their feet in sending money, in making deliveries, in shipping spare parts, etc.; (3)

Savings and loan companies there are in trouble. If pressure were applied they would have to shut their doors, thereby creating stronger pressure; (4) We should withdraw all technical help and should not promise any technical assistance in the future. Companies in a position to do so should close their doors; (5) A list of companies was provided and it was suggested that we approach them as indicated. I was told that of all of the companies involved ours alone had been responsive and understood the problem. The visitor added that money was not a problem." Gerrity responded cautiously to Broe's suggestions because he did not think they would work.[39]

Nevertheless, ITT continued to lobby for greater United States government involvement in Chile and was particularly frustrated by the State Department's hesitancy. As Neal lamented, "Why should the United States try to be so pious and sanctimonious in September and October of 1970 when over the past few years it has been pouring the taxpayers' money into Chile, admittedly to defeat Marxism? Why can't the fight be continued now that the battle is in the homestretch and the enemy is more clearly identifiable?" The State Department's position, ITT Executive Representative for International Trade William Merriam believed, was that "the failure of the Chileans, themselves, to react strongly against Allende is making it difficult for outsiders like the United States and Argentina to move in and try to stop Allende openly or covertly."[40]

On October 5 the Christian Democrats formally decided to support Allende, making it certain that only covert action could block him. A few days later the popular left-wing nationalist General Torres seized power in Bolivia, increasing the fear of the United States that a neutralist or Marxist bloc might develop in South America. The CIA, United States Ambassador Korry, the State Department, and ITT continued to work for economic chaos and a military coup in Chile.[41] In early October the CIA supported the efforts of former Brigadier General Roberto Viaux to kidnap Army Commander in Chief General René Schneider. Such action would remove the man who had insisted on military respect for the constitution and who had thus frustrated the plans of those who sought to block Allende. They also hoped it would lead to a coup. Kissinger was informed of the plan on October 13 but, because he thought it had little chance of success, decided not to give it his support. According to ITT's Hendrix, "word was passed to Viaux from Washington to hold back last week, since Washington felt he was not adequately prepared and the timing was bad. Emissaries pointed out to him that if he moved prematurely and lost, his defeat would be tantamount to a Bay of Pigs in Chile. As part of the persuasion to delay, Viaux was given oral assurances he would receive material assistance and support from the United States and others for a later maneuver." The plan continued anyway. October 22, just two days before the Congress confirmed Allende, Schneider was killed while Viaux's group attempted to kidnap him.[42]

On October 24, 1970, Salvador Allende received 153 of the 195 votes in the Congress and was confirmed as president of Chile. The record of activity during the month and a half between the initial election and the final congressional confirmation shows that : (1) ITT intervened overtly and covertly in the internal politics of Chile but was neither discouraged nor reprimanded by the United States government; (2) ITT officials, who had direct access to the highest officials in the United States government, attempted to determine and implement United States policy toward Chile; (3) high level United States officials, most notably Broe and Korry with the knowledge and approval of Kissinger and the Committee of Forty, participated actively in the plotting to manipulate the outcome of the Chilean election; and (4) the United States opposed Allende in a variety of legal and illegal ways because, although he had been democratically elected, he was a Marxist who sought to bring about fundamental social and economic change. As the Senate subcommittee summed up: "The record of the hearings calls into question the Administration's stated policy that it was willing to live with a 'community of diversity in Latin America: we deal with governments as they are. Our relations depend not on their internal structures or social systems, but on acts which affect us in the inter-American system.' " [43]

Allende and After: 1970–1975

On November 4, 1970, Salvador Allende was inaugurated as president of Chile and initiated an important new phase in that country's history. Allende was the first Marxist to be elected president of a democratic capitalist country and the first to pledge to socialize a country by pacific constitutional means.

The program of Allende's coalition, the Unidad Popular (UP), was designed primarily to improve the quality of life of the majority of Chile's "have nots." It called for the peaceful and democratic socialization of the Chilean economy, the liberation of the country from foreign dependency, economic development at the service of the people (working classes), and political power to the working class and the people. Specifically, the UP pledged full nationalization of natural resources (particularly copper), credit (banks), and major industries; complete agrarian reform including the expropriation of *latifundia* (large estates) and the establishment of government-run cooperatives; the redistribution of income in favor of the working classes; the end to economic dependency on foreign governments and companies; and an independent foreign policy.[44]

During its first year in power, the UP made a major start in accomplishing its objectives. It nationalized the large United States-owned copper companies (Kennecott and Anaconda), the major banks, and many of the major industries. It redistributed income by taxation, freezing prices, and increasing wages; by the end of 1971 the share of wages in the total national income had risen from 51 to 59 percent. Unemployment in the Greater Santiago area dropped from 8 to 5 percent, the lowest it had been since 1963. The redistribution of income increased demand, which in turn stimulated production; agricultural production was up 5 percent, copper production up 8.3 percent, and industrial production up 12 percent. The UP also broadened its political base; in the municipal elections of April 4, 1971, it won 50 percent of the vote. And, despite opposition claims that some newspapers were being harassed, all of this was done in a climate of remarkable freedom.[45]

In 1972 and 1973 the structural reforms continued (nationalization, agrarian reform, redistribution of wealth, and so on), but Chile suffered severe economic problems. New demands for food and consumer goods, stimulated primarily by redistributing wealth, outpaced local production and imports, and this, along with hoarding, speculation, and sabotage resulted in shortages. Spare parts and new machinery were also in short supply. Agriculture, copper, and industrial production declined. Copper prices dropped to their lowest levels since 1967. Investment capital and credit became scarce. And service payments on the large inherited foreign debt of more than $2.5 billion continued. Chronic inflation ensued, reaching 160 percent in 1972 and more than 300 percent in 1973. The government devalued the escudo 30 percent at the end of 1971 and another 50 percent in March 1973. It fell into arrears in its payments to AID and to the Export-Import Bank. And it moved increasingly to control the distribution of food and other items. Middle-class protest demonstrations and strikes became frequent and political polarization intensified.[46]

There is no doubt that part of the problem stemmed from inexperience, bad judgment, and mismanagement as the critics of the UP have pointed out. But there is also no doubt that part of the problem arose as a result of domestic and foreign opposition. Allende with 36.5 percent of the vote in the 1970 election lacked sufficient political support to carry through his program. The Christian Democrats and the National Party controlled 32 of the 50 Senate votes and 93 of the 150 Deputy votes. They also had the sympathy of the courts. Thus, they could block or undermine much of the program of the UP. The National Party, representing the upper classes, sectors of the middle class, and the right-wing groups, opposed the UP in every way possible and in some cases resorted to illegal activity. The Christian Democrats, controlling the balance of power, wavered and then chose to align themselves with the right rather than the left.

Initially, the Christian Democratic Party, whose populist faction sympathized with much of the UP program, established something of a working relationship with the UP. It not only supported the nationalization of the United States-owned copper companies (July 11, 1971), but also the government's decision to deduct excess profits from the value of the copper companies' investments and as a result not to offer the companies compensation (September 11, 1971). Late in September 1971, however, the Christian Democrats formally broke off their working relationship with the government. Eduardo Frei attacked the UP and accused the Communist Party of attempting to impose a dictatorship of the left. Then in February 1972 the Christian Democratic-Nationalist coalition in Congress passed a constitutional amendment that limited Allende's power to impose state controls over private enterprises.[47]

In December 1971 the opposition staged the first of a series of demonstrations to protest food and consumer goods shortages and government policies in general. Allende declared a temporary state of emergency, which banned public meetings and suspended some constitutional guarantees, i.e., the government could make arrests without warrants and the military could impose press censorship. In April 1972 there was another protest march. During August and September small shopkeepers closed down in protest over shortages and taxes. And in October truck owners went on strike to protest the shortage of spare parts and low rates. They were joined by bus owners, doctors, dentists, engineers, shop owners, and other middle-class elements in a protest that greatly increased political polarization and nearly brought down the government. Allende declared martial law and used the army to open up food stores. On November 2 Allende named three military officers to the cabinet. Army Commander in Chief General Carlos Prats became minister of interior in charge of internal security and the number two man in the government (Chile has no vice president and the minister of interior is next in line to the president). On November 6 the strike was resolved and the country returned to work.[48]

The October crisis initiated the campaign for the March 7, 1973, elections in which half the Senate seats and all of the Deputy seats would be contested. The opposition coalition (Christian Democrats and Nationalists), which controlled 32 of 50 Senate seats, needed only one more seat to obtain a two-thirds majority and the power to veto legislation or impeach the president. Frei, the leader of the opposition, claimed that the election would constitute a plebiscite on the UP government's record and campaigned to win an overwhelming anti-Marxist majority. Allende insisted that the elections would not constitute a plebiscite on his government's record and claimed that anything more than the 36.5 percent he had won in 1970 would be a victory for the UP.

In the elections the UP won 43.4 percent of the vote and the opposition 54.7 percent. More importantly, the government gained 2 Senate seats, increasing its total from 18 to 20 out of 50, and 6 Deputy seats, increasing its total there from 57 to 63 out of 150. Both sides claimed victory in these essentially indecisive elections, but the UP did better than anyone had expected: It gained seats in both houses of Congress, and it made impeachment of Allende impossible.[49]

The October crisis also led to the first serious talk among elements of the armed forces of a military coup. The Chilean military had a forty-year record of non-intervention in politics, but as Jorge Nef has shown, the military was not apolitical. The large majority of officers were anti-Marxist and resented Allende's efforts to exploit the natural rivalry between the army, navy, and air force. Most of the officers of the armed forces were pleased when Allende brought General Prats and other military officers into his cabinet, but they soon began to distrust General Prats' sympathy for Allende. Thus, in late November 1972 middle ranking officers of all three services began to plan a coup and established contacts with the business and professional associations that had backed the October strike. Perhaps ironically, the armed forces' long tradition of political neutrality proved to be an obstacle for the plotting officers. As one reported, "I could have pulled my hair out for teaching my students for all those years that the armed forces must never rebel against the constitutional government. It took a long time to convince officers that there was no other way out." [50]

The plotting was temporarily suspended during the weeks before the March elections since the civilian opposition was confident that it could win the necessary two-thirds of the legislative seats to impeach Allende. As one officer said: "It was supposed to be a last chance for a political solution. But frankly, many of us gave a sigh of relief when the Marxists received such a high vote because we felt that no politician could run the country and that eventually the Marxists might be even stronger." [51]

The March 7 election was a critical turning point in the struggle between Allende and his opponents. *New York Times* correspondent Barnard Collier wrote that "the election result was a clear sign to President Allende's political enemies that they could no longer count on the ballot box as a means of bringing him down." The civilian and military opposition increased the pressure on Allende and prepared for the final showdown. The truck owners association carried out a twenty-four-hour strike in May and another crippling strike from mid-July to the September coup. The dominant Frei faction of the Christian Democrats opposed any compromise with Allende and demanded instead increased military participation in the government. And in early September the professional and truck owners associations called for Allende's resignation and military intervention. [52]

After the March election the military members of the cabinet, including General Prats, resigned. On June 29 Lieutenant Colonel Roberto Souper attempted a coup, but was frustrated by the resolute action of General Prats, who still served as commander in chief of the army. Shortly thereafter, the opposition-controlled Congress passed an arms control law and the military proceeded to carry out weapons searches in the factories surrounding Santiago and other leftist strongholds. On August 9 Allende again brought a number of military men into his cabinet, including General Prats, but a week later set off a new crisis by forcing Air Force Commander in Chief and Minister of Public Works and Transportation General Cesar Ruiz Danyou to resign. The air force wanted to initiate the planned coup immediately but was persuaded by other branches of the armed forces to wait until General Prats was removed from the government. On August 23 General Prats resigned under pressure from the military leaders and the final obstacle to the coup was removed.[53]

Allende's supporters responded in kind as the confrontation escalated. They staged a series of pro-Allende demonstrations, workers occupied factories and refused to leave them, and the Chilean labor federation openly urged its members to defend the government by whatever means necessary. Allende shuffled his cabinet several times and vainly sought to work out some kind of a compromise with the military and the Christian Democrats. But once General Prats had resigned nothing could have stopped the coup. On the afternoon of September 10 the order for the coup was given and on September 11 Allende was removed from power and killed himself or was killed.[54]

General Augusto Pinochet Ugarte, the successor of General Prats as commander in chief of the army, was named president of Chile and swore in a new cabinet composed mostly of military men. The Christian Democratic Party and the National Party announced their support of the ruling military junta. The junta proceeded swiftly to carry out a counterrevolution to purge Chile of Marxists and socialism. In a manner similar to that of the Brazilian military in 1964 and the Argentine military in 1966, it outlawed the Marxist parties, prohibited all political parties from functioning, withdrew legal recognition from the Marxist-controlled Central Workers' Confederation, closed Congress, removed all municipal officials from office, purged the universities, shut down leftist newspapers, banned the sale of leftist books, censored all publications, broke relations with Cuba, and detained thousands and killed hundreds of suspected leftists. The junta also moved to restore a free capitalist economy. It initiated an austerity program, returned many of the companies nationalized under Allende to their original owners, restored many of the companies of the pre-Allende managers to their positions in companies that continued under state control, initiated negotiations with the international lending organizations for economic assistance, fired "excess" labor, froze wages, and permitted prices to rise to their "natural" level.[55]

Two years after the counterrevolutionary coup the results were clear: Allende's working-class supporters had been replaced by his middle-class opponents and his brand of democratic socialism had been replaced by an authoritarian and repressive form of free enterprise military corporativism. The greatest beneficiaries under the new military dictatorship were the members of the middle-class associations *(gremios),* the 40,000 truck owners, the 140,000 shopkeepers and small-business men, and the 90,000 professional men. The losers were the poor and the working classes who had been deprived of all institutional participation in the political system. Unemployment shot up, and real wages and purchasing power declined abruptly. Within three months of the coup the cost of bread had risen 250 percent, sugar 500 percent, and chicken 800 percent. In 1974 inflation reached 375 percent and unemployment 9.5 percent. Torture and other forms of repression were used extensively against the opponents of the regime.[56]

The Christian Democratic Party realized too late that it had helped create a Frankenstein Monster by calling for greater military participation in the government and by initially supporting the military junta. The junta's programs not only undermined many of the populist and democratic principles for which the party stood, but also threatened the continued existence of the party. In a January 18, 1974, letter to General Pinochet Ugarte, the party leaders charged that "many Chileans have been or are being deprived of their work, detained, censured, threatened or pressured in different ways without any justification except for the ideas or opinions they profess, or which are attributed to them. . . . The remunerations of workers barely permit them to feed themselves and in many·cases do not permit them to meet the vital needs of their families. . . . Meanwhile, there are businesses whose profits exceed all expectations. Nobody can ignore the injustice of this situation and the dangers which this entails." The leaders then charged that the suspension of political party activity threatened to destroy their party and protested the "systematic and malevolent campaign against Christian Democrats." [57]

Chile today is ruled by a right-wing military dictatorship that has destroyed the institutional participation and power of the working classes and has forced them to bear the brunt of its economic development program. The middle-class Christian Democratic Party, unlike the right-wing opposition to Allende, may now lament the fact, but because it called for greater military involvement in the government and supported the military junta, it must accept a considerable part of the responsibility for the situation.

The United States and the Destruction of Chilean Democracy: 1970–1975

Strong domestic opposition to Allende was a critical factor in his overthrow; had Chileans been united, or nearly united, behind him there would most likely have been no military coup. This must not, however, obscure the fact that the United States government and business interests played a significant part in destroying Allende and with him Chilean democracy. Washington had feared and actively opposed Allende since 1958; it was involved in the political manipulations to keep him from power in 1964 and 1970. And it continued to use vast economic and political resources to undermine Allende while he was president.

Allende's electoral victory was perceived by the United States government and United States business as a threat to their interests. Most importantly, however, Allende's victory and continued rule in Chile destroyed a key tenet of postwar United States ideology—namely, that no Marxist could come to power in a noncommunist country by means of a free and democratic election. As Eric Hobsbawm noted: "Chile is the first country in the world that is seriously attempting an alternative road to socialism. . . . Socialism will never come to, say, Western Europe in the Chinese or Vietnamese way, but it is at least possible to recognize in Chile the lineaments of political situations that might occur in industrialized societies. . . ." *New York Times* columnist C. L. Sulzberger was more specific. The threat of Chile, he argued, is not so

much that it might spread to other Latin American countries, but
that it might spread to Western Europe and to Italy in particular.
"Should Italy be legally taken over by a Communist dominated
government," Sulzberger continued, "there would be little NATO
could do about it. . . . This would virtually destroy the alliance,
undermine the Common Market and drastically alter the tenuous
power balance in the Mediterranean. . . . Thus NATO thinks of
Italy when the word Chile is mentioned." What the United States
faced was the legal take-over of a government by a Marxist coalition with a program of revolutionary but democratic change, and
it was therefore essential to make sure that it failed.[58]

The question for the United States, which particularly during its
early years had done everything possible to make the Frei administration succeed, was how to make Allende fail. The "Bolivian
formula" (see Chapter 4) was unworkable in Chile, since the
Chilean political structure was not similar to that of Bolivia and
Allende was not Paz Estenssoro; Allende feared United States
economic dependence as much as the United States feared Allende's Marxism. Thus, the United States cut its economic aid to
less than $10 million a year from a high of $260 million in 1967
and $80 million in 1969. The United States also rejected direct
military intervention for obvious reasons. Chile was much farther
away than the Dominican Republic, and the Chilean population,
including much of the opposition, simply would not accept American intervention.

The United States therefore developed a dual policy. On the
one hand it restricted credit to Chile in order to create economic
hardship and instability.[59] On the other hand, it supported and
encouraged both civilian (Christian Democrats) and military domestic opposition, making sure that both were strong and ready to
act when the opportunity arose. This policy was possible for a
number of reasons. First, the Chilean economy, long tied to that
of the United States, needed United States parts and equipment to
function. Second, Chile had a large foreign debt ($2.5 billion) and
high service payments. Third, Chile needed foreign credit and
capital to transform its economy and increase production sufficiently to pay for increased social benefits. And finally, the Christian Democrats and the Chilean military were anxious to maintain
their strength.

From October 24, 1970, until mid-1971 the United States pursued an essentially wait-and-see policy toward Chile. There were a few childish rebuffs—Nixon refused to congratulate Allende on his victory and canceled the Chilean courtesy visit of the United States carrier *Enterprise*—but a systematic anti-Allende policy had apparently not yet been formulated and put into practice.

Throughout this period ITT lobbied intensively for a hard-line policy. In January 1971, before Chile had expropriated any United States concerns, ITT Vice President Merriam brought together an *ad hoc* committee of businesses with investments in Chile (Anaconda, Kennecott, Ralston Purina, Bank of America, Pfizer Chemical, Grace & Co.) to apply "pressure on the [U.S.] Government, wherever possible, to make it clear that a Chilean take-over would not be tolerated without serious repercussion following." One purpose of the committee, according to Merriam, was to get the United States government to block loans to Allende by the World Bank, the IDB, and other lending organizations and thus to create economic problems for Chile.[60]

At the time ITT was lobbying to create economic problems for Allende it was also negotiating with the Chilean government regarding the possible nationalization of its holdings in Chiltelco, the Chilean telephone company. Between October 1970 and March 1971 Allende met several times with representatives of Chiltelco to discuss the situation. The Chiltelco representatives described the meetings as cordial and reported that negotiations with Allende were possible. On May 26 Allende informed Chiltelco that it would be nationalized and that a commission headed by the minister of the interior would negotiate a settlement. Chile offered $24 million for ITT's interest in Chiltelco. ITT claimed it was owed $153 million. On September 29 the Chilean government took over the management of Chiltelco with the issue still unsettled.[61]

The nationalization of Chiltelco and other United States companies, and particularly the nationalization of the copper companies in July 1971, marked the turning point in the emergence of a coherent hard-line policy. From then on there were no new AID loans to Chile. The United States-dominated IDB, which had granted Chile $310 million in loans since its establishment in 1959, sent a special mission to Chile in June 1971 and then turned down all requests for development funds. The World Bank, presided over by former United States Secretary of Defense Robert McNamara, sent a mission to Santiago in September 1971 to determine Chile's credit worthiness. The mission reported that declining investment and foreign reserves and inflation made it doubtful that Chile could effectively utilize any loans or continue to pay the service charges on past debts. As a result, Allende's government received no new loans from the World Bank.[62]

Perhaps most importantly, in August, a month after the nationalization of the copper mines and two months before compensation had been determined, the United States Export-Import Bank refused to loan $21 million to LAN Chile for three Boeing passenger jets. The bank's president told the Chilean ambassador in Washington that there would be no new loans or guarantees until the compensation question was settled to the satisfaction of the United States. The Export-Import Bank had provided more than $600 million in direct credits to Chile since 1945, had guaranteed loans by private banks, and had provided insurance for investors against nationalization. The new policy line therefore meant that not only would the disbursement of present loans be cut off and that there would be no new loans, but also that there would be no guarantees or insurance, so that private commercial banks and exporters would also stop granting credit. Private banks, which formerly had granted Chile about $220 million per year in vital short-term credits, limited their commitments to about $35 million in 1971 and $32 million in 1972.[63]

In October 1971, after Chile had taken over the management of Chiltelco and had announced that with the deduction of excess profits it owed no compensation to the copper companies, Secretary of State William B. Rogers met representatives of the major United States companies with investments in Chile to discuss alternatives. After the meeting he announced that Chile's stand threatened United States-Chilean relations, jeopardized the flow of private investment funds, and eroded the base support for foreign aid. At the same time ITT President Geneen met White House advisers General Alexander Haig and Peter Peterson, and, as a follow-up, ITT Vice President Merriam sent an eighteen-point Action Plan to Peterson. The plan proposed credit restrictions, among other things, which would insure "that Allende does not get through the next six months." As the Senate subcommittee summed up: "Thus one year after Broe [CIA] proposed a plan to accelerate economic chaos in Chile, Merriam, on behalf of the company, was proposing to the President's Assistant for International Economic Policy [Peterson] a similar plan to exacerbate the Chilean economic situation. Peterson testified that he took no action to implement the Merriam plan." In December 1971 presidential aides Robert Finch and Herbert Klein returned from a trip through Latin America, which included a visit to Chile, and reported that Allende "won't last long." [64]

On January 19, 1972, Nixon formalized the hard-line policy (credit blockade) in a statement on expropriation of United States property. If a country expropriated significant United States concerns without reasonable provision for just compensation, which the United States alone would decide, there would be no bilateral economic benefits and the United States would "withhold its support from loans under consideration in multilateral development banks." By the beginning of 1972 Chile was cut off from its major sources of both short-term and long-term credits.[65]

In April 1972 Chile did succeed in renegotiating 70 percent of its $3 billion foreign debt and in June it renegotiated outstanding credits with United States banks, but this was done because it was the only way to get back any of the money lent previously to Chile and because several European countries (particularly Italy and Spain) wanted such a settlement. This did not mean that Chile was granted new loans. It meant simply that it had more time to pay off the old loans.[66]

Kennecott added a new dimension to the credit blockade in September 1972 when it successfully got a French court to freeze $1.33 million in payments for Chilean copper. The courts lifted the freeze in November, but Chile was required to keep the amount in escrow pending further investigation. In January 1973 Kennecott attempted the same thing in German courts. The result was to tie up copper sales, hurt Chile's credit rating, and force Chile to spend a considerable sum on court costs.[67]

Allende responded in several ways. He sought and obtained some credit and imports outside the United States, particularly in socialist countries and in Latin America. He negotiated $500 million in short-term credits with Russia, Argentina, Italy, and others, and a like amount in long-term credits from Russia, China, and other socialist countries, plus $40 million from Argentina, $40 million from Peru, and $20 million from Mexico. In addition, he denounced the economic blockade in several international forums. For example, in a speech before the United Nations on December 4, 1972, Allende charged:

> From the very day of our election triumph on September 4, 1970, we have felt the effects of large scale external pressure against us which tried to prevent the inauguration of a Government freely elected by the people and which has tried to bring it down ever since. It is action that has tried to cut us off from the world, to strangle our economy and to paralyze trade in our principal export, copper, and to deprive us of access to sources of international financing. Each and every Chilean is suffering from the consequences of these measures, because they affect the daily life of each citizen. Such misuse [of power] represents the exertion of pressure on an economically weak country, the infliction of punishment on a whole nation for its decision to recover its own basic resources and a form of intervention in the internal affairs of a sovereign state.[68]

In December 1972, shortly after Allende's United Nations speech, the United States and Chile began high level talks aimed at resolving such questions as the nationalization of United States property, Chile's foreign debt, and Washington's blockade of international credits to Chile. Yet shortly after the elections of March 7, 1973, when it became apparent to Allende's military and civilian opposition that he could not be removed from office by legal means, the United States stiffened its position on all of these issues and the talks broke down. The economic and political situation deteriorated, as described above, and Allende was overthrown on September 11, 1973.

The government of General Pinochet Ugarte moved quickly to denationalize a number of companies taken over by the Allende government, to restore a free enterprise economy, to control inflation, to compensate the United States for the expropriated copper mines, and to purge the government of Marxists and socialism. As a result, the credit blockade was ended with both private and government funds from the United States and other sources again becoming available to Chile.[69]

There are many indications that the United States was directly involved in the overthrow of Allende, but it is not necessary to prove direct involvement to make the case for major United States responsibility.[70] The United States did not have to become directly involved in order to bring about the demise of Allende.

Since 1958 the United States government, business, and labor had opposed Allende and his program of revolutionary change in behalf of Chile's "have nots." They had also encouraged and supported the military and civilian opposition to him. In 1970 ITT and high level government officials participated in the manipulations to deny Allende the presidency. The economic blockade of 1971, 1972, and 1973 weakened the Chilean economy, fostered instability, and undermined Allende's chances of carrying out his program.

In September 1974 President Ford confirmed the fact that the Nixon Administration had authorized the CIA to spend $8 million between 1970 and 1973 to weaken Allende and strengthen his opposition. When asked by a reporter under what international law the United States had the right to do this, President Ford responded: "I am not going to pass judgment on whether it is permitted or authorized under international law. It is a recognized fact that, historically as well as presently, such actions are taken in the best interests of the countries involved." The Chilean working class and many others could hardly accept such a statement, but the power realities make it impossible at present for them to do anything about it.[71]

The United States successfully contained Allende and his program of revolutionary change in behalf of the common people, and in so doing it once more demonstrated that it had little interest in improving the quality of life of the South American people. As a well-to-do conservative Chilean lawyer told Robert Kennedy, Jr.: "The military can bring order, but will they try to bring justice? Without justice none of us will really sleep well. And I will tell you this: it does your country, so big and strong and rich, no good to be known by millions in this country and elsewhere as the enemy of the poor. It makes no sense to me either. Your Mr. Nixon shakes hands with Mao and Brezhnev, he sends them wheat and other commodities, calls them his new friends, and then cuts off all aid to this country except to our military. In the long run, America will have to come to terms with Latin America as much as China or Russia." [72]

NOTES

1. Samuel L. Baily (ed.), *Nationalism in Latin America* (New York, 1971), pp. 3–28; Peter H. Smith, "Political Legitimacy in Spanish America" in Richard Graham and Peter H. Smith (eds.), *New Approaches to Latin American History* (Austin, 1974).

2. Federico Gil, *The Political System of Chile* (Boston, 1966); Fredrick B. Pike, *Chile and the United States, 1880–1962* (Notre Dame, Ind., 1963); James Petras, *Politics and Social Forces in Chilean Development* (Berkeley, 1969); Ernst Halperin, *Nationalism and Communism in Chile* (Cambridge, Mass., 1965); the essays of Anibal Pinto, Jacques Chonchol, and Osvaldo Sunkel in Claudio Veliz (ed.), *Obstacles to Change in Latin America* (New York, 1969); Jay Kinsbruner, *Chile, a Historical Interpretation* (New York, 1973).

3. *Foreign Relations*, 1946, p. 616; 1948, pp. 435–437.

4. *Ibid.*, 1946, p. 614; 1947, pp. 497–515.

5. Petras, *Politics*, pp. 167–169.

6. *Latin American and Empire Report* (January 1973), p. 5.

7. Raul Ampuero D., *La izquierda en punto muerto* (Santiago, 1969).

8. Petras, *Politics*, pp. 167–182; Ampuero, *La izquierda*.

9. *Latin American and Empire Report* (January 1973), p. 5.

10. *The New York Times*, September 6, 1964.

11. Barber and Ronning, *Internal Security*, p. 36; Senate Committee on Foreign Relations, *U.S. Foreign Aid in Action: A Case Study* (Washington, D.C., 1966), pp. 114–116.

12. Miles D. Wolpin, *Cuban Foreign Policy and Chilean Politics* (Lexington, Mass., 1972), pp. 87–88, 342; *The New York Times*, February 19, 1967; *Washington Post*, April 6, 1973; *Excelsior*, September 7–17, 1974; *Time*, September 30, 1974; *U.S. News & World Report*, December 2, 1974.

13. Serafino Romualdi, *Presidents and Peons* (New York, 1967), pp. 322–340.

14. *Ibid.*, pp. 332–333.

15. *Ibid.*, pp. 335–336.

16. See also North American Congress on Latin America, *New Chile* (New York, 1972), pp. 54–58.

17. *The New York Times*, September 6, 1964.

18. For an analysis of the Frei administration, see: Albert L. Michaels, The Alliance for Progress and Chile's 'Revolution in Liberty,' 1964–1970," *Journal of Inter-American Studies* (February 1976); Petras, *Politics*, pp. 196–255; *New Chile*, pp. 118–127; Institute of General Studies, *Chile: A Critical Survey* (Santiago, 1972); Victor Wallis, "Imperialism and the 'Via Chilena,' " *Latin American Perspectives* (Summer 1974). My special thanks to Albert Michaels for letting me see an advance copy of his excellent article.

19. Center for Latin American Studies, University of California at Los Angeles, *Latin American Political Statistics* (Los Angeles, 1972), p. 75; *Chile: A Critical Survey*, p. 51; Petras, *Politics*, pp. 204–205.

20. Jaime Castillo Velasco, *Las fuentes de la democracia cristiana* (Santiago, 1963).

21. Petras, *Politics,* pp. 198–199.

22. Michaels points out that there were divisions within the party. See Michaels, "Alliance," p. 79.

23. *Ibid.,* pp. 6–9; Teresa Hayter, *Aid as Imperialism* (London, 1971), pp. 119–134.

24. *Chile: A Critical Survey,* pp. 167–180; Robert R. Kaufman, *The Politics of Land Reform in Chile, 1950–1970* (Cambridge, Mass., 1972).

25. *Latin American and Empire Report* (January 1973), p. 8; *Newsweek,* October 24, 1966.

26. Michaels, "Alliance," p. 85.

27. *New Chile,* pp. 150–167; Fredrick B. Pike and Donald W. Bray, "A Vista of Catastrophe: the Future of United States-Chilean Relations," *Review of Politics* (July 1960), p. 406, n. 25.

28. Quoted in Richard E. Feinberg, *The Triumph of Allende* (New York, 1972), p. 40.

29. Hayter, *Aid,* p. 134.

30. Wolpin, *Cuban,* pp. 88–89; United States, Senate Committee on Foreign Relations, *The International Telephone and Telegraph Company and Chile, 1970–1971* (Washington, D.C., 1973), pp. 3 and 6; *New Chile,* pp. 57–58; *El Día,* September 9–11, 1974.

31. The ITT Secret Documents have been published by the Chilean government and by the North American Congress on Latin America. By far the most complete set of documents and supporting material is in: United States, Senate Committee on Foreign Relations, *Hearings on the International Telephone and Telegraph Company and Chile, 1970–1971, March 20–April 2, 1973* (Washington, D.C., 1973), 2 volumes. Hereafter cited as *ITT Hearings.* The report mentioned in note 30 is a brief summary of the hearings.

32. *ITT Hearings,* p. 102.

33. *Ibid.,* pp. 599–600.

34. *Ibid.,* pp. 282, 290–293, 409–410.

35. *Ibid.,* pp. 608–613.

36. *Ibid.,* pp. 130–132, 285–288, 426.

37. *Ibid.,* pp. 541–544; *The New York Times,* September 23 and 30, 1970, October 4, 1970; *Wall Street Journal,* October 14, 1970.

38. *ITT Hearings,* pp. 622–625. The Chilean government version of the same document differs slightly from that used in the text. It reads: "Despite the pessimism, efforts are continuing to move Frei and/or the military to stop Allende. Efforts are also continuing to provoke the extreme left into a violent reaction that would produce the climate requiring military intervention. Although its chances of success are slender, a roadblock to Allende's assumption of power through an economic collapse should not be dismissed." See *Documentos Secretos de la ITT* (Santiago, 1972), p. 26. See also *El Día,* September 9–11, 1974.

39. *ITT Hearings,* pp. 626–627.

40. *Ibid.,* pp. 630 and 648.

41. *Ibid.*, p. 658.

42. *Ibid.*, pp. 144 and 659. See also Jorge Nef, "The Politics of Repression, *Latin American Perspectives* (Summer 1974). The United States Senate Intelligence Committee *Report on Alleged Assassination Plots* includes a full discussion of the plot. See *The New York Times,* November 21, 1975 for the text of the *Report.*

43. Senate *ITT Report,* p. 19. The quote is from Richard Nixon.

44. *Plataforma de gobierno del partido de la Unidad Popular* (Santiago, n.d.).

45. *Latin American and Empire Report* (January 1973); Enrique Correa Rios, *El primer año del gobierno popular* (Santiago, 1972); Dale L. Johnson, *The Chilean Road to Socialism* (New York, 1973); Pablo Huneeus, et al., *Chile: el costo social de la dependencia ideológica* (Santiago, 1973); *Chile: A Critical Survey;* Feinberg, *Triumph;* Regis Debray, *The Chilean Revolution* (New York, 1971); David J. Morris, *We Must Make Haste—Slowly* (New York, 1973); *Latin American Perspectives* (Summer 1974).

46. Many of the books listed in the preceding note cover all or part of the second year and beyond. In addition, see Enrique Correa Rios, *El segundo año del gobierno popular* (Santiago, 1972).

47. *The New York Times,* September 26, 1971; *Latin American and Empire Report* (January 1973).

48. *The New York Times,* August 29, October 21 and 22, and November 9, 1972.

49. *La Opinión,* March 6, 1973; *The New York Times,* March 11, 1973.

50. *The New York Times,* September 27, 1973; *Excelsior,* August 25, 1974; Nef, "Politics."

51. *The New York Times,* September 27, 1973.

52. *The New York Times,* July 2, August 8, 10 and 18, and September 16, 1973.

53. *The New York Times,* August 19, September 27, 1973.

54. *The New York Times,* September 12, 1973.

55. See the excellently indexed clipping service Information Service for Latin America for the abundance of newspaper articles on Chile from September through December 1973. See also *Latin American Perspectives* (Summer 1974) and Chicago Commission of Inquiry into the Status of Human Rights in Chile, *Report* (Chicago, 1974).

56. *The New York Times,* September 16, October 23 and 28, and December 16, 1973.

57. *The New York Times,* February 8 and 11, 1974; *Excelsior,* July 19, November 29, 1974; *El Día,* January 7, May 8, 1975. See also James Petras and Morris Morley, *The United States and Chile* (New York, 1975).

58. *New York Review of Books,* September 23, 1971; *The New York Times,* January 13, 1971. See also the related articles of C. L. Sulzberger: *The New York Times,* September 25, 1970, April 2 and 4, 1971. Portugal provides another similar example of U.S. fear of potential revolutionary change. See El Día, October 13, November 1, 1974; *The New York Times,* August 8, 1975.

59. Paul Sigmund, in an interesting and provocative article, argues that

there never really was a credit blockade; private and public international capital avoided Chile because the economic environment was unattractive. Perhaps the problem is one of semantics or of deciding which came first, the "unattractive" economic environment or the credit blockade. Nevertheless, as the evidence in the following paragraphs makes clear, the United States did indeed block private and public international capital and credit to Allende. See Paul E. Sigmund, "The 'Invisible Blockade' and the Overthrow of Allende," *Foreign Affairs* (January 1974).

60. *ITT Hearings*, pp. 46–47; Senate *ITT Report*, pp. 12–13.

61. *Ibid.*, p. 14.

62. *Latin American and Empire Report* (January 1973), pp. 17–19; Sigmund, "Invisible," p. 328; *The New York Times*, August 14, 1971.

63. See note 62. See also Petras and Morley, *U.S.*, Chapter 5.

64. *The New York Times*, October 15, December 3, 1971; *ITT Hearings*, pp. 41–42; Senate *ITT Report*, p. 15.

65. *The New York Times*, January 20, 1972, April 3, 1973; *Latin American and Empire Report* (January 1973), p. 13.

66. *The New York Times*, April 20, June 13, 1972.

67. *Latin American and Empire Report* (January 1973), pp. 22–23.

68. *The New York Times*, May 2, September 29, October 7, and December 5, 1972.

69. *Latin American and Empire Report* (October 1973); *Latin American Perspectives* (Summer 1974); Petras and Morley, *U.S.*; *El Día*, April 17, May 8, 1975.

70. *Time*, September 30, 1974; *El Día*, January 17, 1975; Victor Marchetti and John D. Marks, *The CIA and the Cult of Intelligence* (New York, 1974), pp. 14–20.

71. *The New York Times*, September 9, 1975.

72. *Atlantic Monthly* (February 1974), pp. 14–20.

chapter
7

Continuity and Change
in United States
South American Policy

In the preceding chapters I have argued that, despite some
changes in its form, there has been a high degree of continuity in
the substance of United States policy toward South America.
What has sustained this continuity is a set of widely held assumptions about our way of life, our position in the world, our security, our relations with South America, and about the nature of
the developmental process. These assumptions are so much a part
of our thinking that we rarely, if ever, question their validity. We
frequently fail to realize, or perhaps we just ignore, the fact that
the South Americans and others do not always share our
thoughts. Our overwhelming economic and political power has enabled us in the short run to disregard what others think and still
maintain our extensive international influence. There can, however, be no effective and humane long-term United States South
American policy that does not reflect the differences in underlying
assumptions that separate us and that does not permit the South
Americans to assume full control over and responsibility for the
development of their countries. We must evaluate and modify the
assumptions that justify in most of our minds the continuation of

the dependency relationship and the external obstacles to the development of South America.

The Assumptions Underlying Policy

The great imperial powers of history—China, Rome, Spain, England—differed in many ways, but they all shared a belief in their own superiority. In the past the creation and exercise of enormous power stimulated the concomitant development of a cluster of assumptions that might well be summed up by Muhammed Ali's self-appraisal: "I am the greatest." Senator Frank Church called it the "illusion of omnipotence." Former Senator William Fulbright called it the "arrogance of power." "Power," he explained, "tends to confuse itself with virtue and a great nation is peculiarly susceptible to the idea that its power is a sign of God's favor." The arrogance of power, he concluded, is a psychological need to prove oneself bigger, better, or stronger, with force the ultimate proof of superiority.[1]

The United States has also adopted the arrogant attitudes of its imperial predecessors. Those who run the government and a vast majority of citizens view the United States as the richest, most powerful, and most democratic nation in history. They therefore assume that Americans are superior to people of other nationalities and that the American system is the best, not only for the United States, but also for the rest of the world. Nelson Rockefeller expressed this well when he proclaimed: "There is no system in all of history better than our own flexible structure of political democracy, individual initiative, and responsible citizenship in elevating the quality of man's life." [2]

We also assume that the United States must, because of destiny or fate, accept the burdens of world leadership and monitor the international situation. In nineteenth-century England it would have been called the "white man's burden." Today in the United States our leaders talk about the fate of the powerful to dominate or the responsibility of size and power to assume leadership for the good of all. Writing in 1941 Henry Luce captured the essence of the idea: "The twentieth century is the American Century. . . . America cannot be responsible for the good behavior of the entire world. But America is responsible, to herself as well as to history, for the world environment in which she lives. Nothing can so vitally affect America's environment as America's own influence upon it. . . ." Therefore, Luce continued, the United States must "determine whether a system of free economic enterprise . . . shall or shall not prevail," and it must export its technical skills, assume responsibility to feed the hungry, and be "the powerhouse from which the ideals spread throughout the world and do their mysterious work of lifting the life of mankind." [3]

The report of former President Nixon's Task Force on International Development, generally referred to as the *Peterson Report*, stated concisely a more up-to-date version of this assumption: "The United States has an abiding interest in bringing nations together to serve common needs. . . . The size and power of the United States gives us a special responsibility; if this country chooses not to play a major role, it necessarily endangers the succes of such ventures." [4]

Regarding Latin America, the assumption of world leadership means the continuation of the dependency relationship. "It is widely assumed in the United States," wrote Robert Burr in a study for the Brookings Institution, "that the nations of Latin America are an inferior species of states that belong rightfully in the sphere of influence of the United States, existing primarily for the purpose of implementing its foreign policy, contributing to its defense, and serving its economy." [5]

Not only do we assume the superiority of our system, the identification of our interests with those of the world, and our God-given role as world leader, but also that we are exceptional in the exercise of our enormous power. We feel we are not really arrogant, or at least only occasionally so. "Often we in the United States have been charged with an overweening confidence in the righteousness of our own presumptions," admitted former President Nixon, to which he added: "Occasionally we have been guilty of the charge." [6] Essentially, however, we assume we are fair-minded, generous with our wealth, and altruistic. We gave large sums to Western Europe to finance its postwar recovery and to the underdeveloped countries to help them solve their problems. In cases of natural disaster and famine we are always the first to send help. And the *Peterson Report* insisted that the United States continue this tradition; it must "keep to a steady course in foreign assistance, providing its fair share of resources to encourage those countries that show a determination to advance." [7]

Furthermore, we assume that our use of power is judicious, restrained, and beneficial to the world; we use our strength to permit others to live as they choose without external interference. As W. W. Rostow, one of Kennedy's and Johnson's top advisers, put it: "I have for long taken the power interests of the United States to be regulatory: to prevent the dominance of Europe or Asia by a single potentially hostile power; and to prevent the emplacement of a major power in the hemisphere. These objectives demonstrably accord with the interests of the majority of the people and nations of Europe, Asia, and Latin America." [8]

It follows in the minds of most United States citizens that since our system is the best and our leadership wise and beneficial, no one could voluntarily choose any other system or could rationally reject our guidance. Nevertheless, many countries are governed by different political and economic systems and do reject United States leadership. This, we assume, is the result of hostile forces prohibiting free choice. The postwar world has, against our wishes, been divided into two competing blocs: the free capitalist world and the totalitarian communist world. The communist powers, so the argument goes, have used force to prevent countries under their domination from choosing the superior American system and American leadership. To "prove" that this has been the case, American officials were, prior to the Chilean election of 1970, fond of pointing out that no country had ever "gone communist" through free elections.

In addition, according to this view, because the communists use force and deception to pursue their goals, we must protect the weak potential victims. The very security of the United States is at stake every time a country is forced to accept communism. The underdeveloped countries are viewed as a major battleground between capitalism and communism, and any talk of neutrality is therefore considered a threat to the security of the United States. Put in more colloquial terms: If you're not with us, you're against us. Burr summed up the attitude regarding Latin America: "The possible establishment of nonaligned Latin American states represents another potential danger to United States security. By definition such a state would support no particular 'side,' but would vacillate opportunistically in response to momentary individual problems as they presented themselves. Nonaligned Latin American governments . . . could not be relied upon for support but might also at any juncture adopt policies hostile to the United States; moreover, while in a phase of cooperation with the Russians or Communist Chinese, such a nonaligned state might slip beyond the point of no return." [9]

If some person, group or country questions our policies or our leadership, we are inclined to see them as naïve, misinformed, unrealistic, or duped. Thus, in response to United Nations Secretary-General Kurt Waldheim's criticism of the United States' bombing of dikes in Vietnam, former President Nixon simply noted that Waldheim was misinformed and, "like his predecessor, seized upon this enemy-inspired propaganda, which has taken in many well-intentioned and naïve people." Similarly, Nelson Rockefeller dismissed anti-United States sentiments of the church and the youth of South America because their "profound idealism" made them particularly "vulnerable to subversive penetration," [10]

There is in this assumption of our superiority and our destiny to lead the world a sense that we are above the traditional rules of international relations. This sense is symbolically demonstrated every four years at the Olympic Games. The United States alone refuses to lower its flag when it is carried past the head of state of the host nation. Ralph Rose, United States shot-putter, explained in 1908 after he carried the flag erect past King Edward VIII of England: "This flag dips to no earthly king." [11]

United States assumptions concerning the critical question of development in South America flow logically from its assumptions regarding its own superiority and beneficence. Accepting the diffusionist theory, United States policy makers believe that South America is solely to blame for its own underdevelopment and that it must remedy the situation itself. The United States does not accept responsibility for South America's lack of development or for the present low standard of living of its inhabitants.

This view is based partly on the assumption that the reason South America has not developed is because of its culture and background. South Americans, the argument goes, lack the Anglo-Saxon work ethic, Yankee know-how, and the necessary entrepreneurial skills; they are lazy, slow, falsely proud, and unwilling to work with their hands. South Americans, to sum up, lack the "will" to develop. Arthur Schlesinger quotes a now famous aphorism attributed to Johnson's assistant secretary for Inter-American Affairs, Thomas Mann, which reflects this sort of attitude: "I know my Latinos. They understand only two things—a buck in the pocket and a kick in the ass." [12]

In less pejorative and racist terms, the argument is simply that South America is not being held back by any external barriers and therefore must do it itself. The United States can help but not hinder South American development, but it can help only if the South Americans take the initiative and do the main job themselves. Schlesinger criticized the *Consensus of Viña del Mar* because he felt it concentrated on the external rather than the internal obstacles that keep Latin America from selling its goods in the markets of industrialized countries. This, he maintained, is a mistake, because "the contribution of the United States is the lesser part of the problem. Powerful as we are, we can have only a marginal impact. Latin America cannot be saved in Washington. It can only be saved in Latin America. . . . Only Latin Americans can alter the profoundly inequitable distribution of wealth and income." [13]

Our concern with security and our belief that our security and economic well-being demand a South American sphere of influence has led to the assumption that development must be orderly. Washington officials believe that political stability under United States tutelage must precede and must govern the nature of South American economic development, and that economic development must precede social and political development. "One primary purpose of our military assistance program," noted former Under Secretary for Inter-American Affairs Charles Meyer, before a Senate subcommittee, "is to help our Latin American neighbors attain social and economic development by systematic evolution rather than in the volatile atmosphere of destructive revolution." In 1967 Secretary of Defense Robert McNamara told a House committee that "the goals of the Alliance can be achieved only within a framework of law and order." And the Peterson Report noted that "development can help make political and social change more orderly." [14] For the United States, orderly development is the only acceptable form of development.

Our commitment to order is such that we are opposed to violence, even if this is the only way change can be brought about and even if this is the only way to improve the quality of life of such people as the South Americans. This means, of course, that we are opposed to revolution. As William Fulbright noted, "we seem to be narrowing our criteria of what constitute 'legitimate' and 'acceptable' social revolutions to include only those which meet the all but impossible tests of being peaceful, orderly, and voluntary. . . ." Our problem, Fulbright continued, is that we are handicapped when we are confronted by social revolution because we are an unrevolutionary society; we lack "a genuine feeling of empathy for revolutionary movements," and, despite these facts, our mythology holds that we are a revolutionary society. A perceptive Canadian dramatically made the same point in a letter to *Time*:

> In the Bicentennial activities, the U.S. will celebrate 200 years of democracy while supporting dictators round the world simply because they are capitalists. In fact, if the American Revolution were being fought in 1975, the U.S. State Department would probably recommend supporting the British forces against the "insurgents" attempting to overthrow a "constitutional and legal regime". . . .[15]

A third assumption about development besides the need for the South Americans to do it by themselves in an orderly way is that development is essentially an economic or technological matter. "Latin America must be encouraged to see . . . that a society must begin to accumulate wealth," the *Clay Report* of 1963 stated, "before it can provide an improved standard of living for its members." [16] We are to focus on economic and technological problems, the argument goes, if we are to bring about meaningful development. Social and political development will follow in due course once a country adopts the necessary kind of economic reforms and policies.

Furthermore, United States officials see economic development as completely apolitical, something detached from politics and ideology, a process that somehow takes place in a political vacuum. "If the goal is economic development," the *Peterson Report* explained, "the issue is one of efficiency, not ideology." At the same time, we believe that economic development occurs best within a politico-economic system of free enterprise and capitalism, an obvious contradiction to the previous point. The *Peterson Report* noted that "rapid economic progress usually has taken place within a favorable environment for private initiative. . . ." Or, as

Nelson Rockefeller lamented, a major barrier to development "is the failure of governments throughout the hemisphere to recognize fully the importance of private investment." [17]

The United States assumes development is an economic matter somehow separated from politics and ideology and yet to be successful it must be brought about within a free enterprise system. The focus is on economic efficiency with the assumption that in the long run growth will lead to equality and will work to the best advantage of all the people involved. It is an international version of the "trickle down theory": help big business, create a good investment climate, and the economy will expand and provide jobs for the workers who will in turn be able to buy what they want and enjoy a high standard of living.

The United States sees development in terms of the diffusionist theory.

The South American Reaction

By and large, the South Americans reject these assumptions. In the preamble to the *Consensus of Viña del Mar,* the Latin American representatives made it clear that they are pro-Latin America and that being pro-Latin America is not necessarily the same as being pro-United States. The ideas in the document, they explained, "which are not intended to be either negative or hostile, are the logical outcome of the historical process in the course of which the Latin American countries have reaffirmed their own values and become aware of their common interests [vis-à-vis the United States]." [18]

The exiled Brazilian economist Celso Furtado explained the point in slightly different terms. "If the primary concern of the United States in the second half of the twentieth century," he wrote, "is that of its 'security'—that is, of the kind of worldwide organization that will prevail as the result of the technological revolution already under way—the Latin American point of view is different. While Americans desire that the new organizations be compatible with the preservation of the American way of life at home and with the defense of ever-increasing American economic interests abroad, the Latin Americans are faced with the crucial problem of 'development,' or how to open a means of access to the fruits of the technological revolution." [19]

This focus on the Latin American way is fundamental to understanding the difference in assumptions between the United States and South America. "Latin America must find self-expression in the creation of a formula that will reflect its own identity," former Chilean President Eduardo Frei suggested, "and reject foreign transplants or run the risk of falling under 'thought-colonialism' which, in the long run, can only lead to political dependency." Instead of attacking the United States or accepting United States assumptions and policy, the South Americans have been arguing for the right to be different from the United States or anyone else. "We must repeat a thousand and one times," former Venezuelan President Rafael Caldera patiently explained to the United States Congress, "that being different implies neither being better nor worse. We Latin Americans have our own way of life and we have no wish to adopt in a servile manner a way of life which is current elsewhere." [20]

Furthermore, the South Americans reject the idea that no one could voluntarily choose any other system than that of the United States, or that neutrality or nonalignment is tantamount to joining the communist bloc. For most of South America (Brazil, Bolivia, and Chile are currently exceptions) the world cannot simply be divided into two camps. They seek an identity separate from that of the big power worlds of capitalism and communism. Like all Third World countries, the South Americans are acutely aware of the difference between their standard of living and that of the United States, Western Europe, Russia, and Eastern Europe. They want to catch up. They are afraid of big power chauvinism and domination whether from the United States, Russia, or China. But the United States, not the Soviet Union or China, is the dominant big power in the region, and therefore much of their effort is directed against the influence of the United States. Clearly, the South Americans want the technology of the developed world but not necessarily its ideologies. The United States is not a model for the Third World because, as Irving Louis Horowitz pointed out, it developed without a plan, its distribution of income is very uneven, its society is under monopolistic and oligopolistic control, and its cultural pluralism seems to deny national separatism.[21]

Also, most South Americans would question the assumption of United States beneficence. They are obviously aware that the flow of capital from the United States to South America has been considerable during the past two decades. The important questions for them, however, are: Who has benefited from this money and what has been the net flow of capital into their area? Many argue that United States special interests and the tiny South American elites have been the major beneficiaries of aid, and that the United States takes more out of South America than it puts into it. In a recent study for the Inter-American Development Bank, Raul Prebisch demonstrated that over the past two decades the net flow of foreign capital to Latin America has generally been negative.[22]

South Americans agree with the United States view that they themselves must develop their countries, but most disagree sharply with the United States on the matter of external barriers to development. The *Consensus of Viña del Mar* stated that the Latin American countries are "determined to overcome underdevelopment, [and] they reiterate their conviction that economic growth and social progress are the responsibility of their people and that the attainment of national and regional goals depends fundamentally on each country's own effort. . . ." However, it lamented the fact that many changes proposed at the various inter-American meetings over the past decade (1960s) were not passed, since they were based on "the need for a fairer international division of labor that will favor the rapid economic and social development of the developing countries, instead of impeding it, as has been the case hitherto. Now, towards the end of the present decade, the economic and scientific-technological gap between the developing and the developed countries has widened and is continuing to do so, and the external obstacles impeding the rapid economic growth of the Latin American countries not only have not been removed, but are tending to increase." [23]

Few in the area would accept the assumption that the South American character has been an important cause of underdevelopment. Alfonso López Michelsen, the former Colombian minister of foreign affairs, dealt forcefully with the issue at the Viña del Mar conference:

The day is now over when patriarchal societies could treat unemployment in the same way as laziness. . . . The same thing is happening in this century with international relations. We are not poor or backward because of innate incapacity, racial inferiority or our own fault. There is now full and powerful awareness that our efforts at this point in time come up against a world order which continually brings them to nothing. . . . We are hemmed in a structural phenomenon which turns the factors, which in other centuries and in other regions were the spring of development and the prime movers of progress, when they are transferred to our environment, into bonds of our economic serfdom.[24]

Not all South Americans agree that external obstacles are important. The conservative Brazilian economist Roberto Campos viewed the *Consensus of Viña del Mar,* "with its determination to blame 'external factors' for Latin American backwardness, as an exercise in the economics of self-pity." The young MIT-educated Argentine businessman Tomás Fillol blamed the "passive need dependency" of the Argentine character for that country's lack of development.[25] Yet a large and growing number of South Americans, though they accept the idea that they themselves must develop the area, believe that the United States continues to place serious external obstacles in the path leading to their development. They see United States-South American relations in terms of dependency.

Furthermore, most South Americans reject the United States assumptions that development must always be orderly and that it is essentially an economic matter. If we interpret the question of orderly development to mean opposition to violence, then a considerable number of South Americans would support the United States position. Yet this does not mean the rejection of development if at times violence or disorder occur. Many South Americans feel that development is an inherently disruptive process and that if the goals are to be reached, a certain level of disorder must be tolerated.

And finally, most South American officials would reject the notion that development is essentially an economic matter. For them there are fundamental social and political questions that have to be resolved if economic development is to be sustained. The history of the area suggests that fundamental and successful economic reform follows rather than precedes social and political change, as in the cases of Mexico, Bolivia, and Cuba. Celso Furtado explained that economic development under current conditions in Latin America cannot be achieved without cooperation and participation by large parts of the population. "It is for this reason," he argued, "that the most difficult tasks are political rather than technical. . . . All genuine development policies derive their power from an amalgamation of value judgments upon which the ideals of a community are concentrated. And, if a community does not have political organs capable of interpreting the legitimate aspirations of the community, it is not equipped to undertake the tasks of development." [26]

The Possibility of Change

Given the nature of United States society, its still considerable economic and political power, and the assumptions underlying its foreign policy, there seems to be little chance of a fundamental change in United States-South American relations. Yet I believe the reasons for change so compelling that I must, at least briefly, consider how it might come about.

The preceding chapters suggest that United States policy has done the South American countries little if any good in solving their critical social and economic problems, and in many cases has distorted and retarded efforts to overcome them. Most South Americans continue to live in poverty despite repeated statements by the United States that the ultimate goal of all of its foreign programs in recent years has been to improve the quality of life of the inhabitants of that area. In absolute terms there has been some improvement in the situation. In relative terms there has been a steady decline. The United States has assumed that it knows what is best for South America and has argued that the South Americans must just be patient. United States policy, based on the diffusionist theory of development, has served only to reinforce the tiny elite that controls most South American societies and appropriates the "lion's share" of any growth for itself. The continuation of present policy means that the large majority of South Americans will at best have to endure generations of poverty before their circumstances change appreciably. At worst it means they can expect to live in perpetual poverty. It does not seem just nor in our long-run self-interest that the more prosperous North Americans expect Latins who live in poverty to wait patiently for future betterment, particularly when such projected improvement will never permit them to live as well as we do.

United States policy has not only held back South America and apparently condemned its inhabitants to a perpetually inferior standard of living, but it has also done harm to our way of life in the United States. Our verbal commitments to global democracy, human decency and well-being, and respect for the sovereignty of all states have been seriously compromised by our support for military dictatorships, our involvement in Latin domestic politics, and our use of economic and political pressure in the South American countries. The application to foreign policy of ideas and techniques incompatible with what we hold to be our way of life can only lead to a deterioration of such a way of life.

If the chances are not good, there are nevertheless some forces at work that might lead to significant changes in United States South American policy. The near monpoly of world economic and military power that the United States enjoyed for a decade or so after World War II has been seriously eroded. Our percentage of world GNP has steadily declined and our military superiority over the Russians and others has disappeared. In the evolving world situation we will need to rely on the voluntary support of free, independent, and prosperous countries to defend our economic and security interests. If the countries of South America are helped to achieve genuine and rapid development, it is more likely that they would become an important positive force for world stability, prosperity, and security.

Perhaps the changing position of the United States in the world will force us to examine and modify some of our traditional assumptions about South America. We must come to recognize and accept the fact that not all or perhaps any of our ideas and values are relevant to South America today, and that the Latins, not we, know what is best for them. We will have to listen to them, and when we do we will hear that, from their point of view, private investment is not aid, governments can take the leading role in development, immediate improvements in the standard of living of the average citizen may be necessary before economic growth can take place, and that a foreign government cannot interfere in investment disputes between private corporations and sovereign governments. In sum, we will have to recognize that our long-term economic and security interests will best be served by letting the Latins "do their own thing," however distasteful it may seem to us in the short run.

One of the most serious difficulties we face, if we wish to modify some of our traditional assumptions, is that we do not know or understand South America. Our societies and our histories are so different that we simply cannot interpret the actions and attitudes of our southern neighbors as they see them. David Halberstam has effectively portrayed the problem in his book *The Best and the Brightest*; our educational system has not prepared us to understand the reality of the Third World. Hubert Humphrey struck at the heart of the matter when commenting on the "loss" of Vietnam: "What we've learned is that there aren't American answers for every problem in the world. We made judgments about that part of the world based on our experience in Europe. We were a world power with a half-world knowledge." [27] The same is true with regard to South America.

There is, nevertheless, at least one area of verbal agreement that might provide the basis for the reconstruction of United States South American policy. Both parties insist that the responsibility for development lies with the South Americans. Thus why not attempt to build a new policy around the idea that the United States will in fact do everything possible to permit the South Americans to assume full responsibility for their development. If the United States would discard its assumption that it knows what is best for South America and would relinquish its economic and political control over the area, such a policy would practically be a reality.

Specifically, the United States would have to end military aid to the area and withdraw its military missions. It would also have to stay completely out of investment disputes between United States corporations and South American governments, accepting the fact that such disputes are private matters between the parties directly involved. In addition, it would have to terminate bilateral aid and instead contribute increased amounts of development funds to the Inter-American Development Bank and to the fledgling Latin American Economic System. It would have to stimulate trade by actually providing tariff preference for the products of South America and by accepting, at the same time, temporary tariffs to protect South American industry. It would have to increase financial stability by accepting commodity agreements on primary products. And it would have to make more readily available its technology by reducing the length of patent rights and by freely contributing to an Inter-American Technology Bank.

Such a policy would involve some short-term sacrifice on the part of the United States, and many special interest groups would strongly oppose it. Yet the United States would gain a great deal in the long run. It would benefit enormously from the establishment of independent, representative, and genuinely stable governments in South America. Its trade with prosperous neighbors would increase. It would avoid costly, time-consuming, and generally counterproductive involvements in internal disputes in the area. And it would take a major step toward reconciling the debilitating discrepancy between the standards of conduct in foreign and domestic policy.

Many of the ideas that comprise the basis of the above-mentioned policy have been suggested before. In the *Rockefeller Report* and in Nixon's "Action for Progress for the Americas" speech there are numerous references to the need for tariff preference, Latin American initiative, and the improvement of the quality of life. Former United States Ambassador to the OAS Sol Linowitz recommended the termination of military aid and of United States involvement in the internal affairs of the Latin American countries in his October 1974 report, "The Americas in a Changing World." And Henry Kissinger, in his September 1, 1975, address to the United Nations, promised tariff preference, respect for diverse political regimes, trade and commodity agreements, and special funds for the development of the Third World.[28] Nothing, however, has come of most of these suggestions. The United States has always stopped short of fundamental change because it will not relinquish its control over Latin America. It simply does not trust the South Americans enough to let them "do their own thing." Thus, all of the reform proposals reject the idea that the United States must relinquish its control over South America and must rely instead on example and the convergence of interests between the two areas as the South Americans develop and catch up.

Inevitably, these suggestions will be dismissed by many as "naïve," "idealistic," and "well-intentioned but misguided," yet the continuation of present policy will do no good for South America or for the United States. One thing remains certain. Most South Americans continue to live in poverty, and the prospects for meaningful change are minimal. Perhaps the most "naïve" position is to assume that they will wait patiently for a distant and illusory future.

NOTES

1. J. William Fulbright, *The Arrogance of Power* (New York, 1966), p. 3.

2. *Rockefeller Report*, p. 39.

3. Quoted in Green, *Containment*, pp. 113–114.

4. United States, Task Force on International Development, *United States Foreign Assistance in the 1970's: A New Approach* (Washington, D.C., 1970), p. 7. Hereafter cited as *Peterson Report*.

5. Robert N. Burr, *Our Troubled Hemisphere* (Washington, D.C., 1967), p. 48.

6. Gray, *Latin America*, p. 263.

7. *Peterson Report*, p. 2.

8. *The New York Times*, June 22, 1971.

9. Burr, *Hemisphere*, p. 43.

10. *The New York Times*, July 28, 1972; *Rockefeller Report*, p. 31.

11. *Sports Illustrated*, September 4, 1972.

12. Arthur Schlesinger, Jr., "The Lowering Hemisphere," *Atlantic Monthly* (January 1970), p. 81.

13. *Ibid.*, p. 82.

14. Gray, *Latin America*, p. 264; *Peterson Report*, p. 2.

15. Fulbright, *Arrogance*, pp. 72, 76–77; *Time*, June 9, 1975.

16. Quoted in Petras and LaPorte, *Cultivating*, p. 389.

17. *Peterson Report*, p. 18; *Rockefeller Report*, p. 89.

18. *Consensus*, p. 4.

19. Furtado, *Obstacles*, p. 19.

20. Eduardo Frei Montalva, "The Second Latin American Revolution," *Foreign Affairs* (October 1971), p. 92; United States, *Congressional Record* (June 3, 1970), p. 18133.

21. Irving Louis Horowitz, *Three Worlds of Development* (New York, 1972), pp. 8–9.

22. Pearson, *Partners;* Prebisch, *Change;* ECLA, *Survey 1969*, p. 3; *The New York Times*, August 20, 1973. See also Donella H. Meadows, et al., *The Limits of Growth* (New York, 1972), pp. 48–49.

23. *Consensus*, pp. 4–6.

24. *Ibid.*, pp. 33–34.

25. Quoted in Schlesinger, "Hemisphere," p. 82; Tomás Fillol, *Social Factors and Economic Development* (Cambridge, Mass., 1961).

26. Furtado, *Obstacles*, p. 24.

27. David Halberstam, *The Best and the Brightest* (Greenwich, Conn., 1972; *Time*, May 12, 1975.

28. *Rockefeller Report;* Gray, *Latin America,* pp. 262–269; *The New York Times,* October 30, 1974, September 2 and 18, 1975. Levinson and Onis make similar proposals in their book *Alliance.*

bibliography

There is an abundance of material on the United States and the development of South America, but there is still no adequate general survey of the subject. The existing surveys, such as the Gil and Mecham books listed below, provide detailed information about the formal relations among the countries of the hemisphere, but they tell us little about the problems of poverty and development. More satisfactory in this latter respect are the works by Cardoso and Faletto, Furtado, Goulet and Hudson, Levinson and Onis, and Halper and Sterling. Anyone really interested in the subject must of necessity go back to the original sources.

The following bibliography is selective. It includes only the items that I found most useful. Many such items are written in Spanish and Portuguese which, unfortunately, will restrict their value for many readers. They are included, nevertheless, because only in such works does one find some of the important South American points of view. I have in every case cited the English translation if one exists. Especially useful sources for me have been the frequently ignored *Hearings* of the Senate and House Committees on Foreign Relations, the annual *Economic Survey of Latin America* of the United Nations Economic Commission for Latin America, the Organization of American States study *Social and Economic Development of Latin America,* and the Mexican newspaper *El Día.*

OFFICIAL PUBLICATIONS

Brazil, Embassy in Washington. *Brazil Today.* Washington, 1973–.

Chile. *Documentos Secretos de la ITT.* Santiago, 1972.

Chile. *The Latin American Consensus of Viña del Mar.* Santiago, 1969.

Organization of American States. *External Financing for Latin American Development.* Baltimore, 1971.

Organization of American States. *Social and Economic Development of Latin America.* Washington, 1973.

United Nations. *Yearbook of International Trade Statistics, 1970–1971.* New York, 1973.

United Nations, Economic Commission for Latin America. *The Economic Development of Latin America in the Post War Period.* New York, 1964.

United Nations, Economic Commission for Latin America. *External Financing in Latin America.* New York, 1965.

United Nations, Economic Commission for Latin America. *Economic Survey of Latin America: 1969, 1970, 1972.* New York, 1971, 1972, 1974.

United States, Agency for International Development. *Latin America, Economic Growth Trends.* Washington, 1971.

United States, Agency for International Development. *U.S. Overseas Loans and Grants: 1961, 1971, 1972, 1973, 1974.* Washington, 1962, 1972, 1973, 1974, 1975.

United States, Arms Control and Disarmament Agency. *World Military Expenditures and Arms Trade, 1963–1973.* Washington, 1975.

United States, Department of Commerce, Bureau of Census. *Statistical Abstract of the United States.* Washington. Various years.

United States, Department of State, Ninth International Conference of American States, Bogotá, Colombia, March 30–May 2, 1948. *Report of the Delegation of the United States of America.* Washington, 1948.

United States, Department of State, Tenth Inter-American Conference, Caracas, Venezuela, March 1–28, 1954. *Report of the Delegation of the United States of America.* Washington, 1954.

United States, Department of State. *Report of the Delegation of the United States of America to the Inter-American Conference on Problems of War and Peace, Mexico City, February 21–March 8, 1945.* Washington, 1946.

United States, Department of State. *Foreign Relations of the United States: 1894, 1944, 1945, 1946, 1947, 1948.* Washington.

United States, Department of State. *Bulletin.* November 23, 1953. Milton S. Eisenhower. "United States-Latin American Relations, Report to the President."

United States, Department of State. *Report of the Joint Brazilian-United States Technical Commission, Rio de Janeiro, February 7, 1949.* Washington, 1949.

United States, Department of State, Bureau of Public Affairs. *Arms Sales to Latin America.* Washington, 1973.

United States, Department of State, Bureau of Public Affairs. *Secretary Kissinger Proposes New Program for the Americas.* Washington, 1974.

United States, Department of State, Bureau of Public Affairs. *The United States and Latin America: The New Opportunity.* Washington, 1975.

United States, House Committee on Foreign Affairs. *Hearings on The Mutual Security Program, July 25, 1951.* Washington, 1951.

United States, House Committee on Foreign Affairs. *Hearings on New Directions for the 1970's: Toward a Strategy of Inter-American Development, February 25–May 8, 1969.* Washington, 1969.

United States, Office of the President. *International Economic Report of the President.* Washington, 1975.

United States, Senate Committee on Foreign Relations. *Hearings on the Act for International Development, March 30, 1950.* Washington, 1950.

United States, Senate Committee on Foreign Relations. *Hearings on the Ameircan Institute for Free Labor Development, August 1, 1969.* Washington, 1969.

United States, Senate Committee on Foreign Relations. *Background Information Relating to the Dominican Republic.* Washington, 1965.

United States, Senate Committee on Foreign Relations. *Survey of the Alliance for Progress.* Washington, 1968.

United States, Senate Committee on Foreign Relations. *Hearings on United States Policies and Programs in Brazil, May 4–11, 1971.* Washington, 1971.

United States, Senate Committee on Foreign Relations. *U.S. Foreign Aid in Action: A Case Study.* Washington, 1966.

United States, Senate Committee on Foreign Relations. *Hearings on the International Telephone and Telegraph Company and Chile, 1970–1971, March 20–April 2, 1973.* Washington, 1973.

United States, Senate Committee on Foreign Relations. *The International Telephone and Telegraph Company and Chile, 1970–1971.* Washington, 1973.

United States, Task Force on International Development. *United States Foreign Assistance in the 1970's: A New Approach.* Washington, 1970.

United States, Task Force on Immediate Latin American Problems. "Report to the President-Elect, January 4, 1961."

BOOKS AND REPORTS

Alexander, Robert J. *The Bolivian National Revolution.* New Brunswick, N.J., 1958.

American Committee for Information on Brazil. *Terror in Brazil, A Dossier.* New York, 1970.

Ampuero D., Raul. *La izquierda en punto muerto.* Santiago, 1969.

Arévalo, Juan José. *The Shark and the Sardines.* New York, 1961.

Aron, Raymond. *The Imperial Republic, The United States and the World, 1945–1973.* Englewood Cliffs, N.J., 1974.

Arraes, Miguel. *Brazil: The People and the Power.* London, 1972.

Astiz, Carlos Alberto (ed.). *Latin American International Politics.* Notre Dame, Ind., 1969.

Baer, Werner. *Industrialization and Economic Development in Brazil.* Homewood, Ill., 1965.

Baily, Samuel L. *Labor, Nationalism, and Politics in Argentina.* New Brunswick, N.J., 1967.

——— (ed.). *Nationalism in Latin America.* New York, 1971.

Barber, Willard F., and C. Neale Ronning. *Internal Security and Military Power.* Columbus, Ohio, 1966.

Barnet, Richard J. *Intervention and Revolution.* New York, 1968.

———. *The Roots of War.* New York, 1972.

Bemis, Samuel Flagg. *The Latin American Policy of the United States.* New York, 1943.

Berger, Peter, and Brigitte and Hansfried Kellner. *The Homeless Mind.* New York, 1973.

Berle, Adolf A. *Latin America, Diplomacy and Reality.* New York, 1962.

Black, C. E. *The Dynamics of Modernization.* New York, 1966.

Bonilla, Frank, and R. Girling (eds.). *Structures of Dependency.* Palo Alto, Calif., 1973.

Branco, Manoel Thomaz Castello. *O Brasil na II Grande Guerra.* Rio de Janeiro, 1960.

Brill, William H. *Military Intervention in Bolivia.* Washington, 1967.

Burns, E. Bradford. *Nationalism in Brazil.* New York, 1968.

Burr, Robert N. *Our Troubled Hemisphere.* Washington, 1967.

Campbell, Thomas M. *Masquerade Peace, America's U.N. Policy, 1944–1945.* Tallasassee, Fla., 1973.

Cardoso, F. H., and E. Faletto. *Dependencia y desarrollo en América Latina.* Mexico, 1969.

Castillo Velasco, J. *Las fuentes de la democracia cristiana.* Santiago, 1963.

Chicago Commission of Inquiry into the Status of Human Rights in Chile. *Report.* Chicago, 1974.

Chilcote, R. H., and J. C. Edelstein. *Latin America: The Struggle with Dependency and Beyond.* New York, 1974.

Chile: A critical Survey. Santiago, 1972.

Cockcroft, James D., A. G. Frank, and D. L. Johnson. *Dependence and Underdevelopment.* New York, 1972.

Connell-Smith, Gordon. *The United States and Latin America: An Historical Analysis of Inter-American Relations.* New York: 1974.

Cooke, Morris Llewellyn. *Brazil on the March, A Study in International Cooperation.* New York, 1944.

Council for Latin America. *The Effects of U.S. and other Foreign Invest-

ment in Latin America. New York, 1970.

Debray, Regis. *The Chilean Revolution.* New York, 1971.

Dines, Alberto, et al. *Os idos de março e a queda em abril.* Rio de Janeiro, 1964.

Di Tella, Guido, and Manuel Zymelman. *Las etapas de desarrollo económico argentino.* Buenos Aires, 1967.

Dozer, D. M. *Are We Good Neighbors.* Gainesville, Fla., 1959.

Duggan, Laurence. *The Americas.* New York, 1949.

Dulles, John W. F. *Unrest in Brazil.* Austin, Texas, 1970.

Eisenhower, Dwight D. *Mandate for Change.* New York, 1965.

Eisenhower, Milton S. *The Wine Is Bitter.* New York, 1963.

Fann, K. T., and D. C. Hodges (eds.). *Readings in United States Imperialism.* Boston, 1971.

Feinberg, Richard E. *The Triumph of Allende.* New York, 1972.

Fillol, Tomás Roberto. *Social Factors in Economic Development, The Argentine Case.* Cambridge, Mass., 1961.

Frank, A. G. *Latin America: Underdevelopment or Revolution.* New York, 1969.

Freire, Paulo. *Pedagogy of the Oppressed.* New York, 1974.

Freyre, Gilberto. *New World in the Tropics.* New York, 1971.

Fuenzalida, Fernando, et al. *Peru hoy.* Mexico, 1971.

Fulbright, J. William. *The Arrogance of Power.* New York, 1966.

Furtado, Celso. *Obstacles to Development in Latin America.* New York, 1970.

Gallardo Lozada, Jorge. *De Torres a Banzer.* Buenos Aires, 1972.

Gantenbein, James W. *The Evolution of Our Latin American Policy.* New York, 1950.

Gardner, Lloyd C. *Architects of Illusion.* Chicago, 1970.

———. *Economic Aspects of New Deal Diplomacy.* Madison, Wis., 1964.

Garrido, Guillermo Toriello. *La batalla de Guatemala.* Mexico, 1955.

Gil, Federico G. *Latin American-United States Relations.* New York, 1971.

———. *The Political System of Chile.* Boston, 1966.

Goulet, Denis, and Michael Hudson. *The Myth of Aid.* New York, 1971.

Gray, Richard B. (ed.). *Latin America and the United States in the 1970's.* Itasca, Ill., 1971.

Green, David. *The Containment of Latin America.* Chicago, 1971.

Halberstam, David. *The Best and the Brightest.* New York, 1972.

Halper, Stefan A., and J. R. Sterling. *Latin America, The Dynamics of Social Change.* New York, 1972.

Halperin, Ernst. *Nationalism and Communism in Chile.* Cambridge, Mass., 1965.

Hayter, Teresa. *Aid as Imperialism.* London, 1971.

Hirschman, Albert O. *A Bias For Hope.* New Haven, 1971.

Horowitz, Irving Louis. *Three Worlds of Development.* New York, 1972.

Hull, Cordell. *The Memoirs of Cordell Hull.* London, 1948. 2 volumes.

Huneeus, Pablo, et al. *Chile: el costo social de la dependencia ideológica.* Santiago, 1973.

Ianni, Octavio. *O colapso do populismo no Brasil.* Rio de Janeiro, 1968.

————, et al. *Política e revolução social no Brasil*. Rio de Janeiro, 1965.

Jagan, Cheddi. *Forbidden Freedom*. New York, 1954.

————. *The West on Trial*. London, 1966.

Johnson, Dale L. *The Chilean Road to Socialism*. New York, 1973.

Kaufman, Robert R. *The Politics of Land Reform in Chile, 1950–1970*. Cambridge, Mass., 1972.

Kinsbruner, Jay. *Chile, A Historical Interpretation*. New York, 1973.

Kolko, Gabriel. *The Roots of American Foreign Policy*. Boston, 1969.

Kolko, Gabriel and Joyce. *The Limits of Power*. New York, 1972.

LaFeber, Walter. *America, Russia and the Cold War, 1945–1971*. New York, 1972.

————. *The New Empire; An Interpretation of American Expansion, 1860–1890*. Ithaca, N.Y., 1963.

Lambert, Jacques. *Latin America, Social Structures and Political Institutions*. Berkeley, Calif., 1967.

Latin American Center, University of California at Los Angeles. *Latin American Political Statistics*. Los Angeles, 1972.

————. *Statistical Abstract of Latin America, 1971*. Los Angeles, 1973.

Levinson, Jerome, and Juan de Onis. *The Alliance That Lost Its Way*. Chicago, 1970.

Lewis, Gordon K. *Puerto Rico*. New York, 1968.

Loftus, Joseph E. *Latin American Defense Expenditures, 1938–1965*. Santa Monica, Calif., n.d.

Lowenthal, Abraham F. *The Dominican Intervention*. Cambridge, Mass., 1972.

Magdoff, Harry. *The Age of Imperialism*. New York, 1969.

Maldonado-Denis, Manuel. *Puerto Rico*. New York, 1972.

Malloy, James M. *Bolivia: The Uncomplete Revolution*. Pittsburgh, Pa., 1970.

Marchetti, Victor, and John D. Marks. *The CIA and the Cult of Intelligence*. New York, 1974.

May, Ernest. *American Imperialism*. New York, 1968.

————. *Imperial Democracy*. New York, 1961.

McCann, Frank D., Jr. *The Brazilian-American Alliance, 1937–1945*. Princeton, N.J., 1973.

McNamara, Robert S. *The Essence of Security*. New York, 1968.

Mecham, J. Lloyd. *A Survey of United States-Latin American Relations*. Boston, 1965.

Millington, Herbert. *American Diplomacy and the War of the Pacific*. New York, 1948.

Mitchell, Brian R., and H. G. Jones. *Second Abstract of British Historical Statistics*. Cambridge, England, 1971.

Moraes, Marechal Mascarenhas de. *A F.E.B. pelo seu comandante*. São Paulo, 1947.

Morris, David J. *We Must Make Haste—Slowly*. New York, 1973.

Morrison, Delesseps S. *Latin American Mission*. New York, 1965.

Munro, Dana G. *Intervention and Dollar Diplomacy in the Caribbean, 1900–1921*. Princeton, N.J., 1964.

Needler, Martin C. *The United States and the Latin American Revolution.* Boston, 1972.

Nisbet, C. T. (ed.). *Latin America, Problems in Economic Development* New York, 1969.

North American Congress on Latin America. *New Chile.* New York, 1972.

Parkinson, F. *Latin America, The Cold War, and The World Powers, 1945–1973.* Beverly Hills, Calif., 1974.

Pearson, Lester B. *Partners in Development.* New York, 1969.

Petras, James. *Politics and Social Forces in Chilean Development.* Berkeley, Calif., 1969.

———— and Robert LaPorte, Jr. *Cultivating Revolution.* New York, 1971.

———— and Morris Morley. *The United States and Chile.* New York, 1975.

———— and M. Zeitlan (eds.). *Latin America, Reform or Revolution.* Greenwich, Conn., 1968.

Pike, Fredrick B. *Chile and the United States, 1880–1962.* Notre Dame, Ind., 1963.

Potash, Robert H. *The Army and Politics in Argentina, 1928–1945.* Palo Alto, Calif., 1969.

Prado, Eduardo. *A ilusão americana.* São Paulo, 1961.

Prebisch, Raul. *Change and Development—Latin America's Great Task.* New York, 1971.

Quijano, Anibal. *Nationalism and Capitalism in Peru.* New York, 1972.

Radosh, Ronald. *American Labor and United States Foreign Policy.* New York, 1969.

Rios, Enrique Correa. *El primer año del gobierno popular.* Santiago, 1972.

————. *El segundo año del gobierno popular.* Santiago, 1972.

The Rockefeller Report on the Americas. Chicago, 1969.

Rodrígues, José Honorio. *Brazil and Africa.* Berkeley, Calif., 1965.

————. *The Brazilians.* Austin, Texas, 1967.

Roeder, Ralph. *Juárez and His Mexico.* New York, 1968.

Romualdi, Serafino. *Presidents and Peons.* New York, 1967.

Rostow, W. W. *The Stages of Economic Growth.* London, 1960.

Schlesinger, Arthur M., Jr. *A Thousand Days.* Boston, 1965.

Schneider, Ronald M. *Communism in Guatemala, 1944–1955.* New York, 1959.

————. *The Political System of Brazil.* New York, 1971.

Skidmore, Thomas E. *Politics in Brazil, 1930–1964.* New York, 1967.

Spanier, John W. *American Foreign Policy Since World War II.* New York, 1968.

Stacchini, José. *Março 64: mobilização da audacia.* São Paulo, 1965.

Stein, Stanley J. and Barbara. *The Colonial Heritage of Latin America.* New York, 1970.

Stepan, Alfred. *The Military in Politics.* Princeton, N.J., 1971.

———— (ed.). *Authoritarian Brazil.* New Haven, Conn., 1973.

Storrs, Keith Larry. "Brazil's Independent Foreign Policy, 1961–1964." Unpublished doctoral dissertation. Ithaca, N.Y., 1973.

Szulc, Tad. *Dominican Diary.* New York, 1965.

Ugarte, Manuel. *El porvenir de América Latina*. Buenos Aires, 1953.

Veliz Claudio (ed.). *Obstacles to Change in Latin America*. New York, 1969.

Whitaker, Arthur P. *The United States and the Independence of Latin America, 1800–1830*. New York, 1964.

———— and David C. Jordan. *Nationalism in Contemporary Latin America*. New York, 1966.

Wilkie, James W. *The Bolivian Revolution and U.S. Aid since 1952*. Los Angeles, 1969.

Williams, William A. *The Contours of American History*. Chicago, 1966.

————. *The Tragedy of American Diplomacy*. New York, 1962.

Winkler, Max. *Investments of U.S. Capital in Latin America*. Boston, 1929.

Wirth, John. *The Politics of Brazilian Development, 1930–1954*, Palo Alto, Calif., 1970.

Wise, David, and Thomas B. Ross. *The Invisible Government*. New York, 1964.

Wolpin, Miles D. *Cuban Foreign Policy and Chilean Politics*. Lexington, Mass., 1972.

Wood, Bryce. *The Making of the Good Neighbor Policy*. New York, 1961.

ARTICLES

Ayres, Paulo. "The Brazilian Revolution." Lecture at the Center for Strategic Studies, Georgetown University, Washington, D.C., July 1964. Mimeograph copy.

Bodenheimer, Susanne. "Dependency and Imperialism: The Roots of Latin American Underdevelopment." In K. T. Fann and D. C. Hodges (eds.), *Readings in United States Imperialism*. Boston, 1971.

Chalmers, Douglas A. "Developing on the Periphery: External Factors in Latin American Politics." In James N. Rosenau (ed.), *Linkage Politics, Essays on the Convergence of National and International Systems*. New York, 1969.

Dos Santos, T. "The Structure of Dependency." *American Economic Review*. May 1970.

Fernandes, Florestán. "Patrones de dominación externa en América Latina." *Revista Mexicana de Sociología*. November 1970.

Frank, A. G. "Dependence Is Dead, Long Live Dependence and the Class Struggle: A Reply to Critics." *Latin American Perspectives*. Spring 1974.

Frei Montalva, Eduardo. "The Second Latin American Revolution." *Foreign Affairs*. October 1971.

Kaufman, Robert, Harry I. Chernotsky, and Daniel S. Geller. "A Preliminary Test of the Theory of Dependency." *Comparative Politics*. April 1975.

Kenworthy, Eldon. "Argentina: The Politics of Late Industrialization." *Foreign Affairs*. April 1967.

Lowenthal, Abraham F. "United States Policy Toward Latin America: 'Liberal,' 'Radical,' and 'Bureaucratic' Perspectives." *Latin American Research Review*. Fall 1973.

Mayer, Robert. "The Origins of the American Banking Empire in Latin America." *Journal of Inter-American Studies*. February 1973.

Michaels, Albert L. "The United States, The Alliance for Progress and the Revolution in Liberty, 1964–1970." *Journal of Inter-American Studies*. August 1974.

Nef, Jorge. "The Politics of Repression." *Latin American Perspectives*. Summer 1974.

Peregrino, Umberto. "O pensamiento da Escola Superior de Guerra." *Cadernos Brasileiros*. November 1966.

Pike, Fredrick B., and Donald W. Bray. "A Vista of Catastrophe: the Future of United States-Chilean Relations." *Review of Politics*. July 1960.

Ray, David. "The Dependency Model of Latin American Underdevelopment: Three Basic Fallacies." *Journal of Inter-American Studies*. February 1973.

Rowe, James W. "Revolution or Counter-revolution in Brazil." *American Universities Field Staff: Reports Service*. 1965.

Scarone, Hugo. "Latinoamérica se arma." *Excelsior*. November 4–9, 1974.

Schlesinger, Arthur, Jr. "The Lowering Hemisphere." *Atlantic Monthly*. January 1970.

Siekman, Philip. "When Executives Turned Revolutionaries." *Fortune*. September 1964.

Sigmund, Paul E. "The 'Invisible Blockade' and the Overthrow of Allende." *Foreign Affairs*. January 1974.

Soares, Glaucio Ary Dillon. "The New Industrialization and the Brazilian Political System." In James Petras and M. Zeitlan, *Latin America, Reform or Revolution*. Greenwich, Conn., 1968.

Stavenhagen, Rodolfo. "The Future of Latin America." *Latin American Perspectives*. Spring 1974.

Sunkel, Osvaldo. "The Structural Background of Development Problems in Latin America." In C. T. Nisbet (ed.), *Latin America, Problems in Economic Development*. New York, 1969.

Wallis, Victor. "Imperialism and the 'Via Chilena.'" *Latin American Perspectives*. Summer 1974.

PERIODICALS

Correio da Manha (Brazil). 1963–1964 *passim*.

Christian Science Monitor (Boston). 1970–1975 *passim*.

El Día (Mexico). 1970–1975 *passim*.

Excelsior (Mexico). 1970–1975 *passim*.

Jornal do Brasil (Brazil). 1963–1964 *passim*.

Journal of Commerce (New York). 1970–1975 *passim*.

La Opinión (Argentina). 1973–1974.
Latin America and Empire Report (formerly *NACLA Newsletter*). 1970–1975.
Latin American Perspectives. 1974–1975.
Los Angeles *Times*. 1970–1975 *passim*.
Miami Herald. 1970–1975 *passim*.
The New York Times. 1945–1975 *passim*.
O Estado de São Paulo (Brazil). 1963–1964 *passim*.
Time. 1970–1975 *passim*.
Wall Street Journal (New York). 1970–1975 *passim*.
Washington *Post*. 1970–1975 *passim*.

INTERVIEWS

Ayres, Paulo. Interview with Samuel L. Baily. São Paulo, February 1968.
Campos, Roberto. Recorded interview with Dr. John E. Reilly. Rio de Janeiro, May 29, 1964. John F. Kennedy Library Oral History Program.
Pueyrredon, Ricardo H. Interview with Samuel L. Baily. Buenos Aires, August 22 and 23, 1969.

index